STUDIES IN PUBLIC COMMUNICATION

A. WILLIAM BLUEM, GENERAL EDITOR

THE IMPERATIVE OF FREEDOM
A Philosophy of Journalistic Autonomy

STUDIES IN PUBLIC COMMUNICATION

MASS MEDIA AND COMMUNICATION
Edited by Charles S. Steinberg

THE LANGUAGES OF COMMUNICATION
A Logical and Psychological Examination
by George N. Gordon

TO KILL A MESSENGER
Television News and the Real World
by William Small

INTERNATIONAL COMMUNICATION
Media—Channels—Functions
Edited by Heinz-Dietrich Fischer and John Calhoun Merrill

THE COMMUNICATIVE ARTS
An Introduction to Mass Media
by Charles S. Steinberg

PERSUASION
The Theory and Practice of Manipulative Communication
by George N. Gordon

MASS MEDIA AND THE SUPREME COURT
The Legacy of the Warren Years
Edited by Kenneth S. Devol

THE PEOPLE'S FILMS
A Political History of U.S. Government Motion Pictures
by Richard Dyer MacCann

THE IMPERATIVE OF FREEDOM
A Philosophy of Journalistic Autonomy
by John Calhoun Merrill

CONGRESS AND THE NEWS MEDIA
Edited by Robert O. Blanchard

AMERICAN BROADCASTING
A Source Book on the Development
of Radio and Television to the 1970s
by Lawrence W. Lichty and Malachi C. Topping

The Spirit of Liberty

". . . . What do we mean when we say that first of all we seek liberty? I often wonder whether we do not rest our hopes too much upon constitutions, upon laws and upon courts. These are false hopes; believe me, these are false hopes. Liberty lies in the hearts of men and women; when it dies there, no constitution, no law, no court can save it; no constitution, no law, no court can even do much to help it. While it lies there it needs no constitution, no law, no court to save it. . . ."

—Judge Learned Hand
Speech in New York City
1944

STUDIES IN PUBLIC COMMUNICATION

THE
IMPERATIVE
OF FREEDOM

A Philosophy of
Journalistic Autonomy

by

JOHN CALHOUN MERRILL

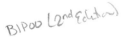
BIPOO (2nd Edition)

COMMUNICATION ARTS BOOKS

HASTINGS HOUSE, PUBLISHERS · NEW YORK

Library of Congress Cataloging in Publication Data

Merrill, John Calhoun, 1924–   The imperative of freedom.
    (Studies in public communication) (Communication arts books)
    Bibliography: p.
    1. Journalism—Philosophy. I. Title.
PN4731.M44   070'.01   74-2064
ISBN   0-8038-3391-1
ISBN   0-8038-3394-6 (pbk.)

Published simultaneously in Canada by
Saunders of Toronto, Ltd., Don Mills, Ontario

Printed in the United States of America
Designed by Al Lichtenberg

To all journalists who commune
with Apollo and Dionysus
and also to
those who choose not to

CONTENTS

ILLUSTRATIONS

PREFACE

For quite a few years I have wanted to write such a book as this. Ideas and concepts which appear on the following pages have undergone considerable change as they have been criticized and challenged by a wide assortment of persons—fellow teachers, journalists, students, and friends at home and abroad. In addition, certain modifications have come about as I have been exposed to an enlarging circle of writers. In a real sense this book objectifies what I feel every journalist should do: develop a philosophy of journalism which is helpful and meaningful. This book presents one such philosophy. Nobody is asked to accept it, but I believe that it should serve as a catalyst for philosophical thinking by other persons.

Areas of philosophy are purposely limited in the book to three. In order of their treatment they are: (1) political philosophy and its relationship to journalism; (2) epistemological concerns—primarily journalistic objectivity and truth-seeking; and (3) journalistic ethics.

I owe a great debt to innumerable persons who have both encouraged and challenged me in this endeavor. A few of these should certainly be mentioned: Russell Neale of Hastings House and Dr. William Bluem of Syracuse University, for their willingness to take a chance on such a book as this; to Dr. Ralph L. Lowenstein (School of Journalism) and the late Dr. Khagendra N. Kar (Philosophy Department) of the University of Missouri at Columbia, for their helpful criticism and ideational stimulation; to Professors Leslie G. Moeller, of the University of Iowa, and William E. Porter, of the University of Michigan, who were instrumental in showing me the importance and delights of philosophizing about journalism; to the late Dr. Wendell Johnson of the University of Iowa who demonstrated to me the value of an eclectic journalistic orientation;

to Professor Alfonso Nieto, dean of the Faculty of Information Science at the University of Navarra, Pamplona (Spain), whose ethical integrity and intellectual autonomy have been an inspiration; to John Whale, editorial writer for *The Sunday Times* of London whose conversations and lectures at Missouri during the summer of 1973 proved most stimulating and helpful; and, finally, to my wife, Dorothy, for her insistence on clear prose and her general intellectual vitality.

A few special acknowledgements should also be made to a group of authors and certain of their works which have had an important impact on my thinking. Although influences from a very large number of authors —many of them in journalism and journalism education—can be found throughout these pages, there are about a dozen writers, not writing specifically about journalism, who have particularly served as catalysts for my thinking and have furnished the basic philosophical foundation for this book. These authors, and a book by each which has especially been helpful to me, follow:

Erich Fromm, *Man for Himself*; Ortega y Gasset, *The Revolt of the Masses*; Karl Jaspers, *Man in the Modern Age*; Friedrich Hayek, *The Road to Serfdom*; Aldous Huxley, *Brave New World Revisited*; John Stuart Mill, *On Liberty*; Albert Camus, *The Rebel*; Gabriel Marcel, *The Philosophy of Existentialism*; Bertrand Russell, *Human Society in Ethics and Politics*; Carl G. Jung, *The Undiscovered Self*; Max Eastman, *Reflections on the Failure of Socialism*; Eric Hoffer, *The True Believer*; Ayn Rand, *For the New Intellectual*; and Jerome Tuccille, *Radical Libertarianism*.

However much the above authors may differ from one another in certain ways, there are important strands of their thought which contribute to the basic journalistic philosophy espoused in this book. The works of Immanuel Kant have also had a profound impact; in fact, certain of his ideas have been merged with several Existentialist concepts and also with various aspects of Rational Humanism to form the basic philosophical base of the book.

Although I find Kant a little too austere and abstract for complete comfort, his fundamentally Christian ethics is generally compatible with mine. And although I find Existentialist thought a little too relative and mystical (or emotional) for my complete acceptance, I recognize many important and helpful concepts in it. And although the objectivistic rationalism and self-interest of Rational Humanism at times seems to go too far and leave me feeling "cold" and "alone," I accept many of its basic tenets. It has been interesting to try to tie many of the compatible strands of these three orientations together into what I consider a reasonable philosophy of journalism.

My orientation, my philosophy of journalism, can be summarized in a few words, words indicating concepts which are found throughout this book: libertarianism, individualism, rationalism, self-interest, self-control, pluralism, competition, duty, sensitivity, and existentialism. Although at first glance some of these concepts may seem contradictory, they really are not, and it is one of the main purposes of this book to show how they can be reconciled and connected in a meaningful and coherent philosophy.

The reader will quickly notice that the term "responsibility" is not in the list. It is purposely omitted, not because I am opposed to responsibility in journalism, but simply because it is implied in the framework of the other concepts. If any journalistic responsibility would have to be expressed explicitly for a journalist or a media unit, it would be the responsibility to remain as free as possible and to determine one's own concept of responsible journalism. This, and nothing more.

—JOHN C. MERRILL
Columbia, Missouri

March, 1974

INTRODUCTION

BY ALL REASONED MEASURE, the main function of "Journalism Educators" is to build programs of study which are designed to create not journalists, but complete human beings. In order to achieve such a significant objective, inquiry in our schools of Public Communication must first review that vision of an ideal world which reflects man's social concern. It is evident that the public media, in exercising their informational as well as diversionary functions, gain increasing influence over the processes by which men arrive at those immediate decisions that govern the social contract. Upon these media may rest the responsibility for change, and perhaps upheaval, in both the policy and organization of our basic social institutions —in government, in education, in our courts and laws, and in all those agencies and systems by which social stability is perpetuated, progress assured and individual liberty guaranteed.

The public media are, without question, persuasive instruments in the social aspect of man's struggle for self-liberation. They select and bring to waiting multitudes a constant flow of detail related to those fruitful dialogues of differences and concordances upon which free societies thrive. It inevitably follows that *what* information is transmitted, and the nature of transmission, will dictate the direction and intensity of change in all other institutions within society. Each of the public media, in varying degrees, in different ways, and in distinct presentational methods, brings us to confrontations with ourselves as social beings. By doing so they shape our collective hopes, aspirations and futures.

Still, a program which directs inquiry and teaching toward those visions built upon the social view of man is less than complete. Self-liberation must also be sought within man's creative spirit and in the

xvii

quality of his life. The study of the public media of communication must be elevated to that high ground overlooking the weary battlers of humanism *versus* scientism, the combatants of individuality *versus* collectivism, and the stubborn defenders of notions that all of man's actions are either mechanically predictable or irrationally capricious.

For if man possesses an awareness of the social necessity to impose order on the world as he finds it, he also cherishes a concept of self, or personal attunement with the cosmos which cannot fade, he must believe, when his physical existence comes to an end. Whatever uniqueness may be attributed to his condition of being more than animal but less than God, man alone is in conscious grasp of the knowledge that while he must live with others, he will die alone. His innate sense of importance in the vast scheme of things underlies all meaning, and remains the very touchstone of what he holds real.

This knowledge commits man not solely to life's immediate decisions, to that necessary involvement with others which enables him to control and direct his social family; it also brings him to that deeper inward searching, to a self-evolved arrangement of his experience. Upon his social action depends his stability in the world; but upon personal pause and wonder depends any true progress. There must be for each man realities which are his alone, and the strength with which he clings to them marks all that is humanly prideful and noble. And it is this sense of wonder that makes the aware human being question all that seems logical in the brief, progressive social view—and come finally to see life with the native and innocent eye of creative, religious and philosophic man.

As we enter the final quarter of this incredible century, all of us are coming to recognize that *communicating man* is either *philosophic man* or he is not man at all. And for many, including John Merrill, the time has come when those who bear responsibility for training young people to enter our vast journalistic enterprise must place first things first. *Studies in Public Communication* is grateful to Professor Merrill for this profound effort.

A. WILLIAM BLUEM, PH.D.
Professor of Media Studies
S. I. Newhouse School of
Public Communication
Syracuse University

THE IMPERATIVE OF FREEDOM

A Philosophy of Journalistic Autonomy

AUTHOR'S FOREWORD
A Revelation of Biases

THIS IS A BOOK with a wide scope. But it is also a book with a rather limited theme or thesis. Its scope encompasses issues and basic principles in journalism, and it is my main concern to raise these issues and reflect on them (philosophize about them, if you will) without going deeply into specifics of individual cases since these are provided on a continuing basis in detail by specialized and even mass media of communication. Although the reader is occasionally referred to a specific case or issue, it is really the philosophical principle of such cases that is the main concern of this book.

The Fundamental Theme

Although various philosophical positions are discussed, or at least mentioned on these pages, a central or basic theme or thesis emerges: that American journalism is becoming so institutionalized and professionalized and so immured with the nascent concept of "social responsibility," that it is voluntarily giving up the sacred tenet of libertarianism—"editorial self-determinism"—and is in grave danger of becoming one vast, gray, bland, monotonous, conformist spokesman for some collectivity of society. As it is the thesis, so is it the warning of the book.

The philosophy of radical or "pure" press libertarianism is not a very popular one in this country at present and I recognize certain risks in basing a book on this concept; the intellectual climate of the times would far more readily accept a socially oriented theory of journalism than one which enthrones individualism. Journalistic philosophy, where it is seri-

3

ously considered at all, is leaning toward a press which has its concept of responsibility socially determined rather than *self* determined.

But it is this very fact that gives rise to this book. The journalistic *self* and the journalistic penchant for media self-determinism must be re-enthroned, and the fuzzy social utilitarian thinking that is undermining journalistic integrity and turning journalists into mechanistic robots must be repudiated. This is the basic bias of the book and it runs throughout: a bias toward journalistic self-determinism, toward individualism and against collectivism, toward personal integrity and self-respect and against altruism, toward responsibility *self*-determined and against social responsibility *socially or collectively* determined.

This bias contributes to the fundamental theme of the book: that American journalism is rapidly losing its freedom, in subtle and often self-induced ways, because of the rise of the philosophy of social or collectivist utilitarianism. Most American journalists think they are free. Actually, they are giving up their freedom, adapting to institutionalism and professionalism, and demeaning their individuality and rational self-interest. They are escaping from freedom and self-responsibility into the comfortable sanctuary of social ethics and fuzzy altruism. American journalists, like most journalists in the Western world, while still chanting the tenets of libertarianism, are marching into an authoritarian sunset under the banners of "social responsibility." They must shake off the benumbing spell that is robotizing them and realize that their only responsibility to themselves and society is the responsibility of breaking ranks and remaining free. For just over the horizon is the World of 1984.

Meta-ethical Emphasis

One of the most important branches of philosophy is ethics, the theory of right conduct. The journalist faces ethical decisions every day; he can better make them if he has a moral philosophy based on a consistent and individually meaningful set of principles.

This broad "principle-based" system of ethics which should guide his day-to-day decisions is actually in the realm of "meta-ethics" (or theory of ethics) since it does not try to provide specific *rules* of moral conduct in every journalistic situation. The journalist must adapt to specifics after he has determined the broad, basic philosophical foundation upon which he will stand.

Morality is a set of basic principles of conduct; if these principles are authentic, they are general, self-imposed and self-regulated. When laws are externalized or passed and imposed from outside the individual person, we have departed the world of ethics and have gone into the world of power and legalism. And this book is not very much concerned with this latter world.

Three Ethical Strains

In the area of ethics, this book takes the position that the journalist should rationally adopt a modified Kantian position of "duty for duty's sake," freely arrived at and individually enforced. Such an ethics would retain the basic Christian aspects of Kantianism while liberating it in important ways by injecting it with certain strains of Existentialism and Rational Humanism. The main characteristic of the journalistic ethics proposed in this book is duty or commitment to a *self*-determined morality, freely and rationally arrived at, with personal responsibility for the consequences of this commitment.

(margin note: ① Kantianism ② Existentialism ③ Rational Humanism)

The three strains, then, which are brought together here are: (1) Kantian obligationism with its emphases of duty, self-esteem, rationalism and self-motivation; (2) Existentialism with its emphases of commitment, freedom and self-responsibility; and (3) Rational Humanism with its emphases of freedom, self-esteem, objectivism and rationalism.

Strain #1: Two of Immanuel Kant's main ideas are of special relevance here. One is his Categorical Imperative which says that a good act is one which the actor would be willing to see universalized. The other is Kant's emphasis on the importance of the person himself, insisting that every man must be considered as an *end*, not a means.

Kant also believed in freedom, but it was a kind of freedom to set rationally for yourself a duty to which you must adhere. For Kant this choice of, and faithfulness to, duty (the Existentialist's "commitment") was a kind of imperative, but one which was not restricting; rather it permitted the fullest exercise of freedom. For Kant thought of man as a "free self-motivated being." [1] Moral actions must be taken for duty's sake—on principle only—and not for something which might result. In this Kant was taking a non-utilitarian approach.

This seems a reasonable approach to ethics: that duty must be done for its own sake and that a person who does what is right because he thinks it will make him happier can claim no moral worth for the action; such ethical maxims as "honesty is the best policy" and "crime doesn't pay" would rob the person's life of any real existential or moral value. Kant would say, for example, that a journalist must write the truth not because a democratic people need to know the truth so they can better govern themselves, *but simply because the journalist has a moral duty to*

(margin note: duty vs utility)

[1] E. W. F. Tomlin, *The Western Philosophers* (New York: Harper & Row, 1967), pp. 220–21.

write the truth. Kant would say that one should be honest for the sole reason that his duty is to honesty.

Kant's concept of "duty" is very important; for those who act from duty are acting morally. In the words of Professor Robert Wolff of Columbia University: "To be truthful from duty . . . is an entirely different thing from being truthful out of fear of disadvantageous consequences, for in the former case the concept of the action itself contains a law for me, while in the latter I must first look about to see what results for me may be connected with it." [2]

Moral duty, as Kant saw it, is a synonym for moral "obligation" freely accepted. It is binding on the individual but it is not binding by external force or threat of external punishment, but, as Ernest van den Haag has said, "because the person obligated *feels* bound without (external) coercion." [3] The person chooses to act in accordance with his freely accepted duty, and even if he does not so act on occasion he may acknowledge it "by regarding his act as immoral, or feeling a conflict about it." [4]

Strain #2: Karl Jaspers, writing specifically of journalism, adds a second strain—that of Existentialism—to the trinary ethical emphasis of this book. He observes:

> The journalist can realise the ideal of the modern universalised man. He can merge himself in the tension and the reality of the day, adopting a reflective attitude towards these. He can seek out that innermost region where the soul of the age takes a step forward. He deliberately interweaves his destiny with that of the epoch. He takes alarm, he suffers, and he balks when he encounters Nothingness. He becomes insincere when he is content with that which brings satisfaction to the majority. He soars towards the heights when he sincerely fulfils his being in the present. [5]

The Existentialist stresses personal commitment and involvement and deplores utilitarian motivation; for being content with that "which brings satisfaction to the majority" makes the journalist insincere. The example of Albert Camus in French journalism (especially as editor of *Combat*) should serve as a worthy model for the person interested in existential journalism. Unfortunately his commitment to, and development of, this kind of journalism was cut short by his untimely death.

[2] Robert Paul Wolff, *Philosophy: A Modern Encounter* (Englewood Cliffs, N.J.: Prentice-Hall, 1971), p. 291.
[3] Ernest van den Haag, *Political Violence & Civil Disobedience* (New York: Harper & Row Torchbooks, 1972), p. 108.
[4] *Ibid.*
[5] Karl Jaspers, *Man in the Modern Age* (Garden City, N.Y.: Doubleday & Co., Anchor Books, 1957), pp. 136–37.

It may seem strange to many readers for existentialist thought to be tied in with Kant and also with objectivists and rational humanists such as Erich Fromm, Friedrich Hayek and Ayn Rand. For Existentialism has the aura of subjectivism, whereas these other two strains (Kant to a lesser degree) enshrine objectivism. Existentialism says in effect that values are made in individual choices; but although it rejects rules and propositions about duty (therein seemingly departing from Kant), one will find a constant and common (universal) emphasis on the essential value of "commitment" or "engagement." Also, respect for personal integrity ("authenticity") is commonly held by Existentialists. These, then, are universal or absolute values which are compatible with both the non-utilitarian "duty" ethic of Kant and the rational "self-respect" ethic of the objectivistic humanists such as Erich Fromm. Kant and Fromm, of course, would insist that the existential commitment or engagement be made freely and rationally.

Strain #3: The rational humanistic ethical philosophy, exemplified by Erich Fromm, adds a third strain to the basic fabric of this book. Fromm refers to his ethics as "objectivistic" humanism and speaks of virtue as being "responsibility toward man's own existence." [6] This ethics is *objectivist* because Fromm rejects subjectivistic humanism which declares that value judgments have no objective validity and are nothing "but arbitrary preferences or dislikes of an individual." [7] He believes such subjectivism to be incompatible with the concept that ethical norms should be universal and valid to all men. In this he is akin to Kant. Fromm says that "in humanistic ethics man himself is both the norm giver and the subject of the norms, their formal sources or regulative agency and their subject matter." [8]

Defining freedom as the "ability to preserve one's integrity against power," Fromm believes this freedom is the basic condition for morality. "Our moral problem," he say, "is man's indifference to himself." [9]

Writing about the importance of reason in the formation of ethical norms and also reason's chief place in humanistic ethics, Fromm says:

> Valid ethical norms can be formed by man's reason and by it alone. Man is capable of discerning and making value judgments as valid as all other judgments derived from reason. The great tradition of humanistic ethical thought has laid the foundations for value systems based on man's autonomy and reason.[10]

6 Erich Fromm, *Man for Himself: An Inquiry into the Psychology of Ethics* (New York: Fawcett Premier Book, 1966), p. 29.
7 *Ibid.*, p. 24.
8 *Ibid.*, pp. 18–19.
9 *Ibid.*, p. 249.
10 *Ibid.*, p. 16.

In many ways the Objectivist ethics of Ayn Rand is similar to that of Fromm, and also to the underlying tenets of such thinkers as Friedrich Hayek and Eric Hoffer. The emphasis here is self-esteem, the competitive spirit and rationalism. About Ayn Rand's ethical man, Nathaniel Branden writes:

mind over matter

> He is the man who holds nothing above the rational judgment of his mind—neither wishes nor whims nor the unproved assertions of others. He is not the man without desires; he is the man who has no desires held in defiance of reason. He is not the man without emotions; he is the man who does not substitute his emotions for his mind. He is not the man without passion; he is the man without arbitrary whims. He is not the man without the capacity to feel; he is the man with the highest capacity for feeling—because his feelings are the product of rational, non-contradictory values.[11]

The Imperative of Freedom

It can be seen that, in each of the three ethical strains introduced above, freedom is the key concept. Freedom is essential to a sound ethics of journalism—freedom to make our own decisions whenever possible, to make our commitments. Responsibility, too, is important, but it is a kind of responsibility for the arrangement of our own lives according to our own consciences and a responsibility for the consequences. As Friedrich Hayek reminds us, this responsibility "is not to a superior, but one's conscience." [12] He continues:

> . . . the awareness of a duty not exacted by compulsion, the necessity to decide which of the things one values are to be sacrificed to others, and to bear the consequences of one's own decision, are the very essence of any morals which deserve the name.

This rational individualism, then, with its foundation of freedom is the ethical imperative of this book and is seen as a way to stop, or reverse, the trend toward journalistic conformity with its social ethics of utilitarianism leading unerringly to journalism's acceptance of "outside" or social determinism of its practices.

Value of Journalistic Philosophy

Many readers will question the value of such a book as this. Philosophy is widely viewed as irrelevant, a kind of pastime for ivory-tower

[11] Nathaniel Branden, *Who is Ayn Rand?* (New York: Paperback Books, 1969), p. 54.
[12] Friedrich A. Hayek, *The Road to Serfdom* (Chicago: Univ. of Chicago Press—Phoenix Books, 1944), p. 212.

dwellers, of little value to the hard and real world of journalism. But such a view is shortsighted. Philosophizing satisfies our desire to know, our curiosity. Philosophy is concerned with our attempt to get at the truth; it might be called, as Bertrand Russell has said, "the art of rational conjecture," and it is interested in "what may be true, or is most likely to be true, where it is impossible to know with certainty what *is* true." [13]

Philosophizing in journalism helps us design meaningful definitions for ourselves which can help us in our work. A few concepts needing defining are "truth," "news," "objectivity," "fairness," "responsibility," "pluralism," "freedom," "interpretation"—and even "journalism" itself.

In addition to wanting to know, the journalist has to act. He has things he wants to do, goals he wants to reach. He needs a consistent plan, a basic set of guiding principles. Philosophy can help the individual formulate a life pattern by which he can assess his progress and correct his direction. Few persons, in a short lifetime, can develop a philosophy which will in all respects be consistent, but they can try; and whatever philosophy journalists build enthusiastically and rationally will help immeasurably in giving their lives a meaning, a framework, a kind of haven in a complex world.

Philosophical Unconcern?

There are those who believe that journalism in America is "aphilosophical"—that is, that it is not guided by philosophy, that it is unconcerned with philosophy. Dennis Chase, for one, has written that when it comes to the matter of philosophy "publishers, editors, broadcasters and journalism educators are virtually unanimous in their conviction that any theories about journalism should take second place to the hard reality of practice." [14]

If Chase is right—and he probably is—such a conviction would evidence more of an *anti*-philosophical orientation than an *a*philosophical one. Chase continues: ". . . journalism is guided by philosophy—but it is whatever philosophy that the culture serves up in any given period. The dominant trends in journalism have always been pragmatism and subjectivism." Chase also believes that in practice journalists participate in "the passive, osmotic acceptance of whatever philosophy is culturally dominant in any given period," and that this is "strangling the chance for a science of journalism." [15]

[13] Bertrand Russell, *The Art of Philosophizing and Other Essays* (New York: Philosophical Library, 1968), p. 1.
[14] Dennis J. Chase, "The Aphilosophy of Journalism," *The Quill* (Sept., 1971), p. 15.
[15] *Ibid.*, p. 17.

This "science of journalism," whatever that might be, may well be strangled, but it is doubtful that osmotic acceptance of culturally dominant philosophies is the cause. Certainly, each journalist must (or should) accept his philosophy of journalism rationally and not osmotically, but even if he were to do so, there would be no assurance that a "science" of journalism would result.

It is true, as Chase suggests, that philosophy is usually considered unnecessary, or at least tangential, by the journalist, and it is not approached systematically and rationally. If the journalist considers it at all, he feels he will be able to function effectively by a kind of spur-of-the-moment philosophy which will come to him intuitively as the need arises. This is especially true in ethics. The rudder is therefore missing; journalistic boats speed off in all directions, not really having a planned destination.

Little wonder the world of journalism is filled with idle chatter, unsynthesized fragments, distorted statements, lies, half-truths and unexplained bits and pieces of information. Journalism creates, even as it reflects, a world of chaos bordering on desperation. Ortega y Gasset, writing on journalism in 1944, put it this way:

> . . . the journalist's profession leads him to understand by the reality of the times that which creates a passing sensation, regardless of what it is, without any heed for perspective or architecture. Real life is, certainly purely of the present; but the journalist deforms this truism when he reduces the present to the momentary, and the momentary to the sensational. The result is that, in the public consciousness today, the image of the world appears exactly upside down. The space devoted to people and affairs in the press is inversely proportionate to their substantial and enduring importance; what stands out in the columns of the newspapers and magazines is what will be a "success" and bring notoriety.[16]

A Summary of Biases

Now a few words are in order about basic biases. I make no claim that there are none, and the nature of the book precludes "objective" presentation, for *philosophy* implies a certain orientation, a certain way of looking at basic concepts, issues and ideas. Therefore, there has been no attempt to give "equal time"—or perhaps even *any* time—to all the prevailing viewpoints, schools of thought, and orientations. I actually feel an obligation to be biased, and hope that I have fulfilled this obligation. So certain

[16] José Ortega y Gasset, *Mission of the University* (New York: W. W. Norton & Co., 1966), p. 90.

fundamental biases or predilections largely shape this book; here are a few of them:

* a bias toward Kantian ethics injected here and there with doses of Existentialism and Objectivism.
* a bias toward libertarian purity or radicalism.
* a bias toward rational self-interest-and-control.
* a bias toward editorial self-determination.
* a bias against all mechanisms, institutions, and systems of ethics which tend to collectivize, neutralize, harmonize or in other ways diminish the Journalistic Self.
* a bias against not only Government interference with journalistic activity, but against *any* interference which comes from outside the individual journalistic media.
* a bias against any program or organization which would tend to constrict the *laissez-faire* pluralism of the media.

Quite obviously the above biases need elaboration and explication; each one is fuzzy, standing in its truncated form. But the temptation for elaboration here will be withstood, for it is felt that as the reader proceeds through the book he will find each of these biases making its appearance; therefore, explication and clarification will follow as ideas, issues and concepts are presented and discussed.

Radical (or "Pure") Libertarianism

One term, however, should be stressed and discussed a little more in detail here: *libertarianism*. It is important because, in a very real sense, it provides the theoretical cement for the whole book. I conceive of myself as a libertarian "purist" in the area of journalism, but realize really there is no *pure* (in the sense of complete) freedom realizable in a social situation. Press libertarianism is "pure" in the sense being discussed here if it is uncontrolled, full, unregulated *laissez-faire* journalism—with a separation of State and press.[17]

Admittedly, a pure system has really never existed, for various degrees of governmental control have always undermined and distorted it; but it is the contention of this book that journalists should dedicate themselves to keeping the system as "pure" as possible *by keeping control of their own*

[17] It is unfortunate that there is no single word to describe this radical libertarianism. At the other end of the freedom-control spectrum, however, there is a term which implies extreme or radical authoritarianism: *totalitarianism*. Its characteristics are well delineated in Hannah Arendt's fine book, *Totalitarianism*, which is the third part of her classic series, *Origins of Totalitarianism* (1951).

journalistic decisions and by thwarting as vigorously as possible any *outside* power or control.

The pure or radical libertarian would return to the *roots*, the basic essence, of libertarianism. In an open society each individual should be free to act in accordance with his own rational self-determinism if his action does not restrain another from doing the same thing. A person should do what he would be willing to have everyone do. This implies *rationalism* on the part of the free-actor; and it is this rationalism that circumscribes individual freedom to the extent that it does not degenerate into nihilism or unprincipled license.

In his catalytic book *Radical Libertarianism*, Jerome Tuccille sees a demise of the basic tenets of libertarianism. He writes:

> The American heritage, our birthright as a society of free individuals, is being trampled by an army of bureaucratic politicians who have been nurtured in the miasma of a philosophical swampland. Relativistic values have displaced absolutes; relativistic ethical codes have displaced moral conviction; pragmatism has displaced objective reasoning as the motive power for human activity. All this must be stopped before we destroy ourselves and the remnant of liberty that remains to us today.[18]

There is little doubt that libertarianism is being compromised; therefore, the libertarian "radical" must keep his "purist" arguments in the public arena even at the risk of exaggerating them on occasion. For example, he must insist that *no* restrictions (repeat *no*) be placed on a journalistic medium's exercise of self-management.

It is recognized, of course, that this is still not complete freedom of journalistic expression, for it does not take into consideration the individual journalist's obligation to take orders from his "superiors" in the journalistic world. Journalists working for somebody must give up some freedom to that somebody, be it a publisher-owner in a capitalistic system or a government-party manager in an authoritarian system. All that is being said here is that the individual journalist should resist any effort to take the decision-making out of the hands of the individual medium and invest it in some "outside" authority. Such outside authorities would include any of the branches of government, advertisers, or pressure groups, including press councils, "professional" organizations and societies of any kind.

In other words, press libertarianism in its "pure" or purest *laissez-faire* form must be defended, and all of us must suffer gladly (or at least,

18 Jerome Tuccille, *Radical Libertarianism* (New York: Harper & Row—Perennial Library, 1970), p. 113.

suffer) those media and journalists which might offend our sensibilities. Of course, we might want to "reform" some of them through discussion or education, but we should respect the right of all to continue in the way they prefer.

If we can remain intellectually free, and it is surely not easy, we will not consciously give up our journalistic self-determinism. But the temptation to do just that seems especially strong at present, even in our democratic society. As Friedrich Hayek has so astutely observed: "Perhaps the most alarming fact is that contempt for intellectual liberty is not a thing which arises only once the totalitarian system is established but one which can be found everywhere among intellectuals who have embraced a collectivist faith and who are acclaimed as intellectual leaders even in countries still under a liberal regime." [19]

Utilitarianism: the Person as a "Means"

John Milton and J. S. Mill are usually held up as great libertarian stalwarts. Maybe so. But I see myself as far more libertarian than these men who brought utilitarian orientations to bear on their attitudes toward the press. They both believed that the truth would automatically emerge victorious in a free encounter of diverse opinions and bits of information. This simply does not follow. Their belief in the value of free expression is certainly commendable, however, and not to be denied. The value, however, is not in the theoretical or utilitarian production of "truth" but rather in the intrinsic value of *free expression* itself. The central value of freedom of expression is in the free expression, not in any *truth* it might somehow unearth, although this might be a peripheral "bonus-value." But we should remember, as Aldous Huxley reminds us, that "an unexciting truth may be eclipsed by a thrilling falsehood" and that "a skilful appeal to passion is often too strong for the best of good resolutions." [20]

Most so-called libertarians today are probably utilitarians, if not on Miltonic principle, then for another reason. Many, for example, say that the press should remain free and give as their justification of such a position a kind of collectivist premise: that society should permit the press to be free *because a free press can best serve the society's needs and interests.* This utilitarian premise implies that the press does not have the right to freedom, but only the right to serve the collectivist interests; in other words, it can have its freedom as long as it serves society in a "responsible" manner.

note rejection of soc. responsibility theory, of Commission Report (1947)

[19] Hayek, *The Road to Serfdom*, p. 163.
[20] Aldous Huxley, *Brave New World Revisited* (New York: Harper & Row—Perennial Library, 1965), p. 104.

These utilitarians masquerading as libertarians are in the forefront of attempts to make the press more socially responsible, in effect taking away the individual, personal freedom of media people to determine their *own* sense of social responsibility. The utilitarians are satisfied only when they can place some kind of obligation on the press—make it serve some social goal. One of their main doctrines is that the people have "a right to know"; they thus justify press freedom so that it can serve the social purpose of "letting the people know."

Such prominent American journalists as James Russell Wiggins, in his *Freedom or Secrecy*, and Kent Cooper in his *The Right to Know*, have postulated (or assumed) a "people's right to know" and seem to equate it with "freedom of the press" or to even place it as a concept *above* press freedom. They believe, and they have many supporters in this belief, that the problem of secrecy poses the greatest threat to freedom of the press. Actually, governmental or other types of secrecy (including secrecy on the part of the press itself) are irrelevant to—or at least tangential to—freedom of the press. Rather, I would say that the greatest threat to freedom of the press is external restriction of, direction of, control of, press *expression*. If the press can freely express itself with what it has to express, then that is the core of press freedom. Secrecy involves something else—another principle—and, important as it may be, it has little or nothing to do with freedom of the press.

Many readers will say that if the press cannot get certain information due to governmental secrecy, let us say, then it cannot have the freedom to express it. I disagree with this reasoning. Of course, the press cannot publish what it does not have; that is a truism. Even if there were *no* secrecy, the press could not know *everything*; therefore, it could not publish everything. Would not having certain information thereby impinge on its freedom? One might as well say that a person does not have freedom of expression because he does not have certain information or ideas to express.

But, the scoffer at this idea will insist, the people have a right to know. What gives them such a right? Where is it found? Certainly not in the Constitution. Yet, an *unabridged* press freedom to publish without prior restraint *is* in the Constitution. About as much as can be said about a right for the people to know (at least, constitutionally) is that they have the right to *want* to know and to *try* to know. Theoretically, they may even have a *need* to know certain things in a democracy, but all of this is not the same as a *right* to know. For such a right, if it existed, would impose an obligation on the press to let the people know; this would thereby conflict with the freedom of the press to determine its own editorial actions. For a "free" press, constitutionally as well as theoretically, is one which can decide what it will publish or *not* publish. A people's "right" to know would abrogate this freedom.

What then, the reader is probably asking, is the valid reason for thinking libertarianism is preferable to some other journalistic orientation? If it does not have a social utilitarian rationale (e.g., to let the people know), then why would libertarianism be considered worthy of support? One answer: It permits maximum *personal* freedom, leads to more informational pluralism, forces the responsibility on the individual medium for its crucial actions, and finally, permits greater creativity—and fun—for those exercising their own freedom.

Conservatism or Liberalism?

Is this position of libertarian purity a liberal or a conservative one? Actually such a question cannot be answered directly because "libertarian purity" is a transcendent term which refers to a position which may be taken by persons in either the "liberal" or "conservative" camps.

Without a doubt, this book will be viewed in the context of current thinking as predominantly "conservative" because it is advocating the retention of, or return to, libertarianism. And this will not be considered "progressive"—and progressivism has "liberal" overtones. Actually, one could just as logically argue that it is really "progress" to recapture as much of the pure essence of libertarianism as possible.[21] At any rate, it should be obvious to any dispassionate reader that persons calling themselves "conservatives" can be just as dedicated to freedom—or as destructive of freedom—as can persons calling themselves "liberals." In fact, it might well be that, in spite of prevailing stereotypes, it is the liberals who are more ready to give away their freedoms—including press freedom—to Big Government than are the conservatives. They apparently have no objection to "social engineering" if it is, in their view, advantageous to society or some minority segments of it.

It must be pointed out, on the other hand, that there are "conservatives" who have elitist and authoritarian dispositions also and would like for some *authority* to control, censor and otherwise regulate the free-working of the journalistic system. Both groups—liberal and conservative —include the elitists, the would-be referees of society, the regulators, the judges who are, at worst, authoritarians and, at best, dupes and pawns of authoritarians.

---

[21] An excellent book which points out the many inconsistencies of liberalism and also highlights the semantic difficulties of using such terms as "liberal" and "conservative" is Robert Paul Wolff's *The Poverty of Liberalism* (Boston: Beacon Press, 1968). Cf. F. Hayek's essay, "Why I am not a Conservative"—chapter 6 in Frank Meyer (ed.),

A pox on both their houses! Rightwing and Leftwing authoritarians are equally obnoxious to the libertarian. Rational sympathies should be extended to those who have no secure home either in the "liberal" or the "conservative" camps; to those who refuse to be tied to labels and loyalties which are thereby forced upon them; to those who revere freedom for what it means to the individual, not what it can do for society or for some other entity; to those who value man as an end in himself, not for what he can do for others; to those who place the responsibility of free choices on the *person* and insist that he shoulder this responsibility; to those who believe that "man thinking" is more truly man than "man feeling"; to those who place rationality or reasonableness over emotions and instinctualism.[22]

Emphasis on Selfhood

This book takes its place on the side of those above, regardless of whether they are called liberals, conservatives, radicals, progressives, reactionaries, moderates, or whatever. Now, this position is often misunderstood. It does not mean that there is no value given to society, or to other people, or to institutions; it does not mean that a person taking this position has no feelings, no compassion, no sensitivities, no public consciousness. It does not mean that such a person does not appreciate the complexities of the freedom-control dilemma, for certainly he must agree with Bertrand Russell that the "problem is one of balance" and that "too little liberty brings stagnation, and too much brings chaos." [23]

I am concerned here with a person who places major and primary emphasis on each individual—on the Self. Society is for the person, not the person for the society. Man is valuable, important, sacred if you like, *qua* man, and he should salvage as much of the essence of personhood from the encroaching embrace of modern society as he can. This "embrace" threatens the existential self and is described by William Barrett in these words:

> The last gigantic step in the spread of technologism has been the development of mass art and mass media of communication: the machine no longer fabricates only material products; it also makes minds. Millions of people live by the stereotypes of mass art, the

What is Conservatism? (New York: Holt, Rinehart and Winston, 1964), and Max Eastman, chapter 6—"What to Call Yourself" in *Reflections on the Failure of Socialism* (San Diego: Viewpoint Books, 1955).
[22] Ayn Rand, *The Virtue of Selfishness: A New Concept of Egoism* (New York: New American Library—Signet Books, 1964), p. 15.
[23] Bertrand Russell, *Authority and the Individual* (Boston: Beacon Press, 1960), p. 25.

most virulent form of abstractness, and their capacity for any kind of human reality is fast disappearing. If here and there in the lonely crowd (discovered by Kierkegaard long before David Riesman) a face is lit by a human gleam, it quickly goes vacant again in the hypnotized stare at the TV screen.[24]

Selfhood, self-esteem, integrity—whatever it might be called—is basic to a humanistic journalism, which is at once free but mature, experimental but moderate, rational but sensitive. When selfhood is minimized, or subordinated to something else, then a totalitarianism creeps into journalism like a cancerous growth insisting that all other cells of the system become like itself. Selfhood does not imply the denial of selfhood to others. I believe, as did Albert Camus, that the perfect society or the perfect journalistic system is one where everyone is assuming his complete potential and individualism without distorting or destroying the selfhood of others.

But society and journalism are not perfect, and certain persons and groups use their freedom to control others. As Camus points out, this authoritarian exercise of freedom from a base of power is usually rationalized by pleading some social good for the future. Camus denounced this concept of the need to tyrannize persons and destroy selfhood for some "cause" related to social utilitarianism. He even broke with Sartre on this issue for Sartre supported the Communist policies of destroying and imprisoning human beings on the grounds that they were necessary for the good of the future society. This "social utilitarian" rationale for authoritarianism is very potent, and very real, and it is mainly against it that this book takes its stand. And journalism, of all areas of human endeavor, is probably most open to the beguiling lure of social utilitarianism.

Observations on Journalists

Journalists in America think of themselves as individualists yet seem to need a sense of unity with other journalists; they worship specifics yet are the great generalizers; they see themselves as social critics yet accept criticism badly; they talk of objectivity while reflecting the world through a prism; they talk of news without really knowing what it is; they see themselves as adversaries of government without knowing just why they should be.

Journalists speak of the people's right to know as they routinely keep the people from knowing certain things; they follow old rules and dig

[24] William Barrett, *Irrational Man: A Study in Existential Philosophy* (Garden City, N.Y.: Doubleday Anchor Books, 1958), p. 269.

about in assigned "beats" and watch their efforts changed, ignored or killed while they talk about freedom of expression; or they get excited about the public not having access to the news media while they themselves submit their own communications and ideas to the authority of their editors and publishers.

Journalists cling tenaciously to old journalistic clichés and practices while excoriating Government for refusing to free itself from reactionary tendencies; they mouth platitudes about the sanctity of free expression and decry a governmental official's exercise of free expression to criticize the mass media; they pay lip service to professionalism without even knowing what it means; they insist they have a right to protect the identity of their sources while they ridicule governmental secrecy.

All of this is not to say that journalists are more unthoughtful or more tradition-bound or more contradictory than other institutionalized persons in our society. It is simply to say that, too often, they do not realize what is happening to them as they routinely "process" the world for others. The fact that they are inconsistent in much of their thinking and conformist in much of their practice is not the most important issue here. What is most important, and rather alarming, is the fact that many of them—probably most—do not realize that anything very significant is happening. Journalism is becoming a depersonalized, mechanistic monster increasingly controlled by outside forces and most journalists appear not to know it or to care about it.

It may well be that a chief reason for the general unconcern about journalism's many inconsistencies and contradictions is that the American journalist is devoid of any serious philosophical awareness or interest. He avoids philosophizing, or as John Dewey has put it—reflecting about the meaning of fundamental ideas. An interest in philosophy might not eliminate inconsistencies in journalism, but it would at least force the individual journalist to look at his work in a deeper, more profound way, questioning many assumptions from a perspective which is beyond the narrow and restricting confines of the prevailing tenets of his pragmatic "professionalism."

The "Parts" of the Book

Part One of this book deals primarily with aspects of journalistic philosophy related closely or directly to the political and social development of a nation, and with several concepts which are especially considered important in modern so-called "libertarian" countries, especially the United States. The concepts of press freedom and social responsibility are discussed, along with three myths—or what I consider myths—which have grown up in American society about press-society relationships.

Part Two of the book relates mainly to the practice of journalism and to the journalist himself, indicating various dangers to autonomy (press freedom) posed within journalism itself. Whereas Part One deals largely with *external* pressures restricting or diminishing journalistic autonomy, Part Two shifts the emphasis to directions and developments in journalism which are contributing to a loss of press freedom. Institutionalization with its dehumanization and emphasis on the "collective good," along with increasing emphasis on *professionalizing* journalism, are forces helping to dissolve journalistic autonomy. A trend toward standardization being brought on by press commissions, councils, journalism reviews, and schools and departments of journalism is discussed as a danger to journalistic autonomy.

Also discussed in Part Two is the growing inclination in journalism toward a kind of *social* ethics of a utilitarian nature and away from an older *personal* ethics of individualistic commitment and responsibility. The last chapters of the book continue the thesis (that journalistic integrity and individuality are in danger before the onslaught of authoritarian tendencies and pressures), discuss various ethical "stances" open to journalists, and present an ethical philosophy which would go a long way toward stopping, or slowing, the contemporary drift toward the total enslavement of journalism.

The reader will probably note that, generally, the development of the book from Part One through Part Two is from an emphasis on institutionalized journalism (or professionalized journalism) to personalized or individualized journalism. The concern shifts from journalistic *media* and their relationship to their government and society to journalistic *persons* and their relationship to their *media* and their society. Integrity and a love for, and dedication to, freedom must finally become a personal commitment. Such a commitment, once made, is not easy to retain in the face of growing forces of dehumanization and "social adjustment," but the journalist must determine to retain it. The alternative is personal slavery and a loss of media independence *vis à vis* the Government Structure.

The autonomous journalist and the autonomous medium: this is really the meaning of libertarianism. Autonomy implies integrity and self-determinism. Integrity implies commitment and freedom. Authenticity (personal and media) results from autonomy and integrity, and gives real meaning to the journalist and to journalism. Freedom is at the root of all this, and it is my contention that for the authentic journalist (or journalistic medium) there is a strong and unwavering imperative of freedom.

Now, with the stage set, the biases out in the open and the basic thesis presented, let us turn to journalism and its relationship to the Government Structure and some of the concepts which have grown up in the Press-Government symbiosis in the United States.

Part One

THE JOURNALIST
AND HIS SOCIETY

I

Political Theories and
The Press

A NATION's press or media system is closely tied to the political system. Although quite obvious—perhaps even a truism—this fact makes it possible to analyze the media system of a society by focusing on the philosophy and structure of government. Since there are many concepts and types of political arrangements, there are many corresponding or related concepts of journalistic relationships to government. Journalism's relationship to government in a very real sense determines its basic function or purpose in the society. Since the total society is influenced most significantly by its political system, this means that journalism relates well to, or functions properly in, a society only if it is compatible with its political philosophy.

When we ask how political theories may be classified, we are also asking how journalistic theories may be classified. And certainly there are many conceptual typologies or models which can be, and have been, suggested for governmental and journalistic systems. In this chapter several old ones and several new ones are discussed.

Regardless of how many typologies may be suggested, there are perhaps only two *approaches* to government-press classification. They might be called (1) the "Pigeon-Hole" Approach, and (2) the "Progression" Approach, and this chapter will explore each. The first tends toward typologies which place government and/or media systems rather snugly in one or another category in a kind of static, "immediate slice of time" way. Actually, however, pigeon-hole classification does imply the potential for change and for category-overlap, but this aspect is minimized. It should also be noted that a dichotomous classification system, such as the one which is discussed first in this chapter (authoritarian/libertarian), is really a kind of continuum or spectrum dichotomy, with possible movement implied on the continuum. However, such models are normally descriptive of a place on a scale, therefore making for a kind of pigeon-hole mode of classification.

After briefly discussing in a general way the symbiosis between a press system and government, this chapter will present several traditional models of political-press theories and suggest several others which are believed to be more realistic and helpful to the student and analyst.

Media Relationship to Government

A media system reflects the political philosophy in which it functions. That is basic. A nation's journalism cannot exceed the limits permitted by the society; on the other hand, it cannot lag very far behind. Journalism is largely determined by its politico-social context, and when it functions basically in accord with this national ideology it is considered—or *should* be, I maintain—socially responsible in a macroscopic sense. Many persons disagree with this, and have, as will be noted a little later, postulated a *separate* theory of "social responsibility."

Certainly there are many ways to think about media or journalistic relationships to government. These could be developed into "theories." We could talk about harmonic versus disharmonic theories; about functional versus conflict theories; about adversary versus supportive theories; about monistic versus pluralistic theories; about self-deterministic versus governmental (or "other-directive") theories; about laissez-faire versus control theories. And when we begin considering these, and there are many other ways to label them, we begin to see that they are really parts of broader or more inclusive theories.

We can also consider journalism's relationship to government in other ways, for example, as: (1) An Equal Contender, (2) A Cooperating Servant, or (3) a Forced Slave. In the first case, the press units are independent of government and each other; there is competition among them; each is a self-developed-and-managed entity. In the second case the press units in a sense form a partnership with government but would cooperate with government voluntarily; government and the "social interest" would be considered synonymous and would motivate the press system into this partnership or cooperative relationship. And in the third case, the press system as a Forced Slave would be subservient to government, would co-operate involuntarily with government out of coercion by the governmental Power Elite.

Out of all the possible symbiotic relationships of government and media systems, a basic dichotomy always seems to emerge. It presents a simple Aristotelian way of looking at differences, and in spite of its dualistic oversimplification and generalized structuring of reality, it is probably still the best way to consider either press theories or political theories.

The Basic A-L Dichotomy

Before analyzing various models describing some of the complexities of government-press theories, it might be useful to discuss briefly the basic "two-valued" typology which underlies all such models. It can be called the "A-L Model" and structures press systems (and political systems) in a dichotomous manner: as either *authoritarian* or as *libertarian*. Actually this A-L model of government-press theories is part "pigeon-hole" and part "continuum" in approach, for the person using these labels normally recognizes varying *degrees* of authoritarianism and libertarianism. Nevertheless, the basic tendency here is to consider various philosophies of government and press as either authoritarian or libertarian.

Press systems, as well as nations and individual persons, tend to be either authoritarian or libertarian. They are all somewhat schizophrenic, of course, but the basic inclination of each is toward either a well-structured, disciplined world-view with explicit patterns of behavior or toward an open, experimental, self-determined, autonomous, non-restrictive society with a minimum of rules and controls. Governments are designed on the philosophical foundation of one or the other of these two orientations. In reality, neither governments nor persons are that simple; authoritarians are open and flexible in many spheres of their activities and thinking, and libertarians are more dogmatic and inflexible than is generally assumed. Nevertheless, governments and persons appear to incline in one or the other of two directions. This is also true of the journalistic systems of the world.

Press systems are conveniently labelled authoritarian or libertarian depending on the degree of their self-determinism. The authoritarian system is the one in which the journalistic media have little or no autonomy in the sense of determining their own editorial policies and activities; the libertarian system is the one in which the media are editorially autonomous and operate in an open, competitive atmosphere.

Obviously there are weaknesses in such a dualistic typology, and perhaps it would be somewhat better to use terms like "authoritarian tending" and "libertarian tending" in describing government-press systems. Some persons, however, would not be satisfied with any such classification, for they maintain that it is impossible to make meaningful statements about freedom in one country as compared to freedom in another. Freedom, they say, means different things in different societies. Such relativistic concepts would make talk about "freedom" in the Soviet Union, for example, meaningless when compared to "freedom" in the United States.

Although it is undoubtedly true that meanings assigned to "freedom" vary in various parts of the world (even among Americans), I cannot agree that there is no validity in describing one country as having a *freer* press than another country. No good reason exists why freedom (of the press, for instance) cannot have a rather pure meaning that can be universalized or applied to the journalistic system of *any* nation. Such factors as how much criticism of government is permitted in a particular country, how many restrictive press laws are found in a country and their frequency of use can be applied universally to get at freedom. Ralph Lowenstein, in his exhaustive PICA studies, has provided a detailed discussion of how this can be done.[1]

In other words, *extra*-press restrictions and controls do indeed vary from country to country; and in this sense (a very legitimate one) press freedom can take on a universal core meaning and comparative statements can validly be made about "press freedom" in countries with disparate governmental philosophies and structures. Press freedom is fundamentally freedom from outside control. The central concept of such freedom used throughout this book—and probably by most Americans—is press *autonomy*. This autonomy would apply most directly to the individual *media units* of the press, although it does (and should) apply to the individual journalist as well. Maximum journalistic autonomy is the imperative for authentic journalism.

The main thesis of this book is that American (and Western) journalism generally is now in a twilight zone between libertarianism and authoritarianism, and powerful forces, both external and internal, are pushing it rapidly into the snugness of authoritarianism. But while saying this, I must admit that we in the United States still have a basically libertarian press when compared to many other press systems of the world. Assuming that there is this basic philosophical dichotomy (A-L) existing among the various national political and press systems, let us look briefly at the two orientations:

[1] Ralph L. Lowenstein, "PICA: Measuring World Press Freedom" (Univ. of Missouri: Freedom of Information Center Pub. No. 666, August 1966). For a far more exhaustive explanation of PICA, see Lowenstein, "Measuring World Press Freedom as a Political Indicator" (Unpublished Ph.D. dissertation, Univ. of Missouri, August 1967).

Authoritarian Orientation. Authoritarianism is appealing; it has a beguiling quality, a neat and disciplined aura, a lure for orderly minds who desire structure, logical progression, and institutional stability. It is a giant invisible sociological magnet which pulls unceasingly at men and nations. Authoritarianism implies an "authority" and basically it is extremely difficult and painful, if not impossible, for the mass of men to be without an authority to direct and lead them. Even for journalists, who theoretically should appreciate and savor the benefits of freedom, self-authority or autonomy is very often a traumatic and unpleasant option. It appears there is a more natural tendency to escape from freedom than to escape from authority. Commitment to freedom and willingness to accept responsibility for the consequences of exercising this freedom is not a dominant philosophical stance today, even though Existentialism has shown that there is a rather large group of devotees to personal autonomy.

It may well be that the philosophical base for authoritarianism can be traced back at least to Plato, the first great proponent of "law and order" and advocate of submission to an *aristocracy of the best.* According to Karl Popper, Plato recognized one ultimate standard: the interest of the State. Everything that furthers this interest, believed Plato, is "good and virtuous and just" and everything that threatens it is bad, wicked and unjust. For Plato, actions that serve the State interest would be moral: actions that endanger it, immoral. So, for Plato, the Moral Code would be strictly utilitarian—a kind of Statist Utilitarianism, where *the criterion of morality is the interest of the State.*[2]

It appears that in recent times there are many national leaders (American presidents included) who have this Platonic notion about morality —about journalistic ethics and responsibility to the State. In fact, it may be said that all forms of political authoritarianism are built on the rationale set forth by Plato: that citizens must submit to the dictates of the rulers of the State who know what is best for the State and who morally can (and must) impinge on the freedoms of citizens in the interest of the State.

In journalism, some manifestations of this can be seen in the increased emphasis on press councils, and other *extra*-press proscriptions and normative "help" given to the mass media. Increasingly media autonomy is being made to appear irresponsible and the old concepts espoused by Plato so long ago are returning to infect us with their anti-democratic and elitist "wisdom"—concepts which do, admittedly, have a very strong appeal to the multitudes who recognize the comfort in being directed "massmen" and also to intellectuals who are titillated by the deterministic ideas of Freudians, Marxists and Skinnerians.

[2] Karl R. Popper, *The Open Society and Its Enemies* (Princeton: Princeton University Press, 1930). See chapters 6, 7, and 8 on Plato.

Many important thinkers since Plato have contributed to the development of the closed, authoritarian, elitist political philosophy. A desire for strong government, a fear of the masses, an inclination to personal arrogance based on felt superiority, a respect for power, a hatred for anarchy, a love for social stability and national objectives commonly sought—all of these are strong forces pulling men away from freedom.

Consistent with such a philosophy, the information media must, of course, be thought of as contributing to social harmony and stability. Certain things the populace should know; other things—harmful things to society—the people should not know. The power elite will either directly operate the mass media, or will control them or dictate their actions, leading to a monolithic journalism of conformity and harmony. The goal is political and social equilibrium brought about by a submission to authority. And this is true whether the country is an authoritarian nation of the right or of the left. Although there are some notable differences between a Communist authoritarian regime and a right-wing one in terms of organization and procedures, they are "basically alike," as Carl Friedrich and Zbigniew Brzezinski contend (1965) in their superb book on totalitarian dictatorship.[3] Friedrich Hayek also demonstrates in *The Road to Serfdom* (1944) that there is no real difference in the basic philosophy of rightists and leftists: both advocate statism and control and both subscribe to a philosophy of political and intellectual arrogance where a small elite group has a deep-rooted suspicion of the masses.

Power, as Lord Acton states, does tend to corrupt. Power is also active and insistent; it must intervene—it must direct, supervise, set standards, define responsibility, eliminate nonconformists and eccentrics, and it must generally make the society march to its unified and regular drumbeat. Alexander Solzhenitsyn was talking about literature in his Nobel Prize lecture (1972), but he could have just as well have been referring to journalism. He said:

> Woe to that nation whose literature is disturbed by the intervention of power. Because that is not just a violation against "freedom of print." It is the closing down of the heart of the nation, a slashing to pieces of its memory.[4]

But this "freedom to print" that Solzhenitsyn sees as being at the "heart of the nation" is seen by authoritarians as potentially bad because it permits error to circulate in the society, damaging the social structure

[3] See especially Chapter 11 ("Propaganda and Monopoly in Mass Communication") in Carl J. Friedrich and Zbigniew K. Brzezinski, *Totalitarian Dictatorship and Autocracy* (New York: Frederick A. Praeger, 1965).
[4] Quoted in John Hohenberg, *Free Press, Free People: The Best Cause* (New York: The Free Press, 1973), p. 511.

and impairing the achieving of social goals. Herbert Marcuse, one of the revolutionary "gurus" of recent years and an example of the Platonic elitists who are always grasping for social control, has been an influential guide for those who are escaping from freedom. Here is what one recent writer says of Marcuse and his idea of freedom:

> Freedom of speech is not an overriding good, for to allow freedom of speech in the present society is to assist in the propagation of error. . . . The truth is carried by the revolutionary minorities, such as Marcuse, and the majority have to be liberated by being reeducated into the truth by this minority, who are entitled to suppress rival and harmful opinions.[5]

People like Marcuse and a whole line of elitists and social engineers before him have a basic suspicion of the masses. People in general are looked upon as not intellectually capable, psychologically rigged, or educationally competent to make crucial decisions for themselves. The masses, in fact, are seen as frightened and frustrated when they are called on to exercise power and, if they do try, pose a great danger to the whole society. Special people must rule—people interested and competent, people dedicated to accumulating and wielding power, people who are ready and willing "to suppress rival and harmful opinions," as Marcuse might put it.

The authoritarian maintains that people in general desire leadership; they like simple, straightforward, easy solutions and actions; they want decisions made for them. Eric Hoffer points out in many of his writings that authoritarianism tries to reduce greatly the variety of aims, motives, interests, human types and, above all, "the categories and units of power." And this being the case, the "defeated individual, no matter how outstanding, can find no redress." [6]

Persons, of course, as well as regimes, are complex and multi-faceted; but in spite of this there does seem to be a general tendency in each political system and individual person: toward authoritarianism. We have looked at some of the characteristics of authoritarianism; now let us turn to its opposite in the basic A-L dichotomy: libertarianism.

Libertarian Orientation. This philosophical stance is as old, and maybe older, than authoritarianism. It has many roots, and Christians and Jews might even trace it back to the Garden of Eden. Undoubtedly "freedom lovers" have always existed, but it was not until the seventeenth and eighteenth centuries that the libertarian orientation took on a philosophical significance and began to have an impact on the press and public expression. John Milton with his "self-righting process" and John Locke

[5] Alasdair MacIntyre, *Herbert Marcuse: An Exposition and a Polemic* (New York: The Viking Press, 1970), p. 103.
[6] Nicholas Capaldi, *Clear and Present Danger* (New York: Pegasus, 1969), p. 269.

with his stress on "popular sovereignty" were seventeenth century pioneers in England, followed by Thomas Jefferson in eighteenth-century America; it was Jefferson who clearly expressed the necessary relationship between a free (even if it seemed irresponsible to him) press and good, sound democratic government. John Stuart Mill in nineteenth-century England (see Chapter 3) added further philosophical status to the concept of press libertarianism.

These men, and innumerable others, propounded a philosophy which was considerably different from authoritarianism. Unlike disciples of Plato, and later Hegel, they basically trusted the "common man" and believed that all kinds of information and ideas should be made public. They despised secrecy; they rebelled against prior censorship and felt that free criticism was essential to personal, as well as national, happiness and growth. They were fundamentally "democrats" and not autocrats, aristocrats, or some other variety of elitists. Of course, there are certain flaws in this generalization—for all of these men would draw the line of freedom at some point—but they determined to keep the idea of expression tied to the concept of personal and press autonomy just as tightly as possible.

A national libertarian orientation is one in which the leadership relates closely with the followship. There is a trust in the citizens, a belief that the majority—even if not always right—should be taken seriously and generally comes closest to the truth and makes sound decisions. This trust of the people is related to the mass media in that it is the media that can best inform the people so they can know enough to intelligently elect their representatives, direct them, and change them when necessary. Many students of the press today erroneously (in my view) see this concept as imposing a responsibility or obligation on the press which, if not fulfilled, will negate or cancel out the press's right to freedom.

Actually, there is a theoretical *assumption* in libertarian theory that a free and unhampered press will serve, at least to a large degree, this idealistic function of adequately informing a democratic people. But in libertarian theory there is no *obligation* on the press that it do so. This would, of course, contradict the principle of press freedom. In spite of many criticisms which can be hurled at a free and autonomous press for avowed "errors" and "excesses" and the like, it is probably safe to say that in the United States, for example, the people are very well informed about the issues of the day, the activities of their elected representatives, and the strengths and weaknesses of their political (and other) institutions.

In a libertarian society—even in one which has compromised many of its freedoms—there is considerable stress on divorcing government from journalism as much as possible. As Franklin Littell has pointed out in his cogent little essay on social pathology, the "existence of strong centers of thought and discipline separate from the state" is especially important to the lover of liberty.[7] This is why libertarian journalists have always—until perhaps recently—shuddered at the thought of government meddling in the affairs of the press, setting goals and standards, and the like.

Unlike authoritarianism, libertarianism is a philosophy revered by non-elitists and democrats—by those who feel that much can be learned from being exposed to ideas and opinions with which they disagree. This concept is basic in libertarian theory. It has, of course, been well expressed by such persons as Milton, Mill, Locke and Jefferson, but here is how a contemporary writer has expressed this symbiosis of free expression and democracy:

> Democracy is based on a profound insight into human nature, the realization that all men are sinful, all are imperfect, all are prejudiced, and none knows the whole truth. That is why we need liberty and why we have an obligation to hear all men. Liberty gives us a chance to learn from other people, to become aware of our own limitations, and to correct our bias. Even when we disagree with other people we like to think that they speak from good motives, and while we realize that all men are limited, we do not let our selves imagine that any man is bad. Democracy is a political system for people who are not too sure that they are right.[8]

It must be admitted that there is, in libertarian press theory, what must be considered a kind of built-in paradox. And it is this paradox which really is at the root of so much of the controversy going on today about press freedom and responsibility. The paradox arises from: (1) the basic philosophical assumption that a democratic people need information upon which to base their decisions, and (2) the basic free press principle built into the First Amendment of the U.S. Constitution (and into constitutions of other nations).

Quite naturally there are many citizens who look at the mass media, or certain of them, and see weaknesses in the way they are informing the public. So, the natural inclination is to evolve such a principle as this: if the press, or any unit of the press, fails to provide the kind of service the citizenry is entitled to in a democracy, it must forfeit its freedom. However worthy or unworthy such a rationale may be, it clearly points out the paradox mentioned above. For quite simply, the press is free and autonomous or it is not; and, of course, if it is regulated, controlled or directed from without (even in the name of "democratic utilitarianism"), it has ceased being free and autonomous.

[7] Franklin H. Littell, *Wild Tongues* (London: Collier-Macmillan, Ltd., 1969), p. 88.
[8] E. E. Schattschneider, *Two Hundred Million Americans in Search of a Government* (New York: Holt, Rinehart and Winston, Inc., 1969), p. 53.

Often the paradox is expressed in other terms; for example, some libertarians refer to two strains of freedom—*positive* and *negative* freedom. Positive freedom is the freedom to achieve some good (generally attributed to Rousseau), whereas negative freedom (usually attributed to Hobbes and Locke) is the freedom from restraint.[9] Many would say that "positive" freedom is responsible freedom and "negative" freedom is not responsible. I have always found this positive-negative dualism troublesome, for it would appear that if a person were not free of restraint, he would not have the freedom to achieve some good (of his own choice). Therefore, it would seem that the heart of the concept of freedom is really what is called "negative" freedom. If one is *free from restraint*, he is automatically free to achieve some good (if he elects to).

This "negative" freedom, then, implies the freedom to act autonomously. And presumably, when one acts autonomously, he at least *thinks* he is acting for *some good*. On the other hand, what is referred to as "positive" freedom smacks too much of the authoritarian concept of freedom, which grants the people the "freedom" to carry out what some elite has decided to be "good." It is little wonder that Rousseau, to whom this positive freedom concept is attributed, is so often considered an authoritarian. It is true that a slave is "free" in the sense that he is free from making choices for himself and, therefore, can provide pre-determined social *good*. But, as Sydney Harris has put it, "People who live in despotic or dictatorial societies have no true security—even though the despot or the state may provide everything they need—because they lack the freedom to make choices." [10]

The libertarians of the "positive freedom" school—which I call pseudo-libertarian—emphasize doing a *good*; they are really utilitarians and have restricted their concept of freedom to freedom to do something "good." This is certainly a very limited view of freedom and one which only elitist descendants of Plato would approve. The libertarian supporting "negative freedom" (regardless of its unfavorable connotation) is, in my view, the valid libertarian for he views freedom as autonomy (freedom from coercion) and knows that autonomy is really basic to *any* concept of freedom; beyond this, he recognizes that the truly free person (or journalistic medium) may choose *not* to act in accord with some social utilitarian objective. The autonomous man or journalistic medium does not have to *do anything* to be "free"; it is only necessary that he be unrestrained so that he can *choose* whether he wants to do anything or not.

Many people today either prefer the "positive freedom" position de-

[9] For a good discussion of this question, see Isaiah Berlin, *Two Concepts of Liberty* (Oxford: Clarendon Press, 1958).
[10] *The Authentic Person: Dealing with Dilemma* (Niles, Ill.: Argus Communications, 1972), p. 29.

scribed above or they say that, really, they cannot see any real difference between the two positions. Those who say either of these things are really the people who are setting in motion the machinery of journalistic control against which this whole book is a warning. For what they are saying, in effect, is simply this: freedom is freedom to do what society (or some instrumentality of society) demands for the good of society. They are putting the "social good" or "social responsibility" (as they see it) above the concept of freedom. This may be all right in the abstract, but in order to make it mean anything, it must be related to reality: in the context of journalism, for example, it implies some *outside* (not the media units themselves) person or group defining for the press what is meant by "the social good" or what is "socially responsible" journalism.

Those who advocate this "positive freedom" for journalism certainly think of themselves as libertarians; or they see themselves as climbing to some level even above libertarianism. Perhaps they are. But I see them, if they are in the sphere of libertarianism at all, as standing in the doorway to authoritarianism urging unsuspecting journalists to enter without warning them what just might be on the other side of the door. They do not call this door, of course, the door to authoritarianism, but the door to social responsibility. This way they can appeal not only to those who desire the comforts of submitting to authority, but also to the many journalists who sincerely want to act altruistically from humanistic motives and are willing to lay aside their freedom and their *autonomous humanism* which they evidently feel is inferior to some imposed, outside elitist power.

Much more could—and will later in this book—be said about the authoritarian and the libertarian orientations or journalistic theories. It has been admitted that this dualistic typology is basic and useful, but not very discriminating. From it, many ways of looking at theories of journalism can be formulated. Probably the best-known typology of press systems is the "four-theories" concept. Let us now look briefly at this popular theoretical model.

The "Four Theories" Typology

In 1956 three professors of communication—Fred S. Siebert, Theodore Peterson and Wilbur Schramm—brought out their *Four Theories of the Press* which went a long way in establishing such a typology in the minds of journalism educators and students. The little volume (in paperback since 1963) [11] has become standard reading in journalism departments and

---

[11] *Four Theories of the Press* (Urbana: Univ. of Illinois Press, 1963). Cf. for a good discussion of the four concepts (and a defense of the social responsibility theory): William L. Rivers in Chapter 2 of Rivers and Schramm, *Responsibility in Mass Communications*, revised ed. (New York: Harper & Row, 1969).

schools and has done much to legitimize the fourth "theory"—social responsibility. Almost every article and book dealing with philosophical bases for journalism has alluded to this book, commented on it or quoted from it. Its impact has unquestionably been great in spite of what I believe are significant weaknesses.

Siebert, Peterson and Schramm discuss journalism philosophy by presenting four theories ("concepts" might have been a more realistic term): 1) the authoritarian theory, 2) the libertarian theory, 3) the communist theory, and 4) the social responsibility theory. Very briefly, here are the main characteristics of each of these theories:

Authoritarian. The state, as the highest expression of institutionalized structure, supersedes the individual and makes it possible for the individual to acquire and develop a stable and harmonious life. Mass communication, then, supports the state and the government in power so that the total society may advance and the state may be viable and attain its objectives. The state (the "elite" that runs the state) directs the citizenry, which is not considered competent and interested enough to make critical political decisions. One man or an elite group is placed in a leadership role. As the group or person controls society generally, it (or he) also controls the mass media since they are recognized as vital instruments of social control.

The mass media, under authoritarianism, are educators and propagandists by which the power elite exercises social control. Generally the media are privately owned, although the leader or his "elite group" may own units in the total communication system. A basic assumption: a person engaged in journalism is so engaged as a special privilege granted by the national leadership. He, therefore, owes an obligation to the leadership. This press concept has formed, and now forms, the basis for many media systems of the world. The mass media, under authoritarianism, have only as much freedom as the national leadership at any particular time is willing to permit.

Libertarian. The "libertarian" press concept is generally traced back to England and the American colonies of the seventeenth century. Giving rise to the libertarian press theory was the philosophy that looked upon man as a rational animal with inherent natural rights. One of these rights was the right to pursue truth, and potential interferers (kings, governors, *et al*) would (or should) be restrained. Exponents of this press movement during the seventeenth century, and the 200 years which followed, included Milton, Locke, Erskine, Jefferson, and John Stuart Mill. Individual liberties were stressed by these philosophers, along with a basic trust in the people to take intelligent decisions (generally) *if* a climate of free expression existed.

In theory, a libertarian press functions to present the truth, however splintered it may be in a pluralism of voices. It is impossible to do this if it is controlled by some authority outside itself. Through the years many new ideas have been grafted onto early press libertarianism; many of them will be discussed later in this book. One of these, for example, is the general acceptance of a kind of obligation to keep the public abreast of governmental activities, of being a kind of "fourth branch of government" supplementing the executive, legislative and judicial branches. This is actually a rather recent concept, having been grafted on to the original libertarian theory. There is a basic faith, shown by libertarian advocates, that a free press—working in a *laissez faire*, unfettered situation—will naturally result in a pluralism of information and viewpoints necessary in a democratic society.

Communist. The communist theory of the press arose, along with the theory of communism itself, in the first quarter of the present century. Karl Marx was its father, drawing heavily on the ideas of his fellow German, Georg W. F. Hegel. The mass media in a communist society, said Marx, were to function basically to perpetuate and expand the socialist system. Transmission of social policy, not searching for the truth, was to be the main rationale for existence of a communist media system.

Mass media, under this theory, are instruments of government and integral parts of the State. They are owned and operated by the State and directed by the Communist Party or its agencies. Criticism is permitted in the media (i.e., criticism of failure to achieve goals), but criticism of basic ideology is forbidden. Communist theory, like that of authoritarianism, is based on the premise that the masses are too fickle and too ignorant and unconcerned with government to be entrusted with governmental responsibilities. Thus, the media have no real concern with giving them much information about governmental activities or leaders. Mass media are to do what is best for the state and party; and what is best determined by the elite leadership of State and Party. Whatever the media do to contribute to communism and the Socialist State is moral; whatever is done to harm or hinder the growth of communism is immoral.

Social Responsibility. This concept, a product of mid-twentieth century America, is said by its proponents to have its roots in libertarian theory. But it goes beyond the libertarian theory, in that it places more emphasis on the press's responsibility to society than on the press's freedom. It is seen as a higher level, theoretically, than libertarianism—a kind of moral and intellectual evolutionary trip from discredited "old" libertarianism to a "new" or perfected libertarianism where things are forced to work as they really should have worked under libertarian theory. The explainers and defenders of this "theory" maintain that they are libertarians, but socially responsible libertarians, contrasted presumably with other libertarians who (if their views and actions do not agree with those of the "new" libertarians) are not socially responsible.

This fourth theory of the press (discussed rather extensively in Chapter 4) has been drawn largely from a report published in 1947 by the Hutchins Commission.[12] Emerging from the Commission's publications and solidified in the literature of journalism by *Four Theories of the Press*, this new theory maintains that the importance of the press in modern society makes it absolutely necessary that an obligation of social responsibility be imposed on the media of mass communication.

Modifications of "Four Theories" Model

It seems very strange that the proponents of the "four theories" can be so well satisfied with their typology, especially with the social responsibility concept which is placed in parallel importance with the authoritarian, communist and libertarian. Actually the four theories are not parallel; logical parallelism holds up pretty well for the A, C and L, but the SR presents some problems. By having an SR theory, implication is given that the A, C and L theories are "irresponsible" theories, and that authoritarian, communist and libertarian press systems cannot be (or are not) responsible to their own societies. There is only one system, really, we are asked to believe, that is socially responsible, and that is the one which is *called* socially responsible by the proponents of this amorphous concept. Model A in Figure 1:1 indicates what I feel is the basic implication of the standard "four theories" model, showing not only that A and C are closely related, as are L and SR, but how the theories have developed (or are said to develop) historically.

The remainder of this chapter will present four modifications of the standard four theories typology—two rather simple ones of mine, a more complex progression model of Ralph Lowenstein, and finally a circular model which is believed to be most realistic of all.

Since the four-theories concept does not seem realistic to me, let us first examine two models utilizing the same four labels which perhaps will be somewhat more realistic. Still there is the problem with SR, but the following two models (see Models B and C of Figure 1:1) use SR (in the four-theories sense) but point up what is believed to be a more valid theoretical construct.

(1) *The "Three-and-One" Model.* As can be seen in Model B, the theories SR, A and C are all interlocking and are above the line separating

12 See Commission on Freedom of the Press, A *Free and Responsible Press* (Chicago: Univ. of Chicago Press, 1947).

journalistic control from journalistic freedom. And below this line is L, all alone. The implication is that social responsibility, authoritarianism and communism are all concepts springing from a belief in the need for some kind of control (from outside the media units themselves) over journalistic activities. The *only* theory which emphasizes freedom instead of control or "direction" is libertarianism.

(2) *The "Developmental Triangle" Model.* Model C depicts a kind of cyclic (or triangular) development or progression from one of the four concepts to another. Presumably, the progression would begin with A, developing into L, then to SR, and then back either to A or to C. It should be noted that in this model L is the highest (because, for me, it is best) concept, and the progression is *downward* to SR (not *upward* or to a higher plane) as in the standard four-theories model (Model A). This triangular model indicates that social responsibility is simply a step in the direction of either an authoritarian or communist system. This is certainly a far different assumption than is implied in the standard four-theories typology, but it seems to be a far more realistic one, and one which is consistent with the basic thesis of this book.

(3) *The Lowenstein Progression Model.* Also dissatisfied with the "four theories" typology, Ralph Lowenstein of the University of Missouri suggested a modification in 1971 and it was incorporated into a book which he and I wrote.[13] Lowenstein made some changes in the titles given to the basic press philosophies. Authoritarian and libertarian, in Lowenstein's typology, remain the same, but he abandoned "Soviet-Communist" (in the Siebert, Peterson and Schramm book) and replaced it with what he called *social-centralist.* The latter term admits a broad enough spectrum to include all the nations of the Eastern bloc, and yet removes the negative connotations of the term "communist" so that his new term may also be used to describe those centrally guided press systems in many developing nations.

The social-centralist philosophy is a modern modification of the communist and the authoritarian philosophies of the standard "four theories" concept. There is government ownership and/or government regulation of the media system. The main difference is that this new (SC) concept, in all its variations, would control the media not primarily to keep them from harming the ruling elite, but to channel the power of the media into what the state sees as constructive educational, developmental and political goals.

Lowenstein also discarded the term "social responsibility" (a wise decision) because it was ambiguous and because he desired to substitute a

---

[13] *Media, Messages, and Men: New Perspectives in Communication* (New York: David McKay Co., Inc., 1971), pp. 185–89.

"FOUR THEORIES" TYPOLOGY

(Evolutionary & Relational Implications):

Standard Four-Theories Model

(Model A):

Authoritarian   Communist   Libertarian   Social Respon.

More Realistic Theoretical Models

(Model B):

-- media cooperation
-- outside pressure &
      coercion of media
-- social determinism
-- monistic concept of
      "good" journalism

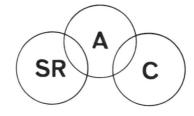

Journalistic
Control

-- media competition
-- no outside coercion
-- self determinism (media)
-- "non consensus" orientation
-- pluralist concept of "good"
                journalism

Journalistic Freedom

L

(Model C):

Developmental Triangle Model

Natural flow: Authoritarian to
    Libertarian to Social Respon-
    sibility and back again to
    either Authoritarian or
    Communist.

more discriminating and meaningful term. So he coined the term *social-libertarian*. His SL concept bears the same relationship to the standard libertarian philosophy as the social-centralist (SC) does to the authoritarian, the main difference being that the SL is only a short step away from the libertarian. The modification is needed only, as Lowenstein sees it, to assure that the libertarian philosophy works as it should work. Self-regulation is preferable, but some government regulation is unavoidable to keep factors such as monopoly and shrinkage of pluralism under control. Lowenstein prefers the SL concept just as Siebert, Peterson and Schramm seemed to prefer the social responsibility theory. He certainly does not think that such a system is perfect; in fact, as Figure 1:2 shows,[14] there is still a Utopian System out there somewhere which provides the maximum of press freedom, social stability, pluralism, public access and medium self-determinism. But, according to Lowenstein, until such a Utopian system emerges—and there are grave doubts that it ever will—the Social Libertarian system will probably be the best.

Actually Lowenstein's developmental typology, so far as what has been said above, is not much different from the old standard "four-theories" approach, except that he hides the old concept of social responsibility under a new label (SL) and the old concept of communism (and authoritarianism) under a new label (SC). But the main contribution of his model, as I see it, is that he ties his press concepts or theories to the developmental stages of society (see Fig. 1:2) and postulates a kind of *forced* libertarianism. His authoritarian system is found in a simple or under-developed society where only a small segment (elite) of the population is literate. From here, the system evolves into a moderately developed system (which is characterized by libertarianism or "uncontrolled" freedom). This is not the ultimate or best stage, for Lowenstein, and the system can either progress in the direction of Social Libertarianism (SL) with an emphasis on private ownership and self-regulation, or it can go toward Social Centralism (SC) with an emphasis on government ownership and regulation.

Although Lowenstein's conceptual model is more sophisticated and realistic than the older "four theories" model, it appears to have the same basic flaw: when a system *forces* libertarianism, for whatever motive, it is no longer libertarian. Forced, or directed, libertarianism presents a logical contradiction. One might ask if this is simply not an authoritarian theory being used to assure (or try to assure) a libertarian system. Lowenstein does, however, appear to recognize the value of basic libertarian tenets, but

[14] Figure 1:2, a conceptual model of Lowenstein's progression typology, was designed by the author and any distortions and incorrect implications which it may contain are not the fault of Dr. Lowenstein.

he assumes their imperfectability if left to the free working of a *laissez faire* system. Or, even more, he assumes the necessity of *perfectability* in libertarianism. He would, therefore, try to provide a system which would, in effect, guarantee the proper working of a libertarian system. But, of course, this same thing could be said of the authors of *Four Theories of the Press* in respect to "social responsibility" and perhaps even to Robert Hutchins and his twelve commissioners back in 1947 when they tossed this whole freedom-responsibility question into the journalistic arena.

(4) *The Political-Press Circle*. Although the three modifications of the regular "four theories" typology presented above are believed to be improvements over their progenitors, they all have basic weaknesses. They are modified pigeon-hole models which tend to treat classifications as largely mutually exclusive and independent. In most such models authoritarianism is one extreme on a spectrum and libertarianism is the other; and with all such models, the extremes with their specific labels tend to become "pigeon-holes" and it is very easy for classification to retrogress into a basic binary type. People and media systems very easily become authoritarian or libertarian, fascist or communist. However the model may be designed, usually it is a kind of spectrum-with-dominant-pigeon-holes with authoritarianism on one end and libertarianism on the other. Probably a more realistic spectrum model would place anarchy over against statism or control (of whatever type).

But instead of a linear pigeon-hole or progression model, a *circle of progression* with the press tied in with political philosophy is more interesting and probably far more realistic. Authoritarianism is farthest away from libertarianism, but they are at opposites of a political-press circle and can be reached by any society by going in *either* direction—right or left. A vertical line through the center of the circle (see Figure 1:3) marks the extremes—at the top of the circle, anarchy, and at the bottom, totalitarianism. As a society or system leaves libertarianism (at the top of the circle), it can either progress down and around the circle toward statism and authoritarianism by going to the left through the route of socialism, or by going to the right through capitalism. In either case it reaches the same destination.

The circle arranged in this manner also indicates that there is a natural tendency toward authoritarianism; communism and fascism (the two faces of authoritarianism) are at the bottom of the circle, whereas libertarianism is at the top, and the implication is that it is harder to go "up" the circle than it is to come "down" it. Freedom is up; enslavement is down.

Consistent with the basic thesis of this book, it must be said that journalism is losing freedom generally and drifting—in some cases left, and

Figure 1:2

LOWENSTEIN PROGRESSION TYPOLOGY

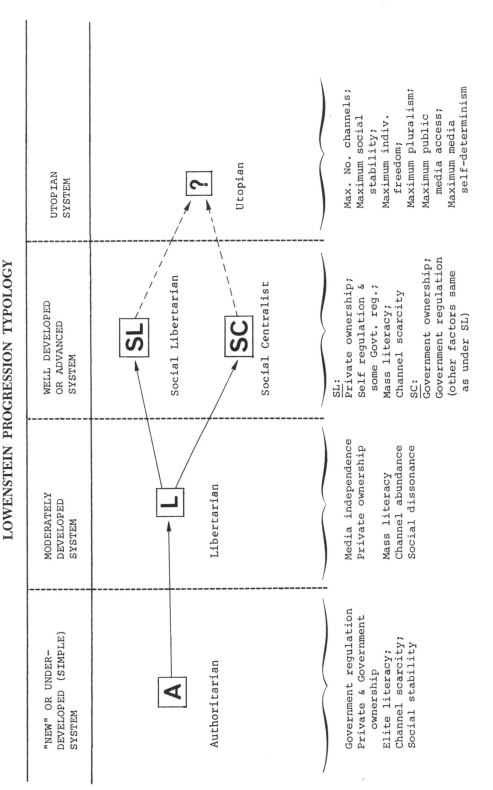

Figure 1:3

THE POLITICAL-PRESS CIRCLE

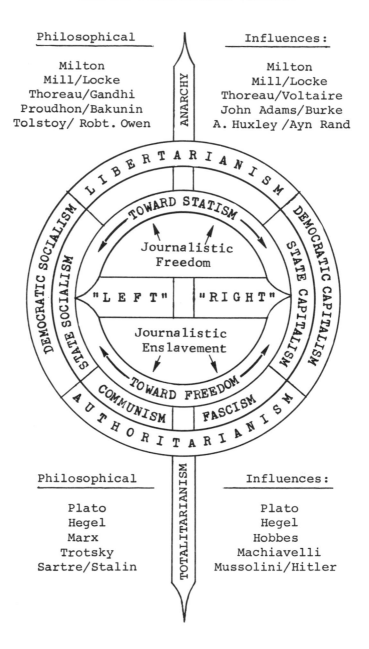

Philosophical _____ | Influences: _____

Milton | Milton
Mill/Locke | Mill/Locke
Thoreau/Gandhi | Thoreau/Voltaire
Proudhon/Bakunin | John Adams/Burke
Tolstoy/ Robt. Owen | A. Huxley /Ayn Rand

Philosophical _____ | Influences: _____

Plato | Plato
Hegel | Hegel
Marx | Hobbes
Trotsky | Machiavelli
Sartre/Stalin | Mussolini/Hitler

in others, right—around the circle toward authoritarianism. As the Political-Press Circle in Figure 1:3 shows, journalistic freedom can be lost in either socialistic (collectivist) societies or in capitalistic (individualist) societies. There is really no one road to serfdom.

As societies grow and get more complex, it is natural for collectivist thinking to dominate over individualistic thinking. This gives a kind of utilitarian rationale for statist control. Social stability and harmony are increasingly glorified and individual deviation is increasingly vilified. The basic fact of social growth and complexity, in a very real way, sounds the death knell for press—as well as individual—freedom. This is indeed a gloomy prospect. What can be done? This drift toward conformity and control cannot really be stopped, but it can be delayed. Libertarians of the "autonomy type" can delay the day of press enslavement, and when that day comes they can go under fighting. It is true, there is a kind of socio-historical determinism implied here, and this will be developed further in the next chapter.

2

Media and
National Development

A NATION'S communication media develop as the nation develops. Significant changes in the scope, sophistication, and purpose of the mass media are evidences of political modification in a society. This is generally known as the "reflective theory" of media-government relationship and was discussed briefly in the preceding chapter. A country's political system (stemming from the political ideology) is obviously related to the direction and speed of a country's total national development. If this basic assumption is true, and it would certainly appear to be, then media and national development join in a kind of symbiotic relationship of a complex and intriguing nature. It is this symbiotic relationship that has been consuming more and more of the time and effort of researchers and theorists in the related fields of journalism, sociology and political science since about mid-point in this century.

All kinds of questions are raised pertaining to the relationship between political ideology and communication philosophy, between political systems and communication systems, between politics and national development, and between communication and national development. This chapter will summarize some of the basic problems in this area of concern, will present many of the conclusions which have been reached by researchers, will offer some fresh insights into the media-political symbiosis, and will present

45

and discuss a multi-factor model of media and national development which is in keeping with the overall thesis of this book: that nations and press systems are becoming ever more authoritarian.

Spurred on by UNESCO and a number of potent "international outreach agencies" (e.g., the U.S.'s Agency for International Development) of the major powers, a fascination with, and emphasis on, communication and national development has ridden into academic and governmental consciousness on the crest of the post-World War II wave-of-concern with international communication generally.[1]

Scholars have made some interesting efforts to fashion meaningful theories about the role of institutionalized communication in the national developmental process, but it is obviously too early for coherent theories of communication and national development to emerge. Their time has simply not arrived, and we are still in a period of unsynthesized case studies, theoretical dialogue, and splintered speculation about this whole area of concern.

Anyone expecting startling insights into the question of media impact on national development is destined for disappointment. At best he may get a few glimmers of understanding from a hodge-podge of theorizing and uneven research done mainly in underdeveloped regions of the world.

Basic Literature

The literature on this subject is far from skimpy. In America alone, scholars such as Daniel Lerner, Lucian Pye, Karl Deutsch, Gabriel Almond, Ithiel de Sola Pool and Wilbur Schramm have produced weighty tomes related to the subject of communication and national development, and many others—such as Everett Rogers, John McNelly, William Hachten, V. M. Mishra, Hamid Mowlana, Vincent Farace and the late Paul Deutschmann have shed further light on this complex subject in books and articles. Their basic conclusions, when there are any, are very similar; and the vast amount of literature which appeared in the last several decades has been largely descriptive, correlational, and speculative—and to a rather great degree, co-terminous.[2]

[1] A few of the UNESCO studies will give an idea of the emphasis in the area of communication and national development since 1950: *Radio in Fundamental Education in Undeveloped Areas* (1950); *Television, A World Survey* (1953); *Developing Mass Media in Asia* (1960); *Los Medios de Informacion en America Latina* (1961); *Mass Media in the Developing Countries* (1961), and *Developing Information Media in Africa* (1962). Since about 1962 developmental studies and works by UNESCO have seemed to disappear, to be replaced by many books and articles by communications scholars of many countries.

[2] A few books contributing to the literature of communication and national development follow: Karl Deutsch, *Nationalism and Social Communications* (1953); Elihu

Most of these studies indicate relationships among such factors as economics, religion, press freedom, industrialization, etc. Several studies, for example, have found a high correlation between the measures of economic growth and measures of communications growth—hardly a finding which would surprise anyone. Daniel Lerner, for example, noted high correlations among four factors: urbanization, literacy, media participation and political participation. Deutsch pointed out a correlation between mass communication of a country and its national spirit and action. Such correlations abound; researchers are constantly finding additional ones. A conclusion emerges: *Communication is necessary, not only for all aspects of a person's development, but also for all aspects of a nation's development.*

So, in a sense we now see that most of the work done in this area has focused on the entire national organism—on the process of *interaction*—and, of course, on *inter-relationships.* What we have had, up to now, have mainly been what might be termed *Gestalt* studies—descriptive, correlational and relational profiles which try to focus on communication networks within nations, while at the same time showing how these networks function in concert with other national institutions.

Lack of Cause-Effect Studies. Notably lacking are credible *cause-effect* studies which give valid insights into the fundamental question that seems to plague us: Do the mass media bring about national development, and if so, how and to what extent?

There is an obvious reason why such a question is difficult (or impossible) to answer, and it lies in the intrinsic weakness of social science research itself: Too many human and social variables impose themselves to make for a neat experiment. How can we have a society working normally and realistically and isolate one variable (the mass media) and test its impact? We cannot really be very optimistic about this type of research.

It could be, however, that one day some researcher or Research Foundation will be able to establish a nation which will agree not to have any communications media for—say—ten years. At the same time, perhaps another nation of equal constituency would be created, but this one *with* primitive communications media from the start. Then we could sit back and happily observe the development of both countries for ten years—

Katz and Paul Lazarsfeld, *Personal Influence* (1955); Daniel Lerner, *The Passing of Traditional Society* (1958); Gabriel Almond et al, *The Politics of the Developing Areas* (1960); Everett M. Rogers, *Diffusion of Innovations* (1962); Wilbur Schramm, *Mass Media and National Development* (1964); Lucian Pye (ed.), *Communications and Political Development* (1963); W. Phillips Davidson, *International Political Communication* (1965); E. Lloyd Sommerlad, *The Press in Developing Countries* (1966); H.-D. Fischer and J. C. Merrill (eds.), *International Communication* (1970); V. M. Mishra, *Communication and Modernization in Urban Slums* (1972).

one nation with communications media at the outset and the other without them; but in all other ways the two nations would be operating and growing naturally. After ten years we might be able to make some valid conclusions as to the specific impact of communications media on national development.

But it is hard to imagine such an experiment developing. And even if it did, I am not convinced such a test would be meaningful for the simple reason that it would seem as unrealistic to isolate a communications system from a nation as it would be to isolate an economic system or a political system from a nation and expect it to function in *any* conceivable manner for *one* year—much less ten.

Some researchers, it is true, have studied the impact of mass media on a small social unit—for example, a village in India.[3] The natural temptation is to project these findings to a *national* context. Certainly such studies have their value, but it is doubtful that their implications for more complex nation-states are very meaningful or valid. One might just as logically study the impact of a message on *one person* and project it to a whole group of people.

McNelly's Four "Positions." John T. McNelly of the University of Wisconsin has written of the contemporary lack of "any full-blown theories of the role of mass communication in the development of nations," but he postulates that at least there are four "general positions"— or points of view—which have emerged relative to mass communication's developmental role.[4]

First is what he refers to as the *Null Position.* This position holds that mass communication has little or no role in national development. Usually those taking this position place great emphasis on literacy and education, or on economics, and not on the mass media.

Second is what McNelly calls the *Enthusiastic Position.* This is usually the position held by UNESCO and academicians of one kind or another. Here the mass media have been assigned a *decisive* role in—not only national development—but in bringing about peace and stability. This is, of course, a tempting position for journalists, but most scholars think it highly dubious.

Third, according to McNelly, is the *Cautious Position.* Supporting

[3] Examples of case studies: Y. V. L. Rao, *Communication and Development: A Study of Two Indian Villages* (Minneapolis: Univ. of Minnesota Press, 1966), and William B. Ward, "Press Media in India's Agricultural Development," *Vidura* (Indian Press Institute, New Delhi), Vol. 18, No. 5, 1971.
[4] John T. McNelly in David Berlo (ed.), *Mass Communication and the Development of Nations* (East Lansing: Michigan State Univ. International Communications Institute, 1968). See Ch. 1 "Perspectives on the Role of Mass Communication in the Development Process."

this position are a number of studies cautioning that mass communication is not omnipotent and that a multitude of social and cultural factors serve to mediate or even nullify the impact of the mass media. The two-step flow hypothesis, proposed by Elihu Katz and Paul Lazarsfeld, relates to this position; it maintains that information and ideas often flow from the mass media to opinion leaders and from them to the general public. Certainly this stress on the importance of opinion leaders in disseminating information would tend to deemphasize the importance of the mass media's *direct* ("hypodermic needle" model) impact on the society and would stress a more complex inter-personal social network.

The fourth and last of McNelly's positions is the *Pragmatic Position,* the one he prefers. Persons accepting this position realize that they do not have adequate theory to predict the impact of information flow for all types of messages on different societies in all situations. McNelly suggests that we might adopt what he calls the "pragmatic" position: Try it and see if it works. Here the researcher seeks empirical evidence on the effects of mass communication in a culture, society or nation. He does not try to set up an *a priori* guide or theory; he simply checks out the consequences case by case as they occur.

This pragmatic position accommodates diverse kinds of data and hypotheses. It leaves open the possibility of *no* media impact, a *limited* impact or a *heavy* impact, depending on the circumstances. If it were to be dignified as a "theory," it might well be called a *situational consequence* theory of mass communication impact.[5]

If we accept McNelly's "pragmatic" position as the most useful, then in effect the admission is being made that each case must be looked at separately and the following question posed: *What has been the observable impact of the mass media in this specific case?* This position is quite satisfying to those who do not demand a predictive theory, but for those who want a more encompassing theoretical framework it will seem nothing more than a continuation of "piece-meal" case studies that generally remain unrelated and virtually meaningless.

A Review of Basic Findings

Let us leave the area of "positions" and theoretical problems of basic research for a moment and turn to a few of the principal conclusions and generalizations which have come from a rather sizable number of tech-

---

[5] By a "situational consequence theory of mass communication impact" is meant that the impact of the media is relative to the particular situation and can only be ascertained empirically by a researcher observing the total message transmission and noting its impact through observable responses and consequences.

nical and observational studies since the end of World War II. Most of these appear to be generally accepted by most students of communication and national development, so in some cases the following statements will not be attributed to any one person.

● Mass Communication is necessary to a national consciousness, spirit, and concerted national action. (Karl Deutsch).

● Social communication's structure is reflective of the structure and development of society. (W. Schramm). Communication grows and changes with society because it is something society *does*; it is the way society lives. And, it might be added, communication is a *function* of society or a *tool* of society with which society constantly fashions and repairs itself.[6]

● Communications media contribute to (a) a people's awareness of potentialities, (b) dissatisfaction and a desire to change, (c) a heightened sense of collective power among the people, (d) either stabilizing or disrupting the society, and (e) either instilling in the people realistic goals or creating extravagant expectations. (It is well to remember that communication activities contribute to these results—but it should be noted that *communication activities* are not necessarily carried on through *mass* media. For example, in early stages of development we can find rather complex networks of informal and personal pre-"mass media" communication working well.)

● Mass media provide information to a nation's people, and the more information people get, the more they are interested in political developments. (Schramm).[7]

● Communication can (a) raise the goals of the society, (b) spread news of these goals, and (c) widen the acceptance of these goals.

● Pye sees the communication process in nation-building as mainly serving an amplifying function, but also as linking the political process to the people, providing the essential bases for rationality in mass polities, and giving form and structure to the political process by reminding politicians that political acts have consequences and the populace of what

[6] Schramm stresses these aspects of social communication which reflect the structure and development of society: *size* of communication activities reflects the *economic* development of the society; the *controls* on communication reflect the political development of the society; the *content* of communication at any given time reflects the *value* patterns of the society, and the pattern of communication networks reflect the homogeneity of culture and geography of a society.

[7] An important consideration in Schramm's statement about information and political development is the stage of development at which the nation finds itself: this largely determines (a) the impact of the media, and (b) the kind of media most effective. Mass media, it would appear, become more and more important in speeding up modernization as the nation rises to ever-higher levels; at the very lowest level, mass media are virtually non-existent, therefore unimportant.

the acts are and what the consequences might be.[8] This, of course, is an important function of communication in advanced or well-developed nations, as was exemplified in the United States by the great "Watergate Story" of 1973.

● Schramm says communication must be used (a) to contribute to a feeling of nation-ness, (b) as a voice of national planning, (c) to help teach necessary skills, (d) to extend the effective market, (e) to help people look to the future, and (f) to prepare people to play their role as a nation among nations.[9]

● In transitional nations (most of the world's nations) the mass media develop almost simultaneously with the new awareness of the outside world and a new national self-consciousness.

● New nations tend to have a one-party press and have media systems of a rather highly authoritarian nature.

● Mass communications can be used either as a national stimulant or tranquilizer. (As Schramm says, the mere presence of a communication system does not necessarily contribute to national development; it depends on the *use of*, and *content of*, the media.) Programs and stories could be largely entertainment and fantasy, for example, and could actually divert attention *away from* national problems. This is exactly what Polynesian media appeared to be doing in the '70's, according to a study by Ralph Barney.[10]

● A rapidly developing mass media system—or a well-developed one, for that matter—does not necessarily contribute to a wider and more democratic political base. (Schramm: Efficient communication works as

[8] At least two things can be concluded about the importance of the mass media to political development and functioning: (a) in small or new nations mass media are not very important in the political realm, and (b) in authoritarian or communist nations mass media are not as important to political functioning as they are in libertarian, democratic nations.

[9] See Schramm's *Mass Media and National Development* (Stanford: Stanford Univ. Press, 1964). As pertains to Schramm's admonition about media use, it should be noted that an important consideration is the *proper* use of media—or the use of the *proper* media. These techniques or media should be meaningful and understandable to people at a certain stage of national development. For example, there is little need to introduce magazines and newspapers into a society that is basically illiterate and isolated geographically. Radio or "wall newspapers" would be much more appropriate and effective.

[10] Ralph D. Barney, "The Mass Media, Their Environment and Prospects in Western Polynesia" (unpublished Ph.D. thesis, University of Missouri, summer 1971). Barney, of the journalism faculty of Brigham Young University, found that the new nations of Polynesia have a sense of cultural and racial "consciousness" but almost no national or political consciousness. At least this was true outside of a very small elite leadership group. And it should be noted that the mass media—if you can call them that—are doing little there to enhance a national consciousness; rather they are hitting their small audiences either with certain kinds of educational programs or with "escapist" entertainment.

well for the dictator as for the democrat—maybe better, because the dictator is likely to have a monopoly on communication; [11] but communication development *provides the conditions* for wider democratic participation— if the political philosophy permits it.)

• More than two-thirds of the world's citizens reside in nations which are normally classified as "emerging," "underdeveloped" or "modernizing." [12]

• The press in underdeveloped nations is almost exclusively the result of Western efforts and influence, says Herbert Passin; no precedent for journalists can be found in traditional (emerging) societies. Journalism develops almost simultaneously with national self-consciousness and growing awareness of the outside world.[13]

• Mass communication has brought to developing nations a "revolution of rising expectations" (in the 1950s) and since the 1960s a "revolution of rising frustrations." People of backward nations suddenly sensed through the mass media that a better life was possible; then they realized, when they began trying to get this better life, that their attempts generally were thwarted, leading to increased frustration.[14]

• Mass communication has often been overemphasized in considering impact on national development, according to Pye. "It is apparent . . . that some governments in new countries once placed excessive faith in the potentialities of modern means of mass communications. Deeper analysis shows that the press and radio can have a profound influence in changing the ways of people only if they are fully supported by the informal, social channels of communication which are intimately related to basic social processes. Rapid national development calls for the coordinated and reinforcing use of both the impersonal mass media and the more personal, face-to-face pattern of social communication." [15]

---

[11] A rapidly developing media system—or a well-developed one—does not necessarily contribute to a wider and more democratic political base. Examples of the USSR, Spain, Egypt, Taiwan, Greece, the Philippines and Israel may be given. Note that all of these nations partially rationalize their press controls and lack of general freedom by pointing to internal and external dangers to their national security. Even such nations as the United States are prone to do this from time to time.

[12] W. Phillips Davison, *International Political Communication* (New York: Frederick A. Praeger, 1965), p. 130. Cf. for an excellent survey of communications in these "emerging" nations: Chapter 3 ("Traditional Societies") in Ronald C. Benge, *Communication and Identity* (London: Clive Bingley Ltd., 1972).

[13] Herbert Passin, in Lucian Pye (ed.), *Communications and Political Development* (Princeton: Princeton University Press, 1963), p. 98.

[14] Daniel Lerner in Pye, *op. cit.*, pp. 327–31. Cf. Ronald Benge, *Communication and Identity*—Ch. 6 ("Development and Communications").

[15] Lucian Pye in Pye, *op. cit.*, pp. 9–10. Cf. Gunnar R. Naesselund, "From Information to Communication Systems in Development," *Vidura* (New Delhi), February, 1973.

"Cause-Effect Interaction"

Having summarized some of the general findings or indicators of the impact of mass media on a nation's development, let me present a few of my observations and reactions. I have always considered media systems mainly as reflectors or indicators of a nation's progress, freedom, sophistication and modernization—and *not as determinants*. But I do not have any more real evidence to back up this notion than do those who are convinced that the media are *change agents*. I see the whole question as correlational or relational. Many social scientists believe, and I concur, that causal proof cannot be obtained in complex social situations.

The safest stance to take is what might be called the "cause-effect interaction" position, a stance which maintains that the media and other factors and forces operating *simultaneously* within a nation bring about growth and progress. They are inseparable—but correlational and relational. This is not nearly as impressive as being able to maintain that the mass media cause or determine national growth, but it is a great deal safer.

To propose *single-factor determinism* is always a great temptation, but much more realistic is the "cause-effect interaction" approach; it is not only safer and more realistic, but undoubtedly it is the most rational approach. In a sense, I am saying that for all *practical* purposes the chicken and egg develop simultaneously and are so interrelated that we must talk about "chicken-egg relationships" and not about chickens causing eggs or eggs causing chickens. The important thing is that we have both chickens *and* eggs. And, where one finds no chickens there are no eggs, and where one finds no eggs there are no chickens. It is largely by using such correlational or interaction concepts and adapting them to normal social progression that I have designed the basic Developmental Model (see Figure 2) presented in this chapter.

Conflict and National Development

Many ways exist for considering the communications media and national development. Several have already been suggested. One way, which I have not seen before, is from the point of view of conflict in the society and communication's relation to it. It is postulated here that as individual, political and press freedom increases, social conflict also increases and as freedom diminishes, conflict decreases. Underdeveloped or *traditional* societies have very little conflict; *transitional* and early modern societies have the most, and late *modern* societies have almost none. The social "conflict cycle," then, is highly correlated to the general political cycle. Let us look a little closer at the three basic stages of development just mentioned:

(1) *Traditional Society:* Conflict (friction) is mainly within the autocratic or elite leadership group; communication, then, is of a personal nature, designed to inform the active agents in governmental military and institutional hierarchies, and to stabilize society. Since there are no true *mass* media (see Figure 2) designed to bring "the people" into a sharing of policy, conflict exists principally among competing elite *persons* who might be competing for power. Communication channels are personal and informal (*elite* media), and are used mainly to try to develop a viable and outwardly stable political system by easing tensions and supporting infant institutions. Communication's main aim is to eliminate conflict and bring social stability.

(2) *Transitional Society:* In this more highly developed society (stage of development), there is likelihood of considerable political power conflict, class conflict, party conflict and institutional conflict. Communication becomes less supportive and monolithic and increasingly becomes more competitive, ideological and pluralistic. Communication is considered a political weapon or tool—a way to gain power for some and dissipate competing and conflicting power. *Mass* media are put in use not simply for solidifying and harmonizing the society, but as propaganda (change) agents—internally and externally. Communication's main function in this stage is to help in political conflict as a means for gaining party, group or personal power.

In the later phase of this stage, libertarianism develops and the media units themselves have maximum self-determinism. Competition and pluralism grows. (See Fig. 2.) Government's control decreases, individual freedom expands and governmental democracy dominates. The mass media spread their general information to medium-sized and large populations.

(3) *Modern Society:* Actually there are two main phases of development in a modern society—a kind of *early* phase where individual and media freedom is still extolled; where ideological conflict among factions, classes and parties is widespread; where the mass media *increase* dissonance and provide a catalyst for change and a pluralism of news and views to all citizens. Then there is a *later* phase flowing into authoritarianism and finally totalitarianism (see Fig. 2) where conflict is discouraged (or banned) and what little there may be is among political factions and strong leaders, and where mass media are mainly used for internal *social control* and external *propaganda*. The overall purpose of the media: to stabilize and direct society and to propagandize other societies.

Profile of a Traditional Society

It might be well to consider further these three "societies" (or developmental stages), first describing the most primitive of the stages—the *traditional* society and its inter-relationship with the mass media.

When we are talking about an "underdeveloped" or traditional society, I would postulate two things about mass media: (1) At this stage of national development there are *really no mass media* (See Fig. 2) within the nation, and (2) The Power Structure or Elite (autocrats) of the nation at this early stage *do not really want a mass media system*.

True "mass" media in this earliest stage are non-existent; only specialized or *elite* media are to be found. No mass media exist mainly because there is no mass literate audience; related to this is the fact that there is a kind of tribal isolationism, poor transportation and communication facilities, and low economic levels. At any rate, media cannot really communicate *with* (or even *to*) the masses of people. What *is* present at this stage of national development are elite lines of communication: from elite to elite within the Power Structure. So it can be reasonably said that the traditional society has *elite* media, not *mass* media.

Emphasis here is on communication of basic policy, aims, objectives, plans, etc. within a rather small select governing group—not on sharing policy material with the general populace. In fact, the leadership elite feel that mass communication is a danger—not an asset—to national growth and cohesiveness. So the elite lines of communication are set up (conferences, luncheons, meetings, workshops, etc.) at a high level on a *personal, seclusive* basis.[16] The object: to rally the elite of the nation to nation-building and loyalty to the ruling Power Structure.

Little attention is given in this developmental stage to the masses—to their participation in government, to their achieving literacy, to their "right to know" and all such things. These concerns appear at a later stage when the nation is fairly well-established, is stable, and has what is considered by the elite a viable political and economic base. But at this very early stage, the elite of the Power Structure do not feel that the nation can "afford" all the trappings of political sophistication and libertarianism.

Authoritarianism is considered not only most expedient at this point, but most rational. The general assumption: the people are unable to rule themselves in a traditional society; they do not even expect to. And, the elite are not anxious to encourage them through mass communication *to*

---

[16] It is obvious that in many nations the *elite media* actually supplement the informal communication activities such as luncheons, conferences, fairs, etc.—not the other way around.

expect to—at least not until the complex foundation of nationhood is worked out by the ruling autocracy.[17] Most of these early leaders (usually military men) are convinced that the people (the masses) want and expect strong rule imposed from the top and these leaders are determined to give it to them. The Power Structure elite, therefore, decide what will be communicated and just how fast lines of communication will be opened to wider and wider segments of the population.

The elite of the Power Structure, then, at this early stage determine the *nature* of—as well as the quality and quantity of—the communication media.[18] Therefore, if anything determines or causes national development at this stage, it is the leadership elite—using informal and specialized media. So it may be said that media in new nations are creatures of a small elite group and develop very slowly and in accordance with careful planning by the elite. As the media *become mass*, the nation is passing from the traditional to the *transitional* stage. (Then, as the media pass through a mass-oriented stage into a more pluralistic or specialized stage, the nation emerges from the upper reaches of the transitional developmental stage into the final or *modern* stage. See Fig. 2.)

In the earliest or traditional stage that I have been discussing, it is not really important to have *mass* support for the leadership—but it is important to control major institutions and to have *military* support. The elite set about slowly instilling in the people the national "consciousness" referred to earlier, giving them a set of common goals, and stressing cultural, racial and religious similarities. Also, it is important at this stage to provide for the people a *common enemy*. This is certainly a potent cohesion factor. A common enemy helps the people subordinate their differences and gives them a common *negative objective*. People can, as Eric Hoffer and others have pointed out, be rallied easiest when they can all be *against* something (some country, ideology, or group).[19] Concern with stressing what the people *are to be for* comes later in the transitional and modern stages of development.

Many persons from countries exemplifying this traditional stage, or even the early transitional stage which follows it, are irritated by the "advanced" nations' tendency to force their conception of *development* upon them. Development, they insist, must take into account the cultural context of a particular country, its traditions, and so forth. And, they insist

---

[17] See William A. Hachten, "Newspapers in Africa: Change or Decay?" *Seminar: A Quarterly Review for Newspapermen* (Dec. 1971) for a look at government press intervention and its harm to national development in new African nations.

[18] By "nature" of the mass media in the primitive society is meant the basic press concept: purposes, aims, objectives; "nature" in terms of guiding philosophy or theory. This is quite different from *quality* and *quantity* of the media.

[19] Eric Hoffer, *The True Believer* (New York: Mentor Books, 1958), p. 86.

with considerable justification, economic and technological growth should not be the main indicator of national "development." Chanchal Sarkar, one of India's most outstanding journalists, recommends a "new journalism of development" which would reflect and lead the public into thinking more fairly and realistically about this subject. He writes:

> In the underdeveloped countries . . . we stand at a crossroad without signposts. We are in search of a new philosophy of development in which GNP is not the king. . . . the philosophy and the strategy must aim to preserve some of the liberation freedoms, which are taken for granted in the advanced social welfare countries but which, in underdeveloped societies, have been enjoyed only by a handful of highly privileged people.[20]

The model of development which I present in this chapter (see Fig. 2) does go beyond the economic factor and postulates several factors—including libertarianism—which are important in the progression of development. Some traditional societies, especially in Africa, appear to be trying to by-pass the newspaper age and go directly into full-fledged broadcast journalism. The British press consultant and critic, Tom Hopkinson, quotes an official of a former French colony as saying: "We shall by-pass the newspaper age just as we shall by-pass the railway age. We shall go straight into radio and television—government-controlled, of course." [21]

Hopkinson frowns on such suggestions, believing that newspapers "are an essential part of the working of a modern democracy"; I tend to agree with him, but I do not assume that *all* traditional societies—or at least their leadership—believe that democracy is best for them. Broadcast media, controlled by the State, can certainly by-pass the imposing barrier of illiteracy and provide cybernetive information directly and effectively. Broadcasting is undoubtedly the most potent control instrument which an elite group can use to give a nation a consciousness and stability.

Apparently recognizing this, Hopkinson admits that "in the special circumstances of Africa today an unusual degree of responsibility is rightly demanded of the journalist," and that press freedom "has clearly got to mean something different from what it means in Brussels or New York." Even though I do not pretend to know what it means even in Brussels or New York, I will readily agree that in a new or traditional society it must, if it is used at all, mean something quite different from independent editorial self-determinism by the media. It is only in the next stage—the

---

[20] Chanchal Sarkar, "Development and the New Journalism," *Vidura* (New Delhi), October 1972, p. 338. Cf. Edward W. Ploman, "New Trends in Communication," *Vidura*, April 1973, pp. 93–97.
[21] Tom Hopkinson, "Africa: Battle for Survival," *WAY Forum* (Brussels), No. 57, Dec. 1965, p. 3.

transitional—that government control slackens and media independence or autonomy has a real chance for viability.

Profile of a Transitional Society

A society passes slowly from the traditional stage, just discussed, into the transitional (or intermediary) stage. It is unreasonable to expect a political or media system to pick up democratic and libertarian philosophies overnight. As Aldous Huxley observes, "No people that passes abruptly from a state of subservience under the rule of a despot to the completely unfamiliar state of political independence can be said to have a fair chance of making democratic institutions work." [22]

As the society becomes more affluent, chances increase for its general progress into new philosophical frontiers of democracy and press libertarianism. As Figure 2 will show, growth and decline of societal prosperity is closely related to democracy and freedom. Huxley makes this point when he says that "liberalism flourishes in an atmosphere of prosperity and declines as declining prosperity makes it necessary for the government to intervene ever more frequently and drastically in the affairs of its subjects." [23]

A very important factor in the transitional society is the natural pull toward democracy and libertarianism. Another characteristic of this society is that media tend to be general or "mass" rather than specialized and elite, although some elite media persist and are supplemented by specialized media reaching segments of the general public.

In the early and middle phases of this transitional stage, circulations of print media are still rather small and lag behind rising literacy. This is largely due to the heritage of elitism and government control which has carried over from the traditional stage. It appears that newspapers, free of controls, can expand and grow much faster than those under government restrictions. Tarzie Vittachi, a noted Indian journalist, is prone to agree.[24] He writes:

> The failure of the newspapers of India and Ceylon to keep pace with the growth of literacy must, in substantial measure, be attributed to state controls. Indian newspaper publishers as well as working journalists have repeatedly demanded the liberalization of government controls on the import of newsprint and machinery for expansion of the press.

[22] Aldous Huxley, *Brave New World Revisited*, p. 31.
[23] *Ibid.*
[24] Tarzie Vittachi, "Asia: A Need for Communication," *WAY Forum* (Brussels), No. 57 (Dec. 1965), p. 7.

It can be said that the transitional stage of national development roughly corresponds to the late autocratic (authoritarian) and the early democratic (libertarian) politico-press developmental stages. See Figure 2 for a schematic picture. In a real sense, then, this transitional stage would seem to be a bridge from one form of authoritarianism across a libertarian river to another form of authoritarianism on the other side. Put another way, in this developmental stage autocracy (personal elitism) merges into democracy and then on into statism (impersonal elitism).

In its earliest phases, the transitional society is still relatively small, autocratic and controlled; in its intermediate phases it becomes larger, democratic, individualistic and pluralistic; and in its later phases it comes even larger and more complex, more mass-oriented, more conformist and more authoritarian. Emphasis begins to shift from individualism to collectivism (or at least statism): the *modern* developmental stage is just ahead.

Profile of a Modern Society

A society in the early phases of its *modern* period still retains many of the democratic and libertarian principles brought over from its transitional stage. There is still some individualism, but it is increasingly suspect. There is still some press freedom, but it is dissolved in the name of social responsibility. There is still an element of *laissez-faire* journalism, but it is increasingly being labelled as outmoded. There is still some ideological conflict and dissonance, but it is increasingly being muted. True "mass" media still exist, but they are being de-emphasized and subordinated to specialized media.

In the later phases of modern society, the tendencies above continue until the growing authoritarianism passes into totalitarianism; partial governmental interference in media affairs becomes total interference; collectivist or statist objectives completely eliminate individual or personal objectives; conflict or social dissonance disappears; media pluralism fades away in the face of State control and domination; and a variety of concepts about responsibility to society are replaced by a single concept of social responsibility.

When the extreme phase of the *modern* stage is reached, national development has, in many respects, come full circle: from authoritarianism through libertarianism and back to authoritarianism. It is true that now the emphasis is on the total society—on the masses—whereas in the autocratic days of the traditional society the emphasis was on the few leaders of the elite. But individual freedom, press self-determinism, competition, ideological conflict and "closed" aspects of the modern society are about back to where they were in the autocratic traditional society.

Far into the final, or modern, stage of development the journalist, and all citizens for that matter, find themselves under a kind of collectivist or statist government, referred to by some writers as "mass" or "corporate." In this stage, as Karl Jaspers says, the "apparatus" dominates and "the importance of the individual leader persists, but peculiar circumstances now become decisive in the choice of leaders." According to Jaspers, "great" men pass into the background and "efficient" men come to the foreground, and the power of the masses remain effective "through the instrumentality of mass-organisations, majorities, public opinion, and the actual behaviour of vast multitudes of men." [25]

Societies (nations) can proceed ever deeper into this mass-oriented, corporate state either through revolutionary (involuntary) or evolutionary (voluntary) processes. One could say that Russia entered it through revolution, for example, and that Sweden entered it through more natural evolution. Although many might disagree with him, one long-time observer of Sweden, Roland Huntford of London's prestigious *Observer*, has contended in his book *The New Totalitarians* that Swedes have quietly and voluntarily given up their freedom and have retired into a conformist, collectivist society.

Writing of the mass media of Sweden,[26] Huntford maintains that

> To judge solely by its mass media, Sweden appears to be run by a tolerant dictatorship. Press, radio and TV show a remarkable similarity, as if guided by some Ministry of Propaganda. . . . It is virtually impossible for anybody opposing the government to get a hearing. Broadcasting has turned into a servant of the party and the State. . . . The Swedish communicators act as a corporate body, collectively following the trend of the moment. They are conformist to a fault, wanting only to promote the concensus.

A Few Conclusions

Assumptions can be made about the impact of mass media on national development, but these inferences must be drawn almost entirely from correlational studies. Little or nothing is known about cause-effect in regard to mass media and national development.

It is generally assumed that a nation's mass communication system is tied in with the nation's general progress. We note that the mass media in well-developed nations are well-developed and that media in new or traditional societies are poorly developed. We can observe also that media in a rapidly changing nation tend to be rapidly changing.

[25] Karl Jaspers, *Man in the Modern Age*, p. 55.
[26] Roland Huntford, *The New Totalitarians* (New York: Stein and Day, 1972), pp. 285–93 *passim*.

figure 2

MEDIA DEVELOPMENT AND NATIONAL AND POLITICAL DEVELOPMENT: A MULTI-FACTOR MODEL

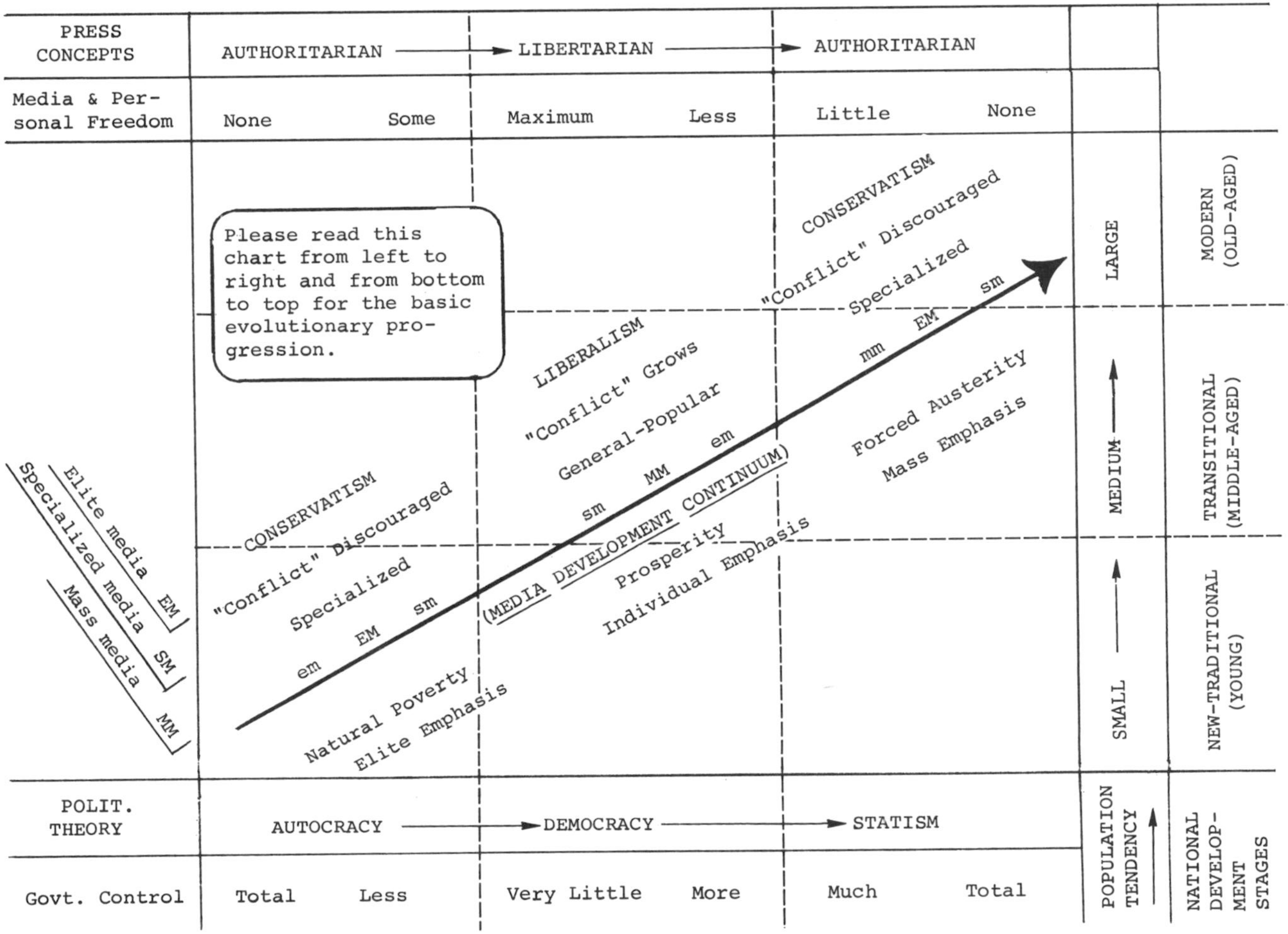

Please read this chart from left to right and from bottom to top for the basic evolutionary progression.

PRESS CONCEPTS → AUTHORITARIAN → LIBERTARIAN → AUTHORITARIAN

Media & Personal Freedom: None — Some — Maximum — Less — Little — None

CONSERVATISM "Conflict" Discouraged — Specialized em — em EM
LIBERALISM "Conflict" Grows — General-Popular — em MM em — (MEDIA DEVELOPMENT CONTINUUM)
CONSERVATISM "Conflict" Discouraged — Specialized em — EM

Natural poverty — Elite Emphasis — Individual Prosperity Emphasis — Mass Emphasis — Forced Austerity

NATIONAL DEVELOPMENT STAGES: NEW-TRADITIONAL (YOUNG) — TRANSITIONAL (MIDDLE-AGED) — MODERN (OLD-AGED)

POPULATION TENDENCY: SMALL → MEDIUM → LARGE

POLIT. THEORY: AUTOCRACY → DEMOCRACY → STATISM

Govt. Control: Total — Less — Very Little — More — Much — Total

Elite media EM
Specialized media SM
Mass media MM

Communication is obviously necessary for a nation to grow and change, just as it is for an individual person. Communication can increase and facilitate personal freedom, but it can also increase and facilitate government control of its citizens.

Media freedom provides a good barometer to a society's general political atmosphere and democratic health.

Societies tend to develop or progress from autocracy, to democracy, to statism, with their media systems going from authoritarianism through libertarianism back to authoritarianism. This is the normal circular progression tendency of social and media development postulated in this chapter—and throughout the book.

Media systems as they naturally evolve, first discourage, then encourage, then discourage social "friction" or dissonance.

Normally media develop from (1) elite (specialized) media, to (2) mass (generalized) media, and finally to (3) elite (specialized) media, although mass and elite media coexist in the last two developmental stages.[27]

Political theory and press ideology are closely related to economic level in a society's natural progression through the developmental cycle; these, of course, are accompanied by other significant factors such as social friction, population size, type of media and age of the society.

The natural tendency of both political and journalistic development in *any* society is toward authoritarianism and state tyranny. This results in increased "social responsibility" and collective consciousness but at the price of the loss of personal and media freedom.

[27] An excellent article which discusses a three-stage theory of media growth and social change-postulating development from elite media through popular (general) to specialized is Richard Maisel's "The Decline of Mass Media," *Public Opinion Quarterly* (Summer, 1973), pp. 159–70.

3

Freedom of the Press

I N A very important sense freedom of the press is the central subject of this entire book. Social responsibility of the press is certainly a major "sub-topic" and, admittedly, is related rather closely to press freedom. But since both terms are vague and are used in so many different ways, perhaps they should be dealt with specifically in separate chapters. So press freedom is emphasized in this chapter, and social responsibility will get special attention in Chapter 4. Dealing with either one of the terms is no easy task, and the discussions which follow bring to the reader's attention only a few of the ways these concepts can be viewed and indicate some of the ramifications for journalism of the semantic-ideological evolution of these concepts.

It might be well to remind the reader again of the basic thesis of this book and the way it relates to the concepts of press freedom and press responsibility. *Freedom is essential to authentic journalism, to creative press systems and to expanding, vigorous and self-assured journalists. Journalistic autonomy is the imperative (the only valid "responsibility") for those who want to participate in journalism on a really human level, and when the philosophy and psychology of "adjustment" begin to make inroads into the philosophy of journalistic autonomy, as is happening in Western nations today, the concept of "press freedom" is changed to journalistic social-determinism or press responsibility.* And we in the United States are entering this period of "responsibility" which, if not arrived at individually and voluntarily through a sense of personal morality, spells the end of press freedom as it relates to journalistic autonomy.

The Concept of Press Freedom

It is quite true that words and terms can mean whatever any person wants them to mean, and certainly this is true with "press freedom." But it is the *what a person wants it to mean* that is important, and it is intellectual cowardice to write the concept off as "really inconsequential" or "simply relative." The concept *is* important; in fact, it is basic to all other journalistic considerations. And it must be dealt with—at least on a personal, individual basis. Fundamental questions must be answered; for example:

Does press freedom belong to the press or to the people?

Does press freedom imply some kind of press responsibility, and if so, what kind of responsibility?

Does press freedom mean freedom of the people to have access to the press?

These questions are basic, but there are dozens of others which will be suggested as soon as answers to the above three are attempted. Each question—or each answer—stimulates many others, and on and on. In this chapter, and in the whole book, many such questions will be brought up and discussed. It is important to make clear at once that the thesis of this book requires that at least the first of these questions be answered directly.

Does press freedom belong to the press or to the people?

Briefly, the answer is that press freedom is the press' freedom; it belongs to the press. The First Amendment to the U.S. Constitution, of course, does provide for other freedoms for the *people*: expression, assembly, redress of grievances, religion. But the explicit provision is made that *freedom of the press* will not be abridged. If this were simply the same as freedom of expression then there really would have been no need to mention press freedom specifically. It is interesting to note, also, that nowhere in the Constitution is there anything about *freedom of access* to the press.

Now, I have not really adequately answered this first question, for even if the freedom belongs to "the press," it must in a sense also belong to "the people"—or at least to some of the people. For *the press* is a "thing" and not a person; it is a social institution or organism composed of people and dealing with people. In that sense, when we think of the *press* being free we really mean that *persons* connected with the press are free; therefore, we can talk of press freedom belonging to people—to some people in the institution of journalism. But note those words: *some people in the institution of journalism.* For here is the key, press freedom is related to, or restricted to, people, of course, but only those who might be considered *press people.* These are the people who determine what to print or not to print; they are the determiners of editorial content; they are the "news managers"; they are the ones who develop their own journalistic ethics and make their editorial decisions. And all of this "freedom" or decision-making is by *press people* independent of other "people" who are *outside the press.* This is the basic and key premise of this chapter and of this book, and if the reader does not really agree with it, then in most respects he will not find the book to his liking.

Quite simply, there are two main ways to consider freedom of the press: (1) as media autonomy with journalistic self-determinism, and (2) as media adjustment to social or political desires. In other words, one can look at press freedom as media-determinism of the content of mass communications or as public (a kind of people's lobby or majority desire) determinism of media content. As has been postulated earlier, the latter view of press freedom (really a pseudo-view) is in its ascendancy and unless it is contested vigorously and constantly by journalists of the Free World, by 1984 the journalism-of-social-adjustment will have triumphed and the editors and publishers, news directors and various media managers will have turned into passive "secretaries for the public" (or for various public pressure groups and lobbies) who will provide the various audiences only with what they want, what pleases them, what reinforces their prejudices and what enhances their social position.

But how, some readers will ask, is this bad? Is it not the "democratic" way? Should not the mass media messages be produced by a kind of public "will"? What is really wrong with news media pleasing outside groups and not necessarily themselves with their message-selection, content and emphasis? Is not anything else merely dictatorial on the part of the media persons?

These are common questions with some rational justification, and lie at the very heart of the problem the Western World faces with the concept of "press freedom." They are questions which are inciting the social responsibility apologists and the social functionalists who are always looking for accommodation, adjustment, stability and social harmony.

The basic question, however, that should be asked is this: Just what does the Social Responsibility devotee mean by the term "social responsible press," and who (or what group) will determine what is socially responsible journalism? And, if the answer is, as it often has been, *that the determination of socially responsible journalism will, of course, be left strictly to the media people themselves, then the question is closed, the debate is over: for this is exactly what we already have in a libertarian, laissez-faire, self-deterministic media system that the Social Responsibility people are trying to discredit and change.*

There are those among us, and they are growing in number very rapidly, who extol harmony over dissonance, adaptation over competition and friction, social stability and viability over social disharmony and contention. And they are wise enough to see that the communications media play a large part in social conflict theory—that is to say that *free* or *autonomous* media play a large part in this theory, and since this disturbs them they have set about to change the whole meaning of press freedom so that autonomous journalism will be considered irresponsible whereas "socially controlled" journalism will be both "free and responsible."

It is interesting that these persons recognize that it is not yet quite the time to drop the term "free" from their catechism, and so they plunge ahead brainwashing others (even themselves, evidently) into believing that a press can be both "free" and "responsible" in some kind of collective, monolithic or commonly-accepted way. This, of course, is a myth and a logical contradiction: if a newspaper, for example, must be "socially responsible" according to some *outside* standard, then quite logically, its editorial freedom is curtailed. It need not accept this-or-that as its responsibility if it is an autonomous and freely acting agent. This is what is interesting about such journalistic clichés as the press "being a fourth branch of government" or a "watchdog on government"; a free press (or units thereof) has no reason to consider itself either of these. Press units of a free journalistic system are *whatever* they want to be; they might even decide to be government supporters and apologists. So be it.

Egalitarianism and Libertarianism

One of the factors which has accelerated a change in the press freedom concept has been the rise of the idea of egalitarianism. It grew rapidly in the latter part of the nineteenth century and has been gaining great momentum in the last generation. Equality—especially equality in social or public institutions—has been the modern watchword, not only in sociology but in various schools of psychology and philosophy. In one sense, egalitarianism has supplanted in the late nineteenth and twentieth centuries the libertarian impulse which was dominant in the late eighteenth and early nineteenth centuries. At least it would appear so on the surface, although as Robert Waelder has observed, this does not mean that people are really becoming more equal; rather, he says, "more realistically it means that such an intellectual climate is conducive to a new elite of intellectuals who are assuming a kind of priestly power.[1] In other words, the very people who do the most talking about equality and equal journalistic rights for all the people, not just the journalists, are the ones who thrust themselves into a kind of position of arrogance and omniscience where they feel they can say with exactitude what the press should and should not do.

All of this is, of course, understandable. If one is for the fuzzy concept of equality, then he must at least make the proper noises to show that he is against any preferred position for journalists who largely control the contents of our mass media. John Doe, the audience member, is envisioned as "equal" to the editor of the newspaper and his voice should be listened to in respect to the newspaper's content and positions; his ideas and information should be considered for publication equally with those of the journalists, and his freedom of access to the press should be equal to the editor's freedom of editorial self-determinism.[2] Forgotten or ignored is the fact that the editor cannot practice editorial self-determinism if he must provide "journalistically equal" members of the public access to his paper's columns.

Egalitarianism, of course, is a curious and even an impossible concept. Like "social responsibility" or "loyalty" it sounds good, but falls to pieces on analysis. And, in journalism, it is ridiculous. We do not have, we never have had, nor will we ever have, an egalitarian press. Even if every citizen had an equal amount of money with which to get into the media business, we would not have any egalitarian press. For there are innumerable other factors which would militate against it. For example, equally wealthy (or equally poor) people would not have the same temperament, or education, or motivation, or talents—or even *opportunity*—to go into journalism.

The word "opportunity" should be noted in the above list; usually it is felt that money automatically provides journalistic opportunity, but it is not that simple. You can have the money—and even the education, ability and motivation—to start a newspaper, but the opportunity may not be present; for example, the community in which you wish to live and work cannot support another newspaper. You are therefore not really jour-

---

[1] Robert Waedler, *Progress and Revolution: A Study of the Issues of Our Age* (New York: International Universities Press, Inc., 1970), p. 53.
[2] See Jerome A. Barron, "Access to the Press—a New First Amendment Right," *Harvard Law Review* (June, 1967); Cf. Barron, "Access to the Press: A New Concept of the First Amendment," *Seminar* (March 1969); Dennis E. Brown and John C. Merrill, "Regulatory Pluralism in the Press?" *Seminar* (March 1969); Mary E. Trapp, "Americans Need Access to Today's Mass Media," *Communication: Journalism Education Today* (Vol. 5, Summer 1972).

nalistically equal to the person who can (and does) start a newspaper. And, even if you were to start one, too, it is a fact that one of the newspapers would have a larger circulation than the other, that one would sell more advertising, that one would have better writers, that one would deal more forcefully with the issues or that one would have more pages than the other every day. Journalistic egalitarianism is only a term, full of noble connotations, but signifying nothing.

Let us assume that "press freedom" is equally available and a rightful commodity of all citizens. Just how would it work? Would every citizen have *equal* access to the press? Would I get fifty words of my side of the question into Newspaper A and every other person with opinions on the matter get an equal fifty words into Newspaper A? And would they all appear on the front page? And would they all have equivalent headlines? And would these "equal" messages get equally into all other media?

A more interesting, but relevant question, would be: Just who would make the decisions as to whose messages got in and what place and emphasis each would get? In other words, who would decide *what* would be given "equal" treatment and *how* it would be done? An arbiter of some kind, presumably. Someone who was qualified (thereby "unequal"?) to make such egalitarian decisions. But, I might ask, are not all persons equally qualified? Why permit some special person to make such important decisions—especially since we are not satisfied to permit editors to make them? Of course, what all this amounts to is a contradiction which might be called the Paradox of Equality. Always there must be decision makers, arbiters, or what you will; they are *more equal* than others, as the old saying goes.

Egalitarianism in journalism is a concept best discarded before it does irremedial harm to freedom and common sense. *Freedom is impossible where egalitarianism is enthroned, and egalitarianism is impossible where freedom is permitted.* Where freedom operates, superior persons and journalistic media are going to emerge, thrive and dominate; where a kind of egalitarianism is enforced, outstanding journalists and media find no real incentive or motivation for individualistic achievement and content themselves with taking orders and keeping out of trouble.

Pluralism and Press Freedom

Another assumption of libertarianism, one which has grown up in the twentieth century, is that a free press must be pluralistic. This assumption, like the one that a free press must be egalitarian, has given birth to much criticism of a press system such as that of the United States. If, for example, the media system is not as "pluralistic" (the term is usually not defined) as certain critics might like, it is indicated as not being truly libertarian and therefore in need of revamping—or scrapping. Most critics of the American press today gather their statistics about mergers, group ownerships, chains and the like, and bemoan what they see as a loss of press pluralism. They even go further: they equate this with a failure of libertarian theory.

Several things are wrong with this kind of thinking: First, the concept of pluralism implied in the above criticism ("unit pluralism") does not assure an informed citizenry—for it is possible for four independent media to provide no greater variety of news and views than two media belonging to the same owner. Secondly, and more important, the contention that pluralism (of any kind) is necessary in a libertarian system is fallacious.

It is amazing how many people—even journalists and so-called communication scholars—use "pluralism" without ever really analyzing its meaning or meanings. Normally they have some vague concept of pluralism as having to do with "great" numbers of media, or a "wide diversity" of ownerships of the media. How great or how wide, they cannot really say. But they have a quantitative concept and generally seem to equate *number of units and ownerships* with diversity and number of different stories and points of view. Yet they have no real basis for this equation. A good example of this kind of assumption is Bryce Rucker's *The First Freedom* in which he presents certain statistics which show a steady growth of newspaper chains and cities with non-competitive dailies.[3] He then bemoans the demise of pluralism and the passing away of libertarianism.

Rucker's thesis is far too broad to be supported by his basic assumption—this basic assumption being that *numbers* of media determine diversity of information and viewpoints. Even if this were proved true (and it has not been), one could still question the tie-in with libertarianism. It should be noted that if we are playing the "numbers game" with pluralism, then we should be able to assume that in an advanced, well-developed closed society—such as the Soviet Union—there is a great pluralism of viewpoints and information *since there are a large number of media.* But we cannot assume this; also we must admit that a large number of media

[3] See Bryce Rucker, *The First Freedom* (Carbondale: Southern Illinois University Press, 1968). Cf. a book by the same title by Morris Ernst (New York: Macmillan, 1946) in which he, like Rucker, contends that pluralism is dying and that "our nation has been put to sleep under the blanket of laissez faire" (p. 41). He adds the prediction, however, that "the public will finally wake up to its mental starvation" (p. 245). In spite of their many statistics related to numbers of media and their many opinions about the state of our media system, neither author actually shows that Americans are being mentally starved and are getting less (or even less varied) information than previously.

units can present very few viewpoints—even if they are under varied ownerships as in Sweden. Perhaps we should, however, recognize the corollary to what has just been said: a few media units can present a very great pluralism of information and viewpoints. Much research needs to be done in this area; so far we can give no clear-cut conclusions.

The only way to really get at pluralism (the significant type: *message pluralism*) is to conduct thorough—and continuing—content analyses. The stress, then, must be on *content*, not on *numbers* of media or ownerships. Unfortunately, the myth persists that press pluralism is shrinking in the U.S. It is, of course, *possible* that it is, but those who say it is have absolutely no evidence on which to base their conclusion. Only content analysis (searching for variety of information and viewpoints) of the total messages today as compared to the total message content at an earlier time can give evidence of shrinking—or expanding—pluralism. As yet, nobody has systematically tackled this difficult task.

Even if we were to make these analyses and were to learn, for example, that there is less pluralism today than in 1900, what would this mean? Would it mean that we do not have "enough" pluralism today and therefore we should change our press system or theory? How much pluralism is *enough*? Nobody can really answer this question because adequacy of message diversification is a meaningless concept. Adequate for what? For whom? In what situation? The concept of pluralism, even "message pluralism," is really a *non-concept* used as a kind of smokescreen behind which to attack a press system. No press system, of course, can *ever* be exempt from attack on this basis—from attack by critics who always see the possibility for ever greater variety of messages and numbers of media.

Press freedom, I maintain, is a far more important and valuable concept than press pluralism. It is true that in theory a free press system (especially one in a large and complex nation) should generate a great pluralism or diversity of media messages. In fact, there has never been any proof that it has not done just that. But it is possible—even in libertarian theory—for a free and self-determined press system under some circumstances to have very little pluralism; in fact, it is possible for free media freely to decide to conform to each other in presenting the same few messages and viewpoints—or even the same message or viewpoint. Since freely operating journalists and media seldom agree on very much (or they naturally tend to disagree in many respects), it is highly unlikely that a free press will result in a monolithic press, but it is a possibility.

Attempts by those in our society to make our press system more "responsible" by *forcing* pluralism are, in effect, repudiating libertarianism. They are doomed to failure, for they can never force "enough" pluralism to please everybody. Libertarianism will probably always result in pluralism, but pluralism (if forced) can never result in libertarianism.

One's thinking about press pluralism would become a little clearer if he had a systematic framework in which to consider the term. Of course, there are obviously many ways to define pluralism, but one typology which has been useful to me and my students is presented below—giving three *types* and three *levels* of pluralism:

(1) *Message Pluralism.* Here the emphasis is on the diversity of messages to which a person is able to expose himself. And it should be realized that this is not the same as the diversity (or number) of media units to which a person may expose himself. The way to get at this is through content analysis, and through this procedure only.

(2) *Media ("Unit") Pluralism.* This kind of pluralism is the one which is usually considered and used by those who would indict our press system for loss of pluralism. Here the quantity of, or diversity of ownerships of, media units is the important consideration. It is assumed here that the more units you have (or the more ownerships), the more viewpoints and stories you will have. This, of course, is not necessarily true.

(3) *Communicator Pluralism.* The emphasis here is on the number and diversity of message-encoders or message-senders. And the assumption is usually that the wider the diversity of communicator "types" and the greater the number of communicators (using the mass media), the greater will be the diversity of information and opinions. This, of course, is not necessarily true, but it would appear to be more valid than the "Unit" Pluralism assumption. The only way to get at this type of pluralism in a sound methodological way would be to study the communicators (their backgrounds, education, religion, etc.) and then study the messages they send, and then see what correlation exists between the diversity of backgrounds and the diversity of messages they communicate.

Of the three types of pluralism briefly discussed above, the most significant one, in my view, is Type I (Message Pluralism). The only way to study it is through content analysis, and this must be thorough and continuing. One must look for the diversity of opinions and information in a certain universe of messages at a particular time for comparison with similar analyses at other times and in other universes. Types 2 and 3 *may* contribute to Message Pluralism, but they may not.

Now, let us consider briefly the *levels* of pluralism:

(1) *System Pluralism.* This level is the one many writers emphasize and, if it is "good" (many media or diversity of messages), it is held up as something very commendable; there are a great many bits of information and viewpoints available in the *total media system* (e.g. in the media system of the United States).

(2) *Community Pluralism*. This level brings the concept of pluralism closer to home, limits it to a smaller geographical or social community— such as a region, state or city. The question of importance here: How much diversity is present at the *local* level? To many persons the System Pluralism is really unimportant when compared to this local Community Pluralism. For example, they will say that the fact that certain viewpoints (or stories) are published in a few newspapers in California is really insignificant if people in the Midwest do not have these items in *their* local media. What counts, then, at this level is that items and viewpoints be available in the media of a specific *locality*.

(3) *Individual (Audience Member) Pluralism*. This, I maintain, is the ideal *level* of pluralism just as Message Pluralism is the ideal *type* of pluralism. At this level, pluralism is related to that information which *gets to the individual citizen* and is not what is available somewhere in the media of a country or a community. In other words, at this level—the perception level of the audience—the amount and diversity of information which the person actually exposes himself to (or assimilates) is the only important consideration. The way to study this level would be to study the individual citizen, trying to ascertain through recall studies, interviews, etc. what he was *getting* from the pluralism of messages revolving about him.

Press Freedom: A Universal?

When a person dares to try to make meaningful and valid statements about freedom of the press in one country compared to freedom in another, he opens himself to academic scoffing. He is told that "freedom" does not *mean* in one country what it *means* in another, and therefore conclusions cannot be made as to which country has the freer press system. Seductive as this argument may be, it may well be simply an intellectual "cop-out"; no reason exists why freedom (of the press, for example) cannot have a rather pure meaning that can be applied to the press system of *any* nation at any particular moment.

Ralph Lowenstein of the University of Missouri, believing that universals exist relative to press freedom, has courageously attempted to devise a formula or standard of evaluating any nation's press freedom. He has called his system the "PICA Index." [4] It is predicated on the assumption that some countries have press systems which have greater degrees of

---

[4] For discussions of the PICA Index for measuring press freedom, see "PICA: Measuring World Press Freedom" (FoI Center Pub. No. 166, U. of Mo., Aug. 1966); "World Press Freedom, 1966" (FoI Center Pub. No. 181, May 1967), and "World Press Freedom, 1967" (FoI Center Pub. No. 201, May, 1968).

independence and critical ability than do other countries. The concept of *autonomy* in journalism (and the differences in degrees of this autonomy) is implicit in his system which has been used several times by the Freedom of Information Center at the University of Missouri. The details of the PICA method of appraising international press freedom will not be given here; suffice it to say that it came under attack by the "relativists" of all types who maintained that Lowenstein forced "Western ideology" and a libertarian concept of press freedom upon all the nations of the world. Here is an instance of an attempt to look *systematically* at various press systems of the world from the point of view of "freedom"; there have been innumerable unsystematic attempts by such organizations as the Associated Press and the International Press Institute to do the same. What is rather strange is that criticism of PICA has come from persons involved in unsystematic attempts who obviously feel that haphazard opining by organization members is as good as (or preferable to) scholarly, systematic probing in this area.

One general finding which seems to be rather common to these "press freedom reports" which are released every year: the world's press is getting less and less free. Admittedly, this finding is based on opinions and conclusions held in the so-called "Free World" where concern over such things as press freedom seems to be considerably greater than in authoritarian societies. For example, International Press Institute annual reports about the status of press freedom do indeed reflect the political bias of those preparing the surveys. Nobody really contends differently. The IPI reports, for example, show a very clear bias against autocratic (socialist or fascist) tendencies toward prior restraint, government-party media control, repressive press laws, governmental control of newsprint, journalistic licensing and the like.

In discussing press freedom within the libertarian context of the West, four ways of considering such freedom suggest themselves. Each one might be considered a different *spectrum* which could be briefly described as (1) the potency or non-potency of government control, (2) the political extremes in governmental philosophy, (3) philosophical or psychological inclination, and (4) governmental and private ownership of journalistic enterprises.

Spectrum 1. At one end of this spectrum is anarchy and at the other total government control. The person who believes in press freedom (at least in the way it is extolled in this book) has a tendency toward anarchy. He rebels against government control—at least very much government control—and wants himself and his social unit (for the journalist: his medium) to be under little or no government compulsion or direction. He would agree with Thoreau, who virtually proclaimed himself an anarchist, that "that government is best which governs not at all." [5] So, on this spectrum "Press Freedom" would be well toward the *anarchy* end and far away from the *government control* end.

Spectrum 2. As has been pointed out earlier in this book, both authoritarianism on the right and on the left tend to stifle freedom of the press and to dissipate media or journalistic autonomy. Therefore, the ideal spot for a free press on a Communism/Fascism spectrum would be in the center. Most journalists (at least in the Western libertarian world) would agree with this if they were using *journalistic autonomy* as the key to their concept. A free press had better attempt to follow a path about half-way between the tempting and ever-beckoning poles of Communism and Fascism.[6] Truly the middle-way here is more compatible with journalistic autonomy and media self-determinism. Both extremes are areas where the press would have to submit itself to an elite, persons or groups, who would dictate to the press and determine its actions in line with their own interests and socio-political philosophies.

Spectrum 3. This is probably a more controversial spectrum than the others for its poles are the semantically difficult terms, Liberalism and Conservatism. A free press, here, is midway between these two poles—the same as it was midway between Communism and Fascism. Although Liberalism, as has been discussed earlier, has the more favorable connotation, the pragmatic Liberal or Liberal government can be just as authoritarian or elitist as can the pragmatic Conservative or Conservative government. In fact, it is quite possible that today's Liberal is tomorrow's Conservative—at least in the sense of wanting to conserve his brand of liberalism. At the extremes, Liberals and Conservatives are arrogant, self-righteous, heavy-handed, dictatorial, and opposed to criticism and open discussion. They know what is best for the society and will enforce their will if they get the chance. The Free Press or the autonomous journalist had best steer a middle course between them so as not to get entangled in the ideological nets thrown far out by the clever ideologues of both groups.

Spectrum 4. It is my opinion that capitalism more than socialism expands the opportunities of personal and media autonomy, competition and the clash of ideas. Therefore, the Free Press finds its most compatible home on this spectrum far toward the capitalistic end. Capitalistic societies have certainly contributed more to personal and journalistic autonomy than any other societies in the world. Capitalism engenders individualists,

[5] H. D. Thoreau, "Civil Disobedience" in M. Meltzer (ed.), *Thoreau: People, Principles, and Politics* (New York: Hill and Wang, 1963), p. 36.
[6] "Fascism" is probably a misnomer here, since unlike "Communism" it has specific reference to a national political ideology (Italy in the 1930's and 1940's). Perhaps "right-wing authoritarianism" would be a better term.

persons who like to compete. Socialism engenders conformists, persons who like to adapt and move along together. Alexis de Tocqueville, writing in 1848, expressed well the danger to freedom found in socialism. He referred to "democracy" (which he contrasted to *socialism*) as an individualist institution standing in irreconcilable conflict with socialism. He wrote, in part:

> Democracy extends the sphere of individual freedom; socialism restricts it. Democracy attaches all possible value to each man; socialism makes each man a mere agency, a mere number. Democracy and socialism have nothing in common but one word: equality. But notice the difference; while democracy seeks equality in liberty, socialism seeks equality in restraint and servitude.[7]

From Freedom to Responsibility

Books and articles tracing the development of freedom of the press (freedom of expression and other related freedoms) abound and there is no need here to examine this subject in great detail. There are many fine sources for the person interested in the historical landmarks of press freedom during its evolution.[8] The literature of press freedom is sprinkled with outstanding writers; one can start with John Milton and his *Areopagitica* in 1644 (licensing impractical, impairing the search for truth; truth arises from the free and open encounter of ideas—his "self-righting process") and proceed through the eighteenth century where John Locke extolled man's natural rights and his rationality and postulated that free expression was a natural right.

Also in the eighteenth century was Voltaire, probably the best known defender of freedom of expression at this time, who accepted the biblical injunction that the "truth shall make you free" but recognized the problem: one had to be free to know the truth. And there was also Adam Smith who proposed his famous concept of *laissez faire* in 1776; the government should keep hands off and let the various business enterprises make their own way in the market place (and this would include the press). In America about this same time, Thomas Jefferson was expressing strong faith in the rationality of man, as Locke had done, and was advocating a minimum of government interference in everyday affairs. For Jefferson, the

[7] "Discours prononcé à l'assemblée constituante le 12 septembre 1848 sur la question du droit au travail," *Oeuvres complètes d'Alexis de Tocqueville* (1866), IX, 546.
[8] For a good discussion of the landmarks of press freedom during its evolution, see Ch. 2 ("Freedom of Speech and Press") in Carl L. Becker, *Freedom and Responsibility in the American Way of Life* (New York: Vintage Books, 1960). Cf. William E. Hocking, *Freedom of the Press: A Framework of Principle* (Chicago: Univ. of Chicago Press, 1947).

free and autonomous press was essential for public enlightenment and as a safeguard of personal liberties.

Another great American spokesman for press freedom was John Adams, who advised journalists in 1765 that they should not "suffer themselves to be wheedled out of their liberty by any pretences of politeness, delicacy, or decency." These, said John Adams, were simply three different names for "hypocrisy, chicanery, and cowardice." [9]

And back in England there was Jeremy Bentham (1748–1832), viewing every law as a restriction of freedom and urging that laws be minimized. He saw society as composed of atomistic individuals pursuing their own happiness. To him, a realization of individual self-interest (of which the best judge is the individual himself) must occur in an atmosphere of freedom. Freedom of the press he defended mainly on the grounds that publicity is necessary to good government, that publicity is the best way to secure and keep public confidence in government.

A close associate of Bentham, James Mill (1773–1836) thought the "middle rank" of society the "most wise" and "most virtuous." He advocated freedom of the press because it made known the conduct of the individuals who were elected to wield power in government, and unless information about their activities was made public the officials might serve their own interests.[10] James' son, John Stuart Mill (1806–1873) solidified his father's ideas on freedom in the nineteenth century and his famous tract "On Liberty" justified free expression on Utilitarian principles. He pointed out that liberty was the right of a *mature* person, and that for the good of society, man must not be restrained. He insisted that intelligence atrophies and initiative dies from overzealous direction by government. One might wonder what might happen to the intelligence and initiative of an "immature" person when directed by government.

It will be noted (see Figure 3) that up until the present century, the emphasis in the discussions of press freedom and freedom of expression generally was on *laissez-faire*, on government separation from the press, on personal and media autonomy, on the elimination of licensing and on the "free" marketplace of ideas individually determined by the various media. In the twentieth century this began to change, and Oliver Wendell Holmes (1841–1935), in a very real sense, set the stage for the new trend toward limited freedom with his "clear and present danger" concept and his implication that the government should be allowed to protect itself. (One is reminded of the statement of President John Kennedy's Pentagon

[9] Reuven Frank, "The First Amendment Includes Television," *Nieman Reports* (Dec. 1971), p. 8.
[10] E. M. Zashin, *Civil Disobedience and Democracy* (New York: The Free Press, 1972), p. 25.

CONCEPT OF "FREEDOM OF PRESS": EVOLUTION

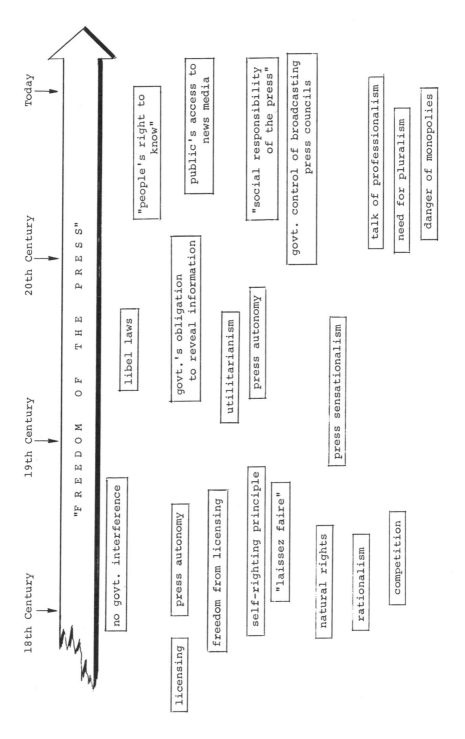

spokesman, Arthur Sylvester, in the early 1960's that the government has a right to lie to protect itself.)

Continuing this trend toward "social responsibility" or limited freedom have been such men as Walter Lippmann, Walter Berns, Robert Hutchins and Jerome Barron who have cautioned the press to be more responsible and to operate in certain ways in order to warrant or deserve its freedom.[11] These are the elitists who would prescribe what the press should do to keep its freedom and whose impact has been great in the recent trend toward such pressure groups and media arbiters as press councils. The broadcast media, of course, have from the beginning operated under the "responsibility" doctrine instead of the "freedom" doctrine; although many broadcasters are agitating for equal freedom with the print media, they are likely to get nowhere as long as the trend continues toward responsibility and away from freedom or autonomy. In fact, what is more likely is that the print media will find themselves one day operating under some type of FPC (Federal Press Commission) in much the same way that the broadcast media operate under the FCC (Federal Communications Commission).

Enter the Platonic Elitists

Although they have always been with us, the twentieth century has spawned a new breed of articulate and very vocal elitists who claim to know what the press should do to be responsible to society. They have shifted, and are continuing to shift, the concept of press freedom from individual media freedom to a kind of conformist press responsibility. Press freedom has all but become, under their influence, the people's freedom to control the press. Here is what one recent commentator, an Austrian editor, has to say about this new trend:

> The great era of press freedom was the great era of liberalism. Accordingly, press freedom was freedom *from* the state and freedom *for* criticism of the state: on one side was the attacking press of ascendant liberalism, on the other, the defensive power of the declining authoritarian state. . . . The old definition was aimed at what the state should not do, the new one should include what the state *must* do.[12]

11 See Lippmann, *The Public Philosophy*; Walter Berns, *Freedom, Virtue, and the First Amendment*; Robert Hutchins *et al.*, *A Free and Responsible Press*, and Jerome Barron, "Access to the Press—a New First Amendment Right," *Harvard Law Review* (June 1967). For further commentary on the press' social responsibility—by 31 leading journalists—see Gerald Gross (ed.), *The Responsibility of the Press* (New York: Simon and Schuster, Clarion Books, 1969). Cf. W. L. Rivers and W. Schramm, *Responsibility in Mass Communication* (New York: Harper & Row, 1957).
12 Günther Nenning, "Negative and Positive Press Freedom," *IPI Report* (Sept. 1966), p. 8.

Along with this new emphasis (often called "positive" freedom) has arisen a companion emphasis on *what the press must* do. Or, put another way, there are things the press must do as a result of the new emphasis on what the state must do relative to the press. The implication is that the state and the press must somehow cooperate to give the people or the society what they need or what they should have "the freedom" to get somehow. It is all a very complicated (and confused) concept, but it is one which apparently has a great appeal for new elitists who would eliminate media autonomy in the name of social responsibility or "people's freedom" or some other equally ambiguous term.

Listen to another journalist, this one from Canada, writing in *The Ottawa Journal* in 1971 and articulating the new emphasis on press freedom:

> The truth about freedom of the press is that it stands for freedom of the people. . . . It is not a special right or cloistered virtue. . . . To deserve its freedom a press should strive daily to be reasonably responsible. . . . Freedom of the press is not a press freedom but a public freedom, a public possession and right, and in some ways its stoutest weapon.[13]

I am happy to see that the Canadian journalist thinks he knows "the truth about freedom of the press." Although his concept makes little sense to me, I must admit that the phraseology which he uses has become a kind of standard incantation for many who are helping to shift press freedom away from the press and to denigrate the concept of journalistic autonomy. Just what he means by "freedom of the people" is anybody's guess, and his admonition to the press that it should strive daily to "be reasonably responsible" (according to whose criteria?) in order to "deserve its freedom" is not only contradictory to his previous statement (that really the press does not have freedom) but is obviously vague due to the adverb "reasonably." It would appear to the libertarian that all free press expression can be defended on the grounds that it is "reasonably responsible."

John Tebbel, a long-time commentator on the American press, has recognized the inroads of forces dissolving freedom (autonomy) in the name of social responsibility. In 1970 he wrote in *Saturday Review*:

> Obviously, in the United States we are witnessing a movement toward some kind of press control, put forward in most cases with assertions of the highest motives and with emphatic denials that any control is

[13] Norman Smith, "Freedom of the Press is a Public Freedom, Not Just a Press Freedom," *Seminar Quarterly* (Sept, 1972), pp. 21–22.

intended. Yet, when the rhetoric is stripped away, the end result is infringement of the freedom guaranteed by the First Amendment.[14]

Tebbel has very succinctly put his finger on what is probably the greatest journalistic issue of the last part of the twentieth century, and certainly he has restated the thesis of this book. Actually, he was referring to the 33-member study group set up by the National Commission on the Causes and Prevention of Violence, which had indicted the press for fomenting violence in the United States. But he could just as well have been referring to the so-called Hutchins Commission report of 1947 which made similar recommendations to the press as to its responsible action. Both commissions were composed of non-journalists who generally believed that the press should submit itself to non-media people who would pressure media to conform to "balanced," "fair" and "responsible" concepts of the news.[15]

Increasingly one hears of freedom *to* as well as freedom *from*. George F. Kennan, in a speech in 1968, made the point that "any freedom from something implies a freedom to something" and that freedom "is definable only in terms of the obligations and restraints and sacrifices it accepts." [16] Let us look at the first part of his statement: Of course, freedom from something implies freedom to something. If, for example, I have freedom *from* government censorship, I automatically have freedom *to* publish. This seems obvious, but it is quite different from saying that freedom from censorship implies a *responsibility or obligation* to publish something. Freedom implies *freedom not* to accept any obligation or particular responsibility. Obligations and responsibilities are contradictory to freedom, for they limit freedom or restrict it and therefore should be anathema to libertarians.

The only obligations acceptable to the free man are those which he chooses to place on himself, and when journalists abide by obligations and responsibilities under any kind of pressure or duress or because they have been led by an outside force to believe that a course of action "is what good and responsible journalists do," then they are no longer free. As a journalist I must do what I think is responsible, not what some other journalist or some outside group thinks is responsible. It is only in this way that our journalism can retain autonomy.

We must assume that in a free society men disagree quite often as to what is responsible journalism, but many of the modern elitists who are flying the flag of "responsibility" seem to be saying that they, and not the individual media people, have the corner on truth in this area. Joseph

14 "Studying the Mass Media," *Saturday Review* (Feb. 14, 1970), p. 69.
15 *Ibid.*, p. 71.
16 "Rebels Without a Program," *New York Times Sunday Magazine* (Jan. 21, 1968).

O'Meara, former dean of the Notre Dame Law School, has dealt with this problem:

> Unfortunately many sincere people do not comprehend the genius of our democracy . . . such people would deny free speech to those with whom they are in fundamental disagreement. . . . They would establish a party line in America—*their* party line, of course. This is an alien concept, a totalitarian concept; it is not consonant with the American tradition; it is anti-democratic; it is, in short, subversive and it should be recognized for what it is.[17]

But such voices are being drowned out in recent years by those who warn against "press abuses" and improper decisions on the part of journalists.

Many of these press critics are politicians whom you would expect to hear blasting free journalism. But an increasing number of them are thoughtful and intelligent non-politicians, people with no apparent personal axes to grind. One such person is Walter Lippmann, one of the foremost of the modern Platonic elitists. He has best articulated his feelings on press freedom (he actually refers to "freedom of speech") in his *The Public Philosophy* where he emphasizes "dialectic" as the prerequisite for such freedom of expression. As Lippmann sees it, the press should "confront ideas with opposing ideas" so that people will get "true ideas," and if this is not done, freedom cannot be defended. For him, when communication is silly or filled with deception, it cannot be "preserved against the demand for a restoration of order or of decency." He goes on to say:

> For in the absence of debate unrestricted utterance leads to the degradation of opinion. By a kind of Gresham's law the more rational is overcome by the less rational, and the opinions that will prevail will be those which are held most ardently by those with the most passionate will. For that reason the freedom to speak can never be maintained merely by objecting to interference with the liberty of the press, of printing, of broadcasting, of the screen. It can be maintained only by promoting debate.[18]

Another elitist, or proscriber for the press, is Walter Berns, a political scientist and lawyer, who would be an apologist for censorship on the grounds that virtue is a higher good than freedom. Of course, like any good elitist, he is certain that he knows "virtue" when he sees it. In his

[17] John Fischer, "The Harm Good People Do," *Harper's Magazine* (Oct. 1956).
[18] Walter Lippmann, *The Public Philosophy* (New York: New American Library—Mentor Books, 1955), p. 100.

Freedom, Virtue and the First Amendment [19] he maintains that the "public interest" requires the law to take a hand in guarding us from "bad" messages, and that First Amendment freedoms are privileges rather than rights. He sums up his position, and evidently the position of most Platonic elitists, with this statement: "Freedom ideally is extended to those we can trust not to misuse the privilege." What I would like to ask Mr. Berns and all of such persuasion is just who the "we" is above—*just who is it* that will make the decision as to which editorial writer, for example, can or can not be trusted? Most likely, he would answer: "the courts." The thought of the already bogged-down court system of this country every day making editorial decisions for the media as to whether they can be trusted in this-or-that-case is almost absurd enough to be funny.

It is very easy to confuse democracy and even responsibility in journalism with "giving the people what they want." But this is a false concept —or at least an erroneous application of the democratic principle, for journalism is something more than a mere public utility that produces a stable, physical staple such as water or electricity. It is at least a quasi-*art*, a creative enterprise whereby individual talents go into its production. Journalism (at least, free journalism) is something other than a fountain which pours forth a predictable and consistent product at the beck-and-call of the consumers.[20]

But many of the attacks on the free press are coming from these "populist" critics as well as from the Platonic elitists. Actually, however, the "populists" are no more than elitists themselves, for they know very well that some group of people's "representatives" must speak and act in the name of the people. These representatives thus become "elitists" and solidify their position as time goes on. But "Give the people what they want" is a fine-sounding slogan, having a more democratic ring to it than "Give the people what our elite group of intellectuals want them to have." Good as it may sound, this kind of public or consensus journalism is the journalism of slave-journalists. It is debilitating to the authentic journalist who wants more than to be at the beck and call of so-called "public opinion."

"Give the people what you want to give them" is the motto for free journalists. *What they want,* if such can actually be ascertained, would become the impersonal decision-maker of the media, turning journalism into a kind of computer-oriented dispenser of messages devoid of individual

---

[19] Walter Berns, *Freedom, Virtue, and the First Amendment* (Baton Rouge: LSU Press, 1957).
[20] See Sydney J. Harris, *The Authentic Person* (Niles, Ill.: Argus Communications, 1972), esp. Chs. 3 and 4.

decision-makers and creative communicators. Journalists would simply become slaves to public opinion or mass desires, giving the "people" what they wanted (or what the journalists concluded they wanted). Many readers will say this is fine; that this is true democracy—that the people *should* rule (not only governmentally but also journalistically). If this is, indeed, what democracy means, then I must cease being a "democrat," for this idea smacks of mass-tyranny or lowest-common-denominator dictatorship and something unsuitable for independent free men.

So, we can see that there is a disposition in many quarters today to "redefine" freedom of the press, to divorce it from independent editorial determinism by the media and to place it somewhere else with a shifted emphasis on the press's obligations rather than on its freedoms. This redefining, whether it comes from politicians or from intellectuals in non-political situations, is limiting the concept and making it into something else. Abraham Lincoln in his statement that a nation cannot exist "half slave and half free" pointed out the fallacy of trying to tamper with the definition of freedom. If freedom of the press is to have any real meaning —the kind that has to do with autonomy—then it means freedom from outside (non-journalistic) forces and nothing more.

Any power to make the press "responsible" or "accountable" is the negation of liberty; if society, or a press council, or a judge, or a jury, or any other non-journalistic group assumes the power to define for the press what "responsible" journalism is, then liberty is surrendered. It is just that simple.

De Tocqueville recognized the fallacy of setting up a group or even a society to impose opinions on others. He wrote in his *Democracy in America:*

> A majority taken collectively is only an individual, whose opinions, and frequently whose interests, are opposed to those of another individual, who is styled a minority. If it be admitted that a man possessing absolute power may misuse that power by wronging his adversaries, why should not a majority be liable to the same reproach? [21]

It is interesting to note that Arthur Hays Sulzberger, for twelve years publisher of *The New York Times,* pointed out in 1947 that there is "no *quid pro quo* written into the Constitution," that "freedom is granted— responsibility is not required." He also stressed that "you cannot have outside control of a free press and have it free. Control must come from within." [22] Sulzberger saw clearly two important realities: (1) that free-

[21] Alexis de Tocqueville, *Democracy in America,* ed. by Phillips Bradley (New York: Vintage Books, 1959), I, p. 269.
[22] *Seminar* (Dec. 1969), pp. 3–4.

dom is not responsibility, and (2) that editorial self-determinism or autonomy is the essence of press freedom. It is amazing how many Americans have blinded themselves to these two fundamental facts.

Although Eric Hoffer did not write specifically about press freedom, I would like to take the liberty (at the risk of being thought "irresponsible" by someone) of adapting to press freedom what he did say about personal freedom in *The True Believer*. He would apparently believe that media must have freedom to develop their own characters and their own sense of responsibility. It is true that bad, inferior and sloppy media will develop. And there is a tendency to judge a press system by its least worthy units; but this is generally unfair. But it does have some justification—for quality in a total press system is determined to a considerable degree by its inferior elements. However, it is well to remember that the superior media—and journalists—play a major role in shaping a nation's press system as well as the nation itself.[23]

Perhaps it is well to end this chapter with a reference to Friedrich Hayek and his feelings about "social responsibility" or "public obligation" on the part of the press. Warning against collectivist tendencies which would tend to organize or plan or direct intellectual pursuits (and certainly journalism is one such pursuit), he wrote:

> It may indeed be said that it is the paradox of all collectivist doctrine and its demand for "conscious" control or "conscious" planning that they necessarily lead to the demand that the mind of some individual should rule supreme—while only the individualistic approach to social phenomena makes us recognize the super-individual forces which guide the growth of reason. Individualism is thus an attitude of humility before this social process and of tolerance to other opinions and is the exact opposite of that intellectual *hubris* which is at the root of the demand for comprehensive direction of the social process.[24]

[23] Adapted from Eric Hoffer, *The True Believer*, pp. 29–30.
[24] *The Road to Serfdom*, pp. 165–66.

4

Social Responsibility
of the Press

THE IMPACT of the many Platonic elitists who have concerned themselves with guiding journalism has been great. They have, indeed, all
but reversed the eighteenth and nineteenth century emphasis and have
given a new definition to the term "freedom of the press." Just when this
trend began is debatable; Gene Gilmore and Robert Root, and others,
have mentioned the 1930's in the United States as the concept's genesis;
some students of the press would go back much further.

Gilmore and Root in a 1971 book, which I consider a notable contribution to journalistic literature, wrote: "Increased pressure to make newspapers more responsible has been increasing since the days of the New
Deal. The trend has been toward more and more government control. Intellectual pressures behind many of these moves have been those religious and philosophical concepts of the Golden Rule and utilitarianism." [1]

It may well be, however, that the trend began the first time somebody
set down some specific "duties" or "responsibilities" for the press, or implied that individual journalists must (or even *should*) conform to some
set of guidelines. This, of course, would place the beginning of such a
concept well before the 1930's. In fact, it would make the roots of the

[1] Gene Gilmore and Robert Root, *Modern Newspaper Editing* (Berkeley: Glendessary
Press, Inc., 1971), p. 248.

concept coexistent with the rise of the authoritarian press. For, of course, the authorities who would guide and control the authoritarian press used the very same rationale of social responsibility to justify their practices.

Within the last few years hundreds of articles and books have been written, and probably thousands of speeches have been made, by persons who set out to define what "responsible" journalism is; the whole subject has been discussed and debated in great detail, and seemingly everyone knows what a responsible press should be like. Listen to this: "What is the mission of the media in a Republic? To tell the people the truth, of course." Then we are informed that the U.S. media have "singularly failed to meet this responsibility . . . to stress to the people the simple truth that democracy demands a price for those who would enjoy its fruits . . . a willingness to surrender some personal benefit for the common good." [2] Here John E. Tilton has given us the "simple truth" of the matter, as he puts it.

Talking about the press's responsibility is quite popular. Listen to Clark R. Mollenhoff, a long-time Washington correspondent, in a speech in 1964:

> The future of the American Democracy is contingent upon the performance of the American press. If the newsmen of today and tomorrow are diligent workers and balanced thinkers on problems of governing our society, then I have no doubt that the American Democracy will survive and flourish as a symbol to the whole world. If the press fails in its responsibility—if it founders in a quagmire of superficiality, partisanship, laziness and incompetence—then our great experiment in democracy will fail.[3]

So, we are led to believe that if democracy fails, it is the fault of the American press. If our democracy fails, then it means that the press has been "superficial, partisan, lazy and incompetent." Why, we might ask Mr. Mollenhoff, has not our democracy already failed, for certainly many feel the press has been all of these things? And, certainly *parts* of the press have been—at least in *somebody's* opinion. Free presses are not monolithic presses, and when Mollenhoff and others talk of *the press* being "superficial, partisan, lazy and incompetent," they are simply uttering good-sounding words, well-meaning, perhaps, but not very meaningful or helpful.

Even Arthur Hays Sulzberger, who was quoted in the last chapter as generally believing in journalistic autonomy, wrote in 1947 that he held

[2] John E. Tilton, *Blind Behemoth: A Critical Study of News Media Performance* (Minneapolis: Sun Press, 1972), p. 79.
[3] Clark R. Mollenhoff, "Life Line of Democracy" (15th annual William Allen White Memorial Lecture, Feb. 10, 1964, University of Kansas).

that it was "the duty of every newspaper of general circulation to inform its readers on *all* sides of *every* important issue, and that it fails in its responsibilities when it does not do so." [4] He says this seemingly without realizing that it conflicts with his statement a little later that "control must come from within" the press. His statement also makes one wonder just how many "sides" *every important issue* has and how one determines just what an "important" issue is. Like so many others, he champions *self-control* of the press and at the same time seems able to know what is the "duty of every newspaper." It could just be that my newspaper would not see it as its duty to inform its readers "on all sides of every issue"—even if it felt it could do it. What then? Is my newspaper therefore irresponsible? Yes, according to Mr. Sulzberger, who really (in my opinion) did not believe what he was saying.

Stalwarts of press freedom who have been quoted earlier—men like James and J. S. Mill—themselves evidenced the schizophrenia prevalent in this whole area. James Mill, maybe the conceiver of the "watchdog" function of journalism, advocated liberty of the press because it made "known the conduct of the individuals who have been chosen to wield the powers of government." [5] Would he, then, have cancelled liberty of the press for those press units which failed to live up to his rationale for such freedom? We are left to speculate about the answer to that question. And James Mill's son, John Stuart Mill, wanted to hold the individual to a high standard of responsibility to his fellow men; but he was a freedom-lover to the extent that he did prefer that "the conscience of the agent himself" should enforce a person's responsibility and that a free society should put few restrictions on its members' behavior.[6] And, if the *agent's conscience* did not enforce the person's responsibility as Mill saw it, then what? Again, we must speculate.

As has been mentioned earlier, Walter Lippmann has maintained (1955) that the justification of free expression is to provide a clash of opposing ideas.[7] Therefore, we see that Lippmann has added his name to a list of those who make press freedom contingent on some responsibility of the press.

And by a Marxist journalist, Melor Sturua, correspondent for the Soviet daily *Izvestia*, we were told in 1972 that "We must remember that our responsibility is greater than our rights." [8] He was speaking to the Deadline Club, a journalistic organization in New York City. Although he

4 Harold L. Nelson (ed.), *Freedom of the Press from Hamilton to the Warren Court* (Indianapolis: The Bobbs-Merrill Co., Inc., 1967), p. 410.
5 Zashin, *Civil Disobedience and Democracy*, p. 25.
6 *Ibid.*, p. 49.
7 Lippmann, *The Public Philosophy*.
8 "Russian Correspondent Speaks of Responsibility," *The Quill* (May 1972), p. 26.

did not spell out for his audience just what that responsibility should be, those familiar with Communist press ideology might very well guess what it would be.

The remainder of this book could be taken up citing a whole series of persons who have duties and responsibilities in mind which they feel the press should accept. And there is nothing inherently wrong with persons having opinions relative to duties, responsibilities, obligations and the like *if they are aware of, and make clear to others, the fact that these are no more than personal opinions of what they might do if they were engaged in journalism and not what should be done by the press generally.* But it appears that most of these commentators like to universalize, like to go beyond permitting each journalist and each medium to frame an individual sense of responsibility in journalism. There is not only something arrogant about most of these non-journalistic responsibility-definers, but also something of a spirit of authoritarianism.

A New Theory Emerges

Increasingly one hears reference to the responsibility of the press and less and less about its freedom to react independently in a democratic society. Not only has the concept permeated the authoritarian countries, where it is an expected development, but in recent years it has made notable incursions into the press philosophy of the United States and other Western libertarian countries.

The book, *Four Theories of the Press,*[9] published in 1956, attempted to put in intelligible language this new concept of the press which had been developing at least since World War II. It dealt with "social responsibility" as a press theory alongside the theories of communism, authoritarianism and libertarianism. And from this book the new "theory" has made its way, largely unchallenged, into innumerable books, articles, speeches and academic dissertations. On the surface this new emphasis appears noble. Writers and speakers enthusiastically expound its virtues. And, of course, it is difficult for anyone to take issue with any concept which is wrapped in the glittering garments of "people's freedom" and "public good" and "social responsibility."

Although journalists, statesmen and academicians have for years (actually centuries) been thinking in terms of "responsibility" as well as freedom for the communications media, there had really been no significant effort to place the concept as a serious theory—parallel in importance to "libertarianism"—until 1947 when the Commission on Freedom of the

[9] Fred S. Siebert, Theodore Peterson, and Wilbur Schramm, *Four Theories of the Press* (Urbana: Univ. of Illinois Press, 1956), pp. 73–103.

Press, headed by Robert Hutchins, discussed it in A *Free and Responsible Press*.[10] Previously, it had been thought that responsibility was somehow a *personal* concept or somehow automatically built into a libertarian press, or that various of the media units would interpret "responsibility" in their own ways. Actually, it had generally been felt that the multiplicity of interpretations was what actually constituted not only a free press, but also a responsible press. At least it was felt generally in the Western world that a "free press" in a democratic sense was responsible *per se* to its social system.

But the Hutchins Commission thought differently. After seeing a very clear danger in growing restriction of communications' outlets and general irresponsibility in many areas of American journalism (the criteria for responsibility, of course, set up by the Commission), it offered the ominous warning that "If they [the agencies of mass communication] are irresponsible, not even the First Amendment will protect their freedom from governmental control. The amendment will be amended." [11] Another blast: "To the extent that the press does not assume its responsibility, some other agency must see that the essential functions of mass communication are carried out." (Would this be only for those of the media which do "not assume their responsibility" or for the *entire press?* The Commission did not see fit to get into that.)

Two basic assumptions (and conclusions) stand out in the Hutchins Commission Report: (1) That the press has a responsibility (defined by the Commission) to society; and (2) That the libertarian press of the U.S. is not meeting this responsibility, therefore a need for a new press theory exists.

For a while, it seemed that the majority of United States publishers were quite excited over the Commission's report and the implications which they read in (or into) it; but by 1950 the issue had largely settled down, the journalists perhaps thinking that the best policy was to ignore it. Certain ideas inherent in the report, however, had taken root in journalistic soil which was already well-fertilized with the philosophy of Welfareism and egalitarianism and a readiness to accept ever greater governmental power.

Here is what a press scholar wrote about the Hutchins Commission report in the 1960's:

> In 1947 the Commission on Freedom of the Press—thirteen men, of whom most were scholars and none was connected with the mass media—reported the results of several years' deliberations on freedom

10 Commission on Freedom of the Press, A *Free and Responsible Press* (Chicago: Univ. of Chicago Press, 1947).
11 *Ibid.*, p. 80.

and responsibility in mass communication. Their central theme was not the need for a rebirth of competition, but for a greater sense of responsibility on the part of the owners and personnel of the mass media. They said that the people would surely demand regulation of a press that did not meet more fully the needs of society for mass communication services. The fullest, most orderly, and perhaps most basic statement of the problem and of suggestions for change among American analyses, the report was attacked heavily by the press as unfair, badly informed, and unfriendly to freedom of the press. Much of the world of the press was to mellow somewhat in its attitude toward the Commission; some publishers even came to agree with most of its report.[12]

Some Implications of the Theory

Just what does "social responsibility" mean as used by the Hutchins group in 1947, nine years later in *Four Theories of the Press*, and by many others who have become attached to this new theory? It is really difficult—or even impossible—to answer such a question largely because its proponents do not seem to know the answer themselves. At any rate, it is interesting to try to *assume* what they might mean. One thing is certain: they do not mean "libertarianism" (for they see social responsibility as a theory growing out of libertarianism), nor do they mean media autonomy or editorial-determination of what is responsible (for that is what we theoretically have in libertarianism already).

Proponents of "social responsibility" see their theory closely related to the libertarian press system, but they see it as going beyond the free press theory, in that it places many moral and ethical—and conceivably, legal and other—restrictions on the press. It is a restrictive theory although its devotees do not stress this point. Instead of emphasizing "freedom," it stresses "responsibility" to the society of which the press system is a part.

If this responsibility is not forthcoming, voluntarily, then in time it will be absolutely necessary that it be imposed on the communications media by the government. According to the Hutchins group, press freedom is limited by a social responsibility to report facts accurately and in a meaningful context. Since such thinking inevitably leads to the advocacy of a regulatory system to watch the actions of the press and to keep it functioning "properly," the Hutchins Commission suggested that some

[12] Harold Nelson, *op. cit.*, xli–xlii. For other comments on the Hutchins Commission report, see *Columbia Journalism Review* (Summer 1967) for a long section—"The Hutchins Report—a Twenty-Year View," pp. 8–20. Cf. Frank Hughes, *Prejudice and the Press* (New York: Devin-Adair Co., 1950), a strongly worded attack on the Hutchins report, *A Free and Responsible Press*.

type of government regulation might be needed to assure that the press accept its responsibility.

The social responsibility theory implies a recognition by the media that they must perform a public service (of some specific "responsible" kind—that, presumably, they are not already performing) to warrant their existence. The main parts of the Commission's report which seemed to have antagonized many Amercian editors and publishers were those that intimated possible government involvement in the press system. Also there was the basic arrogance of this self-appointed "commission" which set up its own standards for press responsibility and then found the American press unable to meet them.

This "theory" of social responsibility has a good ring to it and has an undeniable attraction for many. There is a trend throughout the world in this direction, which implies a suspicion of, and dissatisfaction with, the libertarianism of *press*-related journalism. Implicit in this trend toward "social responsibility" is the argument that some group (obviously a judicial or governmental one, ultimately) can and must define or decide *what* is socially responsible. Also, the implication is clear that publishers and journalists acting freely cannot determine what is socially responsible nearly as well as can some "outside" or "impartial" group. If this power elite decides the press is not responsible, not even the First Amendment will keep the publishers from losing this freedom to government, we are told.

Nobody would deny that the press, in one sense, would be more "responsible" if some type of governmental supervision came about; indeed, reporters could be kept from nosing about in "critical" areas during "critical" times. The amount of sensational material could be controlled in the press, or eliminated altogether. Government activities could always be supported and public policy could be pushed on all occasions. The press could be more "educational" in the sense that less hard news (crime, wrecks, disasters, etc.) would appear, while more news of art exhibits, concerts, speeches by government personages and national progress in general could be emphasized. In short, the press would stress the positive and eliminate, or minimize, the negative. Then, with one voice the press of the nation would be responsible to its society; and the definition of "responsible" would be functional in a monolithic way—defined and carried out by government or by some non-journalistic power.

Many persons will object to this line of analysis and will say that "social responsibility" of the press of a nation does not necessarily imply government control. I contend that ultimately it does, since if left to be defined by various publishers or journalistic groups the term is quite relative and nebulous; and it is quite obvious that in the traditional context of American libertarianism no "solution" that would be widely agreed upon or practiced could ever be reached by non-government groups or individuals.

The only way a "theory" of social responsibility could have any significance in any country is for the governmental power elite to be the definer and enforcer of this type of press. Since in any country the organization of society—its social and political structure—determines to a large extent what responsibilities the press (and the citizen) owe society, every country's press quite naturally considers itself (or might logically be considered) as being socially responsible.

Assuming that a nation's socio-political philosophy determines its press system, and undoubtedly it does, then it follows that every nation's press system is in one sense socially responsible. For example, the Marxist or Communist press system considers itself socially responsible,[13] and certainly it is responsible to its own social system. A capitalistic press, operating in a pluralistic and autonomous context, would be diametrically opposite to what the Soviets consider a socially responsible press. It would be to the Soviets the most irresponsible press system imaginable, since "social responsibility" is roughly synonymous in Marxist theory to "party/government support." The Communist press *is* government, *is* reflective of the society, *is* an instrument for social harmony, conformity and support. As such it is "socially responsible."

The same thing might be said of the so-called "authoritarian" press system, exemplified for so many years in Spain. A critical press, a press which by its autonomous and pluralistic nature would tend to undermine national policy and disrupt national harmony, would be anathema in an authoritarian nation like Spain. It would be considered quite "irresponsible" in that context. As it is with the Marxist press, the so-called authoritarian press is conceived as an instrument of government—although in this case it might be privately owned. For the authoritarian press theory revolves around the idea that a person engaged in journalism does so as a special privilege of the National Leader. It follows that this journalist is under the obligation to the leader and his government. The authority of that state, the national equilibrium, the status quo, must be supported and preserved under this theory. This is social responsibility of the press—in an authoritarian context.

All this brings us back to the point about all press systems conceiving of themselves as socially responsible. This does not mean that every citizen (or journalist) in every country *approves of* everything the communications

[13] It is interesting that the Communist press considers itself, not only socially responsible, but free; and it considers the American press a typical "enslaved" press.

media do; many individuals may well wish for something else, but so long as a socio-political reality exists in a particular country, the press will support it. This is the simple fact of responsibility which follows from the basic *reflective* theory of press-government nexus discussed in some detail earlier in Chapter 2. Actually any other possibility would be unimaginable —at least over any substantial length of time. For the press of a nation is caught up in the governmental philosophy and fits into the structure of its society. If it does not, then the politico-social structure of the country is in flux; either the government must change to fit the press (unrealistic) or the press must change to fit the government (realistic).

Those who say that the press of the United States is "irresponsible" are seeing in it some real or imaginary danger to the national society—or those aspects of the society which appear to these critics as most important. Those who might view the press of the Soviet Union or Spain as irresponsible would do so if in their views the press was exhibiting mannerisms which endangered the equilibrium and on-going of their respective national societies. Responsibility and irresponsibility are not only relative to the particular national society under consideration, but even within an individual society the terms have a multitude of meanings depending on the degree of pluralism present.

It is significant, looking at the question from another perspective, that in an authoritarian country nobody believes (or makes a big issue of it) the press to be socially irresponsible. At least, if such brave critics exist, their complaints are made to one another and are not aired before the public. Only in a libertarian nation, or in a quasi-libertarian nation such as France, are there persons who criticize the function of the press and condemn it for its "irresponsibility." This might lead one to think that in order to be "responsible" a press system *must* be authoritarian; and this is a valid assumption if one is to pursue this idea of social responsibility very far.

Following from what has just been said, the following hypothesis could be made: The amount of social responsibility present in a press system is closely correlated to the amount of "control" some outside group exercises over that press system. Of course, such a hypothesis could be taken seriously, but only in the sense of considering "responsibility" as a kind of commonly-accepted or "socially-imposed" monolithic concept. Naturally, I do not accept such a hypothesis, for a libertarian press system (even one like we have in the United States) *is* (for me) socially responsible *for the very reason that it has little control from outside and much autonomy*. But my reason for considering the American press "responsible" is the very reason many of my colleagues consider it "irresponsible."

The new "Social Responsibility" theorists say that government should intervene "only when the need is great and the stakes are high." [14] They assure us that the government should not be heavy-handed. The question arises, however, as to just when is the need great enough and the stakes high enough for government to intervene. And just how much intervention by government is enough to be "heavy handed"?

According to *Four Theories of the Press* a "duty to one's conscience is the primary basis of the right of free expression under social responsibility theory." [15] This is all very well, but what relation does this have to the question of government intervention "if the need is great"? It would seem that "duty to one's conscience" is extremely relative and that one editor would feel he had one duty to *do* something that another editor in good conscience would feel he should *not* do. Which is irresponsible to society? I feel certain the Social Responsibility advocate could tell us; I cannot. In fact, I am prone to say (not knowing anything really about the journalistic action in question) that neither was *irresponsible*—that, in fact, in a free and autonomous press system they were both *responsible*, regardless of which action I might personally approve.

The American press had largely been proceeding on unregulated initiative up until about World War II. But the Hutchins group and other elitists have put this libertarian concept in question. For them it is certainly questionable, if not unwise, for unregulated initiative in journalism to continue, for the "citizen has a moral right to information and an urgent need for it" [16] and the implication is that the United States press is not giving it to the citizen. A moral right to *what* information? This is a significant question. Or, probably a better one: To *whose* information? Evidently the Hutchins group and other elite critics do not think that a libertarian (autonomous) information system is good enough. No proof, of course, is ever produced; it is just a "feeling" or "opinion" of those who believe that libertarianism has outlived its usefulness and should be replaced by "social responsibility." Admittedly, there are gaps in the information which our press gives the public; everyone in our society does not get the kind and amount of information he prefers in all cases. The gaps, indeed, are there. But anyone vaguely familiar with information theory and semantics knows that there will always be gaps, and if different reporters observe and communicate it, there will also be variant versions. And, what's more, changing from a libertarian press system to something else where different editorial decision-makers come on the scene will not

14 *Four Theories of the Press*, p. 95.
15 *Ibid.*, p. 97.
16 *Ibid.*, p. 101.

eliminate "the gaps" in public information. In fact, chances are that the gaps will become "chasms."

It is certainly not contended here that all information coming to the public from all mass communication outlets in a libertarian society is reliable, honest, complete, fair and "socially responsible." Nobody really knows just how much of it is—or if any of it is. Since, in a nation such as the United States, there is no ready definition for "social responsibility," there is really no standard to which our media seek to conform—even though, without a doubt, they would all conceive of themselves as socially responsible.

Their very pluralism, their very diversity is the base of their nebulous idea that in our society they are responsible. This is based on the concept of autonomy. Responsibility to our society implies a continuance of this very pluralistic (and autonomous) communication—with all of its virtues and evils—and a constant guard against any encroachments by government on any level to "define" what is "responsible" to society and further to align the press to its definition.

This concept of "press autonomy" seems much sounder (and easier to grapple with) than "social responsibility." All press systems can claim to be responsible to their societies, but the idea of autonomous media injecting a variety of opinions and ideas into the social fabric is one which only the libertarian system can reasonably claim. Libertarianism, or press autonomy, then, if it is to be considered as a separate theory must embrace the right of, or at least the possibility for, some press units to deviate from others to the degree that they will be considered "irresponsible." When the term and concept of "irresponsible journalism" disappears from the United States—or even comes close to disappearing—then will be the time when journalistic freedom and autonomy are dead.

Self-Respect and Freedom

As a kind of footnote or suffix to what has been said above about "social responsibility," the matter of *self-respect* on the part of the journalist should be touched upon. Respect for one's self, or self-esteem, is closely related to the autonomous kind of freedom discussed in this book. Those persons, or those media, desiring freedom and cherishing it must also respect themselves and the capacity they have to contribute to the total pluralism of viewpoints and information in their society. Actually, the journalist who does not operate in freedom (who cannot make his own decisions) will find it difficult to have much respect for himself. Freedom is closely related to self-respect.

What Kant calls the "dignity of ends" is possible only through personal autonomy, or the freedom of will, and it is this autonomy that is the ground of absolute value of the person. Dignity or worthiness comes from self-respect and has no substitute.[17] At least it may be said that the person who has no freedom or little freedom cannot have very much self-respect. It is possible, I suspect, for a person who has freedom to act in such a manner that he will lose his self-respect, but probably he had little to begin with. Quite likely, the inheritance of freedom will enhance the self-respect of those who have had little or none in a situation of no-freedom. Freedom at least gives a person the chance to be himself, to do positive and self-rewarding acts, and to learn by his misadventures. If a person is free, he is free to make choices—and many of these choices may well be considered "irresponsible." [18]

Freedom is to self-respect what water is to a flower; in general it nourishes it and makes it grow. Of course, a flower can get too much water; but with too little (or none), it will surely die. It is the same with a person. A person with too much freedom—or with more freedom than he is able to control—becomes psychotic and his creativity or positive activity begins to wither. Too much freedom, then, can harm a person—if he is not mentally, emotionally and spiritually capable of handling it. And, of course, what harms a person can, if projected, also harm his society. This admitted possibility is, of course, the rationale used by the anti-freedom social controllers to tamper with the liberty of individuals. It seems to me, however, that it would be better that a society tolerate the small amount of harm it might suffer from those of its members who are harmed by too much freedom than to "protect" them at the expense of the general freedom among all the citizens.

Actually, if I had no self-respect, I would care little whether I had freedom. In fact, the person with no self-respect is happier when he has his decisions made for him; as Eric Hoffer has pointed out, he finds satisfaction only by losing himself in a mass movement or attaching himself to an organization. Self-respect makes a person believe that he can do something with freedom, and even if his freedom leads him into trouble and causes him pain, his self-respect is enhanced by the realization that he has at least put himself into a position where he must take the consequences. Self-respect grows with freedom, and freedom grows with self-respect.

Freedom leads to what I call "psychic openness"—a level of awareness or consciousness which makes it possible for a person to "let himself go"

17 H. J. Paton, The Categorical Imperative: A Study of Kant's Moral Philosophy (New York: Harper Torchbooks, 1967), pp. 188–89.
18 Harris, The Authentic Person, p. 29. Cf. Nathaniel Branden, The Psychology of Self-Esteem (Los Angeles: Nash Publishing Corp./New York: Bantam Books, 1971).

in the sense of permitting himself to respond to the creative urge which comes when he realizes that his actions and thoughts are not determined by forces from without. Psychic openness allows a person to realize his potential through confidence in himself. This condition flourishes in an atmosphere of freedom.

William Ernest Hocking has emphasized that freedom is necessary both for personal and for national development; in addition, journalists must be free if a nation's press is to be healthy and develop properly. In his *Freedom of the Press* he maintains that freedom is a necessity of one's being like breathing and that one suffocates when his freedom is taken away. Further commenting on the value of freedom to the individual, he says:

> To the individual the value of his freedom lies simply in the enjoy-
> ment of his capacity for self-direction. It is not separable from the
> value of being alive; for to live is to act, and action *means* free action
> —the adjective adds nothing to the natural fact. It is only as spon-
> taneous action is interfered with that the notion of freedom comes
> to consciousness or receives a name.[19]

The libertarian is one who knows there are always some kinds of restrictions on his freedom, but he constantly "pushes" back these limits. He is committed to expanding his area of free choice and self-determinism just as far as possible. This provides creative tension for his life. This desire for freedom and autonomy will, of course, for the *rational* person go beyond simply fighting for freedom for the sake of freedom, although freedom in itself is good; it will be tied to creative action, rational thought, and basically selfish motivation.

If a person wants to be truly himself—"if he craves for self-expres-sion," as Karl Jaspers puts it, then there "arises a tension between his self-preservative impulse, on the one hand, and his real selfhood, on the other." [20] A person, then, must be willing to gamble, to take a chance, to accept the possibility that self-expression is a kind of commitment, and that he may suffer in various ways by this self-expression. As Jaspers says: "Immediate self-will is what primarily moves him, for he is animated by a blind desire for the advantages attendant on making good in the strug-gle for life. Yet the urge to self-expression drives him into incalculable hazards which may render his means of livelihood perilously insecure." [21] Certainly this danger related to free expression applies to the press and to

[19] W. E. Hocking, *Freedom of the Press* (Chicago: University of Chicago Press, 1947), pp. 56–57.
[20] Karl Jaspers, *Man in the Modern Age* (Garden City, N.Y.: Doubleday and Co., Inc.—Anchor Books, 1957), p. 43.
[21] *Ibid.*

the individual journalist. The journalist with self-respect who is proud of the freedom which gives him the chance for self-expression, regardless of its hazards, will be eager to have his say, take his stand, commit himself—and be willing to take the consequences for this exercise of freedom. This is nothing less than the Existential Journalist, and his commitment to freedom, his desire for authenticity, and the general expansion of life which results are well worth the dangers referred to by Jaspers.

If a journalist does not respect himself, he cannot really respect anyone else, nor can anyone else respect him. Without freedom (autonomy) there is really nothing a journalist (or a mass medium) can do that warrants respect. There is little real respect, dignity or sense of progress that comes from being a puppet or slave, whether this servitude is voluntary or forced by some brute Power. So it is the fight for freedom and autonomy—even if it is never really won—that gives a person respect for himself and drives him ever deeper into creative thought and action.

The journalist who stops fighting for increased self-determinism and autonomy is the journalist who has capitulated to the comfortable world of slavery where his only commitment is the vapid commitment to conformity and indecision. Although this subject will be explored further in the last part of the book, suffice it to say here that freedom is the spring from which self-esteem, authenticity and creativity bubble. And, without freedom, one becomes a zombie, and zombies have no self-respect.

5

Three Libertarian Myths

R ELATED directly to both freedom and responsibility of the press are many glittering platitudes or slogans which, through constant and uncritical use, have taken on a kind of sanctity in America. And, rather strangely, libertarians—or many who like to call themselves libertarians—evoke these slogans with great assurance and abandon, not recognizing the subtleties lying beneath their sugar-coated exteriors. Actually, many of these oft-used sayings are even more than platitudes and slogans: they are myths. They are accepted and trusted although they have no real substance and no rational foundation.

Three of the most popular and sacred of these myths are: (1) that the "people have a right to know"; (2) that the people have a right "of access to the press"; and (3) that the press is a "fourth branch of government." All of these slogans are used by those who call them into service in "defense" of freedom of the press. But, actually, they are destructive of press freedom; in fact, they are subtle myths which contradict journalistic autonomy by placing obligations on the free press.

All three of these myths, as "American as apple pie," are extremely popular today and one opens himself to charges of seditious activity, disloyalty to journalism, acute myopia—of even insanity—when he dares to question one or all of them. But even at the risk of spoiling the "pie" by looking at the apples in it, let us consider briefly these three myths and their relationship to libertarianism.

MYTH # 1: "THE PEOPLE'S RIGHT TO KNOW"

The idea is prevalent today, particularly among journalists in the United States, that the people have a right to know what is going on in their Government. In the foreword to his book, *The Right to Know*, Kent Cooper says that "the right to know" has been adopted generally by newspapermen as "a slogan in the cause of conserving and broadening the right which has commonly been called 'press freedom.'"[1] Mr. Cooper is correct; the term has indeed almost become synonymous with "press freedom." To use the term in this way, however, is a mistake; it leads to a problem and poses a danger. Many defenders of press freedom have appropriated the expression "the people's right to know" because it sounds more democratic than the simple term "freedom of the press" and shifts the theoretical emphasis from a private and restricted institution (the press) to a much broader base—the citizenry.

The Concept's Fuzzy Shape

Walter Lippmann has spoken of the "perennial" conflict between "the public's right to know" and governmental secrecy,[2] and Walter Cronkite, as late as 1973, posed the question: "Why can't the American people see that freedom of the press is not some privilege extended to a favored segment of the population but is purely and simply their own right to be told what their government and its servants are doing in their name?"[3] Even Secretary of Defense Robert S. McNamara, in 1968, asserted that the American people "have both the need and the right to be thoroughly informed" on governmental decisions.[4] And in 1973, among the many voices which were extolling the people's right to know, was that of Congressman Charles W. Whalen, Jr., who warned that because reporters were being asked to reveal their sources "the people's right to know" was at stake.[5] The Ohio representative expressed hope that "the general reader" would be alerted to dangers to his "right to know" which were inherent in the subpoenaing of reporters and their notes by grand juries.[6] Whalen was

[1] Kent Cooper, *The Right to Know* (New York: Farrar, Straus and Cudahy, 1956), xiii.
[2] John Luskin, *Lippmann, Liberty, and the Press* (University, Ala.: University of Alabama Press, 1972), p. 241.
[3] Charles W. Whalen, Jr., *Your Right to Know* (New York: Vintage Books, 1973), x.
[4] James Aronson, *Deadline for the Media: Today's Challenges to Press, TV and Radio* (Indianapolis: Bobbs-Merrill Co., Inc., 1972), p. 62.
[5] Whalen, *op. cit.*, 186. It is interesting that Congressman Whalen, being so interested in the "people's right to know," desires legislation which would permit reporters to *keep the people from knowing the sources* of their stories and quotations.
[6] *Ibid.*, xiii.

busy at the time trying to pass a "Shield Law" which would permit reporters to protect their sources by not letting the people know who they were.

On and on we could go for many pages indicating a growing concern in the United States for "the people's right to know," but it is really not necessary. As Hillier Krieghbaum pointed out in 1972 the slogan has been "a rallying cry during the past decade or longer." [7] And it has been primarily an *American* rallying cry. The concept is not important, for example, in Britain. Here is what Anthony Howard, Washington correspondent for *The Times* of London, has to say on this subject:

> . . . despite the occasional rousing declarations on editorial pages, the people's right to information in Britain is nowhere taken seriously. One only has to look at the catalogue of complaints to the Press Council to notice that the automatic instinct of the British citizen is to identify not with the press, but rather with the victims of its curiosity. . . . For it is precisely the public's right to know that politicians of all parties in Britain join together in a collective phalanx to resist. . . .[8]

In Britain, it seems, the public and press people alike reject any concept of a *right* to know what their Government representatives are doing. At any rate, most of them fail to see where they get such a right. In the United States, on the other hand, large numbers of citizens and journalists (and occasionally, even a government official) assume the "right" and believe they have a basis for it (even a legal one). But if such a "right" does exist, what is its source? Is it implicit in the First Amendment to the Constitution as we are often told? Where is there the slightest insinuation in the Bill of Rights that the people have a *right* to know? The right of the press to freedom is there; the right of the people to know is not there. But the myth persists. And related to it is another assumption: that the press has the obligation (responsibility) to see to it that the people know. Where did the press acquire this obligation? The First Amendment only forbids laws abridging press freedom; it places *no* obligation on the press—not a single one! If there is some theoretical right of the people to know, the obligation to grant it would fall on Government, not on the press.

Although many press people in America still believe in the older

[7] Hillier Krieghbaum, *Pressures on the Press* (New York: Thomas Y. Crowell Co., 1972), p. 54. Cf. John L. Steele, "The People's Right to Know: How Much or How Little? (*Time* Essay), *Time* (Jan. 11, 1971), pp. 16–17; Bud Schauerte, "Yes, There is the Right to Know" (FoI Center Report No. 003, May 1967, U. of Missouri); Francis Williams, "The Right to Know," *Twentieth Century* (Spring 1962), pp. 6–17.
[8] Anthony Howard, "Behind the Bureaucratic Curtain," *The New York Times Magazine* (Oct. 23, 1966), pp. 34–94 *passim*.

concept of *their* rights as representatives of "the press," they realize that by the simple semantic trick of bringing "the people" and their supposed rights into the picture, they tend to dissipate some criticism from intellectuals that the press has only selfish motivations in its continual quest for freedom. (This is, of course, exactly the kind of motivation the press *should* have.) "Non-press" libertarians, often as suspicious of the press as they are of Government, like the idea of a "people's right to know" for other reasons. In terms loaded somewhat against the press, these "democrats"—often found on university faculties—say that if anyone should have a "right" in this area it should be the "people," not institutionalized units like newspapers. So the argument goes, and with it a de-emphasis of the older concept of press freedom and a growing emphasis on the press's (and Government's) responsibility to give the people what they presumably have a right to know.

Editors and publishers criticize the Government for restricting the people's right to know, and the people, if they are concerned about it at all, usually blame the editors and publishers for lack of initiative on one hand or some kind of bias on the other. Also in the United States today editors and publishers are lamenting governmental secrecy while the Government is decrying press irresponsibility, general meddling and the endangering of national security. So "the people" blame the press; the press blames the Government, and the Government blames the press.

One group of critics, the libertarian intellectuals, are divided: one branch berates the press for not giving the people what they should have, for its inaccessibility to minority viewpoints and its general apathy, while the other faction makes Government its main target. The first group might be called the *press responsibility* group, placing the main burden of fault upon the press, and the second group the *Government obligationists*, believing the main trouble lies with the increasing sensitivity and secrecy of Government. Both groups, of course, obviously believe that the people have a right to know—not merely a desire or need to know. It is just that the first group blames the press, while the second group sees Government as the main restrictor of this "right" of the people.

Most journalists (especially those in the broadcast media) like to equate the "people's right to know" with the traditional concept of "freedom of the press." And most Government officials, looking at the situation from another perspective, are not so sure; they tend to have questions about a people's right to know and wonder just where the people get such a right. Government tends to conceive of press freedom as basically *no prior censorship by Government*—or at least by the legislative branch of Government, and that is about the scope of it. Government sees nothing in the Constitution or anywhere else—except perhaps on editorial pages—that says that it should give out to the press (or to the "people") everything that goes on in its complex institutionalized system. It seems that Government, at least, takes the press-Government "adversary" concept seriously: the press has a right to *try* to get information, and the Government has a right to *try* to keep certain of it secret.

Should Government be a Publisher?

A very strange thing about all this is that if the people really do have a right to know Government business, then the Government is initially and chiefly responsible (maybe totally responsible) for fulfilling this right. Not the press. The press cannot really do it, even if *it feels it must*, for it is impossible for the press to provide this "people's right" as long as even one Government official is "unavailable for comment," is secretive or evasive, or classifies one document so as to withhold it from release.

If, therefore, the Government is principally (or totally) responsible for permitting the people to know (after all, the Government, and *not the press*, represents the people), certain interesting potentialities arise: For instance, should not the Government—having such a responsibility to let the people know—actually get into the mass communication business? Should not the Government take the initiative and make the people know what is going on in its massive workings, not waiting for the commercial press to ferret it out? And, could not the Government through its own publications and resources fill in a multitude of gaps with information and viewpoints which the people have a right to receive, but presumably are not receiving? In other words, if such a right to know does in fact exist, should not the people's government—and not a theoretically free and independent press—bear the responsibility for fulfilling or granting this right? Why should the *press*, any more than any other private or commercial institution, be saddled with the awesome responsibility of providing Government information to the people?

Undoubtedly many will say that the Government has no right competing with private media. But, strangely, many of these same persons are the ones who talk of the "people's right to know" and bemoan the fact that they are not knowing nearly enough. If the people have such a right, what difference would it make how the right were fulfilled? One answer might be: Freedom of the press in the context of the First Amendment implies a press which is a non-Government press, a commercial press, a libertarian press, a pluralistic press. Although this answer itself is open to argument, let us assume that it is valid; one might then ask: But if the country's non-Government press is not permitting the people "to know" and the people have a right to know, what other alternative is there?

It is at this point that the "press responsibility" devotees mentioned earlier would reply that the press should be made more enterprising, less monopolistic, more imbued with its obligation to let the people know. Who would make the press more responsible in this sense? Certainly not the Government which cannot make even itself more responsible in this respect. Why do these social responsibility people think it is any easier to reform the press and make journalists see the error of their ways than it is to make the Government decide to change its ways and inform the people? In short, the argument runs again to a critique of the press, and the brunt of the burden falls again on the reporters, editors and publishers.

So we have a circular, never-ending theoretical game and the emphasis is taken off of what precipitated the discussion in the first place: *the people*. If the people really have this right to know, it should be enforced even to the point of disciplining uncooperative or irresponsible journalists and Government officials. If the people really do *not* have such a right (and it is my position that they do not), then there is really no need to try to enforce—and the situation stays exactly as it has been: the press trying to get some information; the Government trying to keep some away from the press and the people; and the people trying to get some information from both the press and the Government.

Many readers will think the preceding paragraph at best, facetious, or at worst, extreme. It is not meant to be; it is stated quite deliberately and seriously, for if the people's right to know is really to be taken seriously, we must not let anything (such as press autonomy or Government secrecy) stand in its way or subvert its intention. If this right exists, it must be a civil right of great importance. Why, then, one might ask, has not the Supreme Court (or even the Constitution itself) dealt with it? (Congressional "laws" as shown in certain civil rights cases, are not enough by themselves; they must be "enforced" by the Executive branch of government. Would not this also be true of "Right to Know" legislation—if any really existed? But it is rather interesting to speculate about the Executive Branch enforcing such legislation *on itself* when it wants to keep something secret in line with some kind of "executive privilege.") Why is it that such a "right" (to know) is only mouthed and is ignored in actual practice, unrecognized and unenforced and unappreciated on the pragmatic level, not only by "the people" who are supposed to have it, but also by the press and Government who are supposed to grant it?

Who Believes in "The Right to Know"?

This much is obvious: The Government does not really believe in such a right, for in spite of the 1966 Freedom of Information Bill—opposed as it was by powerful forces within Government and containing numerous "loopholes"—Government persists in exercising all the secrecy and restraint that it possibly can, feeling that either the people do not need to know many things or they have no right to know them. Something else is equally obvious: The press itself does not take this "people's right to know" very seriously in spite of its incantations, for its persistence, enterprise and independence in seeking news from Government and in attacking Government secrecy leaves much to be desired—this in addition to the press's own restriction and censorship of Government information through its own editing processes.[9] If American journalists *really* believe in the people's right to know, they would insist that Government give them everything—and, beyond that, they would insist that Government force the media to withhold nothing of what they did get.

And "the people" themselves—what of them? Do they feel that their "right" is being taken from them or subverted? Do they write letters to their Congressmen and to their newspapers demanding the granting of this right to know? Do they write the President or his cabinet officers protesting that this important right is being lost? How many governors, state legislators, congressmen and other Government leaders in Washington receive messages from indignant citizens demanding their "right" to know? How much real pressure is being applied to Government or to the press, for that matter, by citizens insisting on their "right to know"? The answer: very little. And the reason is that *the people* really think that the only right they have is the "right to want to know or to try to know."

The people hope they will find out enough—from the press or from other sources. But they do not spend much time writing the President or his cabinet officers protesting that their "right" is being withheld; nor do they contact the Supreme Court justices and insist that their "right" to know be protected. Nor do they make it an issue in elections. Nor do they march, picket, protest or otherwise publicly demonstrate for this allegedly important civil right. If they really thought they had such a right—or if they cared about it—they would surely show more interest in it. Perhaps it is that they are smart enough to sense that they really have no rights except those which can realistically be delivered to them by their Government apparatus; and they know that Government cannot, and will not, ever deliver this "right to know" to them.

The concept of the people's right to know has mainly been promoted in America since World War II; books such as Kent Cooper's *The Right to Know* (1956) and Harold Cross's *The People's Right to Know* (1953)

---

[9] Let me emphasize that I am all in favor of the press's determination of what it will and will not print about Government activities—this is in line with journalistic autonomy; but if the press insists on a "people's right to know" it must take note of this basic philosophical (and practical) problem.

and numerous articles have been printed declaring such a "right" and usually castigating Government for infringing on it. Involved is some type of theory that the people have an inalienable right to know what is going on in Government—because it is their Government.

Such a concept implies, further, that Government is under an obligation to satisfy the public's right to know by revealing *all* of its information. (*Part* of its information will not suffice, for if the Government decides which of the information it will keep back, it will be accused of censorship.) It follows that, if this is the case, the press is essentially excluded from the process (except in a kind of transmission sense). No wonder, then, that many persons have difficulty equating "freedom of the press" with "the people's right to know." The people would have their "right" *even without a press*; therefore, freedom of the press could hardly be the same as the people's right to know. The Government, therefore, would really be the responsible party and the press theoretically would be superfluous to, or at least peripheral to, the concept.

The Press as a Gatekeeper

Although it is doubtful that they *really* believe in the "right to know," journalists manifest a devotion to this people's right—evidencing, in so doing, a repudiation of their own editorial "freedom." This journalistic criticism of Government for not letting the people know, many will say, is quite logical and understandable. But is it really? Would it not be just as logical and justifiable for Government officials to complain that the press is infringing on this same theoretical right? If the people have such a right, then why should Government be the only recipient of adverse criticism? In effect, the editors and publishers imply that Government alone keeps the people from "knowing" governmental business. But this implication should not be permitted to go unchallenged.

What about the press itself? If there is a right to know, then what of the press's obligations and activities in this respect? This is what the Government might ask. Why do we not hear journalists dealing with this aspect of the "problem"? For certainly any person vaguely familiar with the typical news operation of both the print and broadcast media must recognize that only a very small portion of Government-related information available to the editors ever gets to the audience member. Many of the news people who evidence such concern about Government's part in keeping the people from knowing show very little concern about their own parts in keeping Government information from their readers, listeners and viewers. (If anyone has so lost touch with the news operation of a news medium as to doubt the veracity of these statements, he should visit the newsroom and note how much news goes into the wastebaskets instead of into the columns or newscasts. And, he might also notice how little agonizing there is on a day-to-day basis about keeping the readers, listeners and viewers from knowing this "scrapped" information.)

Press people will in all likelihood reply to this by saying that it is the press's prerogative to make decisions as to what will and will not be published. I wholeheartedly agree with this reply, but if one supports a "right to know" this does not appear a logical argument; it simply is a substitution of press-determinism or press news-management for Government-determinism or Government news-management. Another response might be that even though *some* media here and there restrict or censor information which the people have a right to know, *other* media elsewhere fill in these gaps. So, they may say, *somewhere* in the complex and sprawling press of the nation *some* people are granted their right to know. This, too, seems a poor argument and tends only to place the burden on the reader to dig out the complete picture of what is going on in Government from a reading of *all* the publications and exposing himself to *all* the broadcast media of the land, an obvious impossibility.

Conclusion

It might be well to summarize the main points which have been made in the preceding paragraphs: (1) nobody is quite sure just where this "right to know" of the people comes from or who should provide it; (2) the press generally blames the Government for the poor situation; (3) the Government does not indicate in a systematic and pragmatic way that it even believes in such a "right"; (4) "freedom of the press" and the "people's right to know" are often used synonymously but they should not be; (5) a "right to know" places an obligation on the press, thereby contradicting the libertarian concept of *not* publishing something; (6) if the "right to know" is actually a people's right, the people do not realize it or are not concerned with it; (7) if such a right exists, the Government is logically responsible for seeing that the people have it because the Government is in the critical position and legally represents the people; and (8) the press itself withholds Government information from the people, thereby evidencing that it does not *really* believe in a people's right to know.

Such a discussion as has been presented in regard to this "myth" always gets around to the question: "*Right to know what?*" This leads to the next question: Who, then, will decide *what* is appropriate for the people to know? For certainly somebody or some group must, since all information cannot be disseminated, make this determination. If this is true, the concept of the "people's right to know" is already abridged, for it simply means now the "right to know" *certain* things that *certain persons* want us to know. We already have that kind of right, and always have had it—but a "right" to know only certain things selected for us by others is hardly more than a mythical right and one which should be erased from our journalistic lexicon.

MYTH # 2: "RIGHT OF ACCESS TO THE MEDIA"

Another myth has grown up in the United States, having been nurtured by the same type of libertarians that instituted the "people's right to know" myth. This second myth goes a step further and suggests that the people also have the right to get their information and opinions into the press. It adds to, or completes, the concept of the *people's press* which has been grafted onto the tree of press freedom in America. People—all people—we are told, should have the right to have their voices heard in *their* press. Increasingly we hear that the press does not belong to the press people, but to all the people.

Stimulating, although perhaps not initiating, this myth was the Hutchins Commission of the 1940's which reported that the press "is not free if those who operate it behave as though their positions conferred on them the privilege of being deaf to ideas which the processes of free speech have brought to public attention." [10] Since this 1947 pronouncement there has been a whole rash of related opinions filling the lecture halls and literature of journalism, all reiterating a basic theme: that journalists have no preferred or special position *vis à vis* the Constitutional provision of press freedom.

The Barron Proposal

Exactly twenty years after the Hutchins Commission report, a professor at George Washington University's Law School, Jerome A. Barron, published an article in the *Harvard Law Review* advocating public access to the media which he referred to as a "new First Amendment right." [11] Barron derided the "free marketplace of ideas" as nothing more than a "romantic conception" that permitted the press to indulge in its own information control and censorship. He called for an interpretation of the First Amendment which goes beyond restraining government interference with the press and focuses on the restraint of access exercised by the

[10] Commission on Freedom of the Press, A *Free and Responsible Press*, p. 9.
[11] Jerome A. Barron, "Access to the Press—a New First Amendment Right," *Harvard Law Review* (Spring, 1969).

press itself. And what is Barron's cure for such an evil in our press system? It is the judicial forcing of the press to give space to every variety of opinion.

Barron insisted in 1967 and has continued to insist since—most recently in a 368-page book, *Freedom of the Press for Whom?*,[12] published in 1973—that public access to the media would give the First Amendment a positive, rather than a purely negative dimension. All minority opinions and what he calls "unpopular" points of view should be legally admitted to the press. Barron has also called for the mass media to begin the practice (to be enforced by the courts) of the right to reply to attacks and the right to purchase advertising space or time for expression of opinion.

It is rather surprising that the American Civil Liberties Union, vigorous defender of First Amendment rights, jumped in very quickly to help fight for Barron's 1967 ideas about a "right of access." It is also interesting to note that the ACLU was among the greatest supporters of the Hutchins Commission suggestions along the same line twenty years earlier. Even Barron was somewhat surprised by the ACLU's support, for he had supposed that the group's oft-enunciated belief in government-hands-off-the-press would have made him a foe, not a friend, of the organization.

At an ACLU biennial national conference in 1968, Barron's ideas were lauded by the ACLU's Communications Media Committee, and members of a press workshop at the conference reported back to the full conference that "denial of access to newspapers and magazines is a civil liberties problem, and that the ACLU should initiate and support efforts to open access to these media." [13] So it was all coming up again, although Prof. Zechariah Chafee of the Harvard Law School had noted the Hutchins group's toying with a similar proposal for government-imposed "responsibility" and had rejected it as dangerous and untenable.

Reflecting Chafee's views in 1969 was the press critic, Ben Bagdikian, who clearly saw the danger in Barron's proposal. He pointed out that "one function of news is the professional judgment of what is more and what is less important at any given hour." He also noted that "despite all the flaws in these decisions, someone has to do it, and judges and legislators are not able to do it better." [14]

Despite a few scattered warnings such as were offered by Chafee in

[12] Barron, *Freedom of the Press for Whom? The Right of Access to Mass Media* (Bloomington: Indiana University Press, 1973). This book brings up to date some of Barron's earlier writings and attempts to answer some of the criticisms of his proposals.

[13] Gilbert Cranberg, "New Look at the First Amendment," *Saturday Review* (Sept. 14, 1968), p. 136.

[14] Ben Bagdikian, "Right of Access: A Modest Proposal," *Columbia Journalism Review* (Spring, 1969), pp. 10–13.

the 1940's and Bagdikian in the 1970's, the force of intellectual opinion has been running with Hutchins-Barron & Company. The rationale for increased "public" or outside control of media content is usually that the people cannot make themselves heard. Listen to what is probably a typical expression of this new Barronite emphasis. John Hohenberg, professor of journalism at Columbia University, is speaking about the "role of a free press"; and specifically he is deploring the lack of public access to the media:

> The press, of course, continues to publish a handful of letters to the editor daily, and usually more on Sundays. But for all practical purposes, public access to the news media is even more limited than public access to office-holders. People do have a chance to see a congressman or an alderman, a mayor or a judge, at election time, but how many—outside small towns—have ever seen the editor of their local newspaper? Let alone talk with him! . . . . The fact is that, with a number of brilliant exceptions, too many newspapers in every open society still pay insufficient attention to minority causes and unpopular opinions generally. Righteousness is rationed in too large a section of the press and the unpopular critics and the minorities are the first to say so.[15]

Writing in a publication of the University of Missouri's Freedom of Information Center in 1967, Dennis E. Brown also bemoaned the shrinking of pluralism and rationalized the "right of access" due to this "increasing paucity of intellectual wares, hawked by a diminishing number of vendors." [16] He went on to reiterate the *people's press* "myth" by saying: "In effect, freedom of the press—a right granted to all of the people—becomes the privilege of media managers and owners. A romanticized theory of the marketplace of ideas fails to take into account the increasing inequality of access that prevails in modern society."

One other interesting statement from Brown's article, one which typifies the Barron redefinition of press freedom, should be noted; it shows how the Barronites are focusing on pragmatic *access* to media instead of editorial self-determinism. After lamenting the growth of monopolies in mass communication and pointing out their dangers, Brown suggests a generalized guideline: "that the test of a community's opportunities for free expression should be based not so much on the availability of alternative media but on the abundance of opportunities to be heard in media with the greatest impact." And, then, comes Brown's clincher—which must cause a smile to cross the faces of all scholars who have recognized the terrific problems connected with media impact or effect studies; Brown

15 John Hohenberg, "The Free Press on Trial," *Current* (June 1971), p. 44.
16 John C. Merrill and Dennis E. Brown, "Regulatory Pluralism in the Press?" (FoI Center Report No. 005, Oct., 1967, University of Missouri-Columbia), p. 1.

concludes that "community control of a particular medium, therefore, would be proportionate to the impact of that medium on the community." It is interesting to imagine the makeup and functioning of such a Community Control Group regulating its degree of control over various media on the basis of the community impact each of these media has.

Ayn Rand: An Opposing Perspective

The whole attempt to "redefine" the First Amendment press freedom since about the time of the Hutchins Commission has stemmed from the belief that the "people" have some kind of inalienable *right* to have someone else publish their opinions. This "myth" of people's rights in this area is increasingly potent in America, but it is not accepted by everyone. One of the foremost writers in recent years to take issue with it is Ayn Rand. In her *Virtue of Selfishness*, she writes:

> The right of free speech means that a man has a right to express his ideas without danger of suppression, interference or punitive action by the government. It does *not* mean that others must provide him with a lecture hall, a radio station or a printing press through which to express his ideas.[17]

As Ayn Rand sees it, there are no "rights" for the consumers of journalism if no journalist chooses to produce particular kinds of journalism certain consumers *want*. There is only the right for any citizen to be a journalist and produce them himself—or for him to *try* to get the kind of journalism he desires, or to *try* to get his ideas into journalism. "Remember," writes Ayn Rand, "that rights are moral principles which define and protect a man's freedom of action, but impose no obligations on other men." [18] A case in point would be Ayn Rand's own book in which these words appear; she had the freedom to write the book, but she had no right to force it to be published by her publisher. It was published *voluntarily* by the publisher.

She notes that the Bill of Rights reads that "Congress shall make no law . . . abridging the freedom of speech, or of the press. . . ." and that it does not "demand that private citizens provide a microphone for the man who advocates their destruction." [19] This whole subject of the people's right to access is, to Ayn Rand, contrary to the concept of individual freedom. Carried very far this "right of access," as Miss Rand sees it, would mean that a publisher has to publish articles (or books) he considers worthless, false or evil, and that the owner of a newspaper must

[17] Ayn Rand, *The Virtue of Selfishness*, p. 97.
[18] *Ibid.*
[19] *Ibid.*, p. 99.

turn his editorial pages over "to any young hooligan who clamors for the enslavement of the press." [20]

Although Ayn Rand perhaps loses some support for her case by focusing on "young hooligans" and "radicals" and the like, her philosophical base seems sound enough. For certainly the First Amendment gives no evidence of sanctioning the *forcing* of people's ideas into the private media of the country, of forcing the editors to relinquish their editorial functions to the courts, or of even hinting that the people have more than the right to speak freely. Freedom of expression is indeed there; but the right to talk freely is not the same thing as the right to have that talk publicized or amplified through someone else's private media. I may *want* to get my ideas into *The New York Times*, but where do I think I get the *right* to have them printed there?

It is amazing how many normally sensible people condemn the principle of press self-determinism on the grounds that everybody and every group does not get equal access to the press. Friedrich Hayek deals with this very issue when he writes cogently about intellectual freedom:

> To deprecate the value of intellectual freedom because it will never mean for everybody the same possibility of independent thought is completely to miss the reasons which give intellectual freedom its value. What is essential to make it serve its function as the prime mover of intellectual progress is not that everybody may be able to think or write anything but that any cause or idea may be argued by somebody. So long as dissent is not suppressed, there will always be some who will query the ideas ruling their contemporaries and put new ideas to the test of argument and propaganda.[21]

The most interesting sentence in the quotation from Hayek above is this one: "What is essential to make it serve its function as the prime mover of intellectual progress is *not that everybody may be able to think or write anything but that any cause or idea may be argued by somebody*" (emphasis added).

A Few Basic Considerations

Let us consider a few journalistic ramifications inherent in this concept of "right of access." The First Amendment provides that the government *will not pass any laws* which abridge press freedom. Although press freedom is not defined in the Bill of Rights, an explicit concern with not passing laws which might diminish press freedom appears to be quite clear.

[20] *Ibid.*
[21] Friedrich A. Hayek, *The Road to Serfdom* (Chicago: Univ. of Chicago Press— Phoenix Books, 1944), p. 165.

When any group—even Government seeking to remedy certain suspected evils in the press—tells a publisher what he must print, it is taking upon itself an omnipotence and paternalism which is not far removed from authoritarianism. And, if the courts involve themselves in determining what will be printed, this would have to be approved by legislation; so it would, in effect, be a case of government-sanctioned (legislative branch) and government-implemented (judicial branch) control of editorial content of the press. Apart from the danger of editorial dictatorship of journalism from outside forces implied in Barron's concept, it is interesting to speculate on the physical and very practical problems which would face the courts—in making these editorial decisions as they arose in a news-hungry world.

"Freedom of the press" *must* mean something; obviously it does in the sense that it means almost anything at any time in any context which a particular person using it wants it to mean. The publisher, of course, stresses the fredom of the *press*, while the reader, seeking sometimes in vain for his viewpoint or orientation in certain newspapers, stresses the freedom of *information* concept. The Government official who attempts to keep certain information from the press, has his own definition: the newspaper has a right to print something if it can get it—a kind of "freedom to print" but not necessarily a "freedom to get" concept.

Perhaps we try to make the term "freedom of the press" cover too much. If we were to understand it narrowly, in the sense clearly indicated by its syntax, we would emphasize the *press* and its *freedom* from restraint or control. This would mean that the "freedom" belongs to the "the press." The press alone, in this definition, would be in the position of determining what it would or would not print. The press would have no prior restrictions or directions on its editorial prerogatives; this would be press freedom.

Some Perplexing Questions

The person, however, who is concerned about what does not get into the press is not primarily a supporter of the concept of press freedom stated above; he is not overly concerned that the press should make editorial determinations. However laudable his reasons for such a stance might be, he must recognize that his position is potentially *authoritarian*—or even basically authoritarian—just as the existing libertarianism of the press (the *press's* freedom) is potentially *restrictive*. Naturally this "anti-press's-freedom" person justifies his position on the basis that it is what is "best for society" and contends that the press must be willing to give up its freedom in order to be socially responsible.

Few sincere and concerned persons would quarrel with the position that "the good of society" is important or that the press should be "responsible to society." However, trouble arises when these theoretical concepts are applied to the actual workings of the press in society. What, for instance, is the best way to do the most good for society, and what is the best way for the various segments of the press to be socially responsible? Nobody quarrels with the goal, only with the idea that there are definite and set ways of reaching it. There are many who would feel very strongly, for example, that forcing minority opinions (especially "certain" opinions) into a newspaper would be very harmful to the "social good," and that this would be the epitome of social *irresponsibility*. It obviously depends on one's viewpoints and values as to what he feels is "responsible" or "irresponsible" to get into the press; this would be as true with court-coerced material in the press as with press-determined material.

In addition to the *what* of the concept mentioned above, the *how* of the concept adds further complications. How will decisions be made about what shall or shall not be printed under a Barron-type system? What would be a fair and rational manner of making such determinations if we were to take them out of the hands of individual editors and publishers? A federal press court of some type? A national *ombudsman?* An FPA (Federal Press Agency) organized along the lines of the Federal Communications Commission?

From among all the "minority" positions in a given community or in the nation, which ones would have a "right" to be published and which ones would not? Which spokesman for any one "minority" or "constituent group" in the society would be published as representative of that minority or group? Or would all of them—or many of them—be published, since undoubtedly there is a pluralism in minority opinions even on a single issue? Would all minority opinions forced into the press be given equal "space" and emphasis? How would such things be determined in any more objective and fair way than they are by the diversity of media managers? These are basic and important questions—questions which would constantly plague the *authority* (presumably a legal one) which would have to make such decisions. It is said that the press (or the various units of it) are irresponsible in making such decisions; what would keep this new authority from being just as irresponsible?

Minority viewpoints which one membership of some extra-press authoritative body would deem valuable and beneficial to society might well be irresponsible, inane and irrational to another equally perspicacious authoritative body. Undoubtedly, even among the staunchest advocates of minority rights there is preference for *some* minorities over others. Some, for instance, would find the views of the Congress of Racial Equality more to their liking than, say, those of the John Birch Society or the Ku Klux Klan. Do they all get equal treatment as they appeal to the "Barron

Courts" for forced access to the press? Biases being what they are among human beings (journalists *or* judges), some minorities will always get preferential treatment. To deny this is to deny the reality of human nature.

Beyond the actual "access" to the press of minority opinions, there is another rather perplexing and closely related problem. What emphasis should various minority views receive in press, or even in a single newspaper? Would this be decided by the proportion of the total population which the "minority" under consideration comprises? Would it be decided on the basis of the "worth" or "intrinsic value to society" of the viewpoint espoused? If so, how would such worth be ascertained? Would it be decided on the basis of the economic or political pressure which a particular "minority" group might bring to bear on the press Authority?

We now come to another question. To some it may not appear to be important, but it certainly would cry out very quickly for an answer under a coercive-publishing system. This is the problem of defining a "minority" group or a "minority" viewpoint. Just what is a minority in the sense of seriously considering the forced publication of its opinions or positions? Just as the majority is composed of many minorities, there are minorities within minorities. How does one determine which of these minorities should be heard? Or are they all to be heard with equal force?

Many persons will reply that these are really unimportant and theoretical questions that should not be permitted to interfere with the serious consideration of a forced-publishing system. Sure, they will say, there will be problems and weaknesses, but we must push on in spite of obstacles toward a New Journalistic Day when all opinions are recognized as equal and get equal treatment in the press. This is a beautiful and idealistic aim, indeed, but one which appears extremely naive in the light of the practicalities of day-to-day journalism.

It seems likely that a forced-publishing concept will take root only when our society has moved much farther along the road to Orwell's 1984, where a paternalistic and omnipotent Power Structure makes our individual decisions for us so that we shall be responsible to society. But even then, I would wager that somewhere amid all the opinions which theoretically would be blending deliciously into one big View-Stew there would be some "minority" fretting away—misunderstood, misused and hoping for a greater voice in social affairs.

MYTH # 3: THE PRESS AS "FOURTH BRANCH OF GOVERNMENT"

The third myth, which has by now acquired a large following in the United States, is that the American press is somehow an unofficial, but very real, part of the governance of the country. Related to this are similar concepts of the press being a "watchdog," a "check" on governmental excesses, and an adversary of Government. Journalists especially are fond of wrapping themselves and their "profession" in these glittering generalities.

Books and articles abound propagating these related myths; so intense and profound has been the bombardment of such ideas in journalism schools, in newspaper and broadcast offices, in journalistic groups of one kind or another, that surely a person stepping into American society for the first time and not knowing any history would think that U.S. journalists are elected by the people to fulfill some specified public function. What seems to have started these myths was a reference to the reporters' gallery of the English Parliament as the "fourth estate" by Edmund Burke or Thomas B. Macauley.[22] So from a casual reference by an Englishman, whoever he may have been, the myth arose, crossed the Atlantic to America where "estate" became "branch" and now we live with the belief—fuzzy as it may be—that the press is a kind of fourth branch of government, checking on the other three branches—the Executive, Legislative and Judicial—as each of these supposedly check on one another.

Governmental Branch or Check?

Usually when the term "fourth branch of government" appears in articles, books and speeches, it is used in a casual and vague way with no real attempt made to clarify its meaning. Douglass Cater's popular book, *The Fourth Branch of Government* (1959) is a case in point. It covers the usual press-government relationships and highlights certain problems and tensions always creeping into such relationships; but it never really gets around to discussing the real topic of its title. What exactly does Cater mean by the press being the fourth branch of government? What is the justification for the press's being this, and what are the ramifications of it? Who gave the press this status? Does the press really want it or accept it? These and a dozen related questions present themselves to the reader of the book, but Cater fails to come to grips with them.

Related to the general assumption (at least among journalists) that the press is a "fourth branch of government" is the belief that the press is a "check on government." This would, of course, put the press *outside* government, would exclude the press from government and would place it in a position of watching and criticizing government. Would this not contradict the "fourth branch of government" concept which would imply that the press is *part* of government—one of its branches? Certainly the press cannot be both government and a check on government. Of course, what is really the case is that the press is not part of government; it is

[22] Herbert Brucker, *Freedom of Information* (New York: The Macmillan Co., 1949), chapter 4.

private enterprise. It is true that portions of the press—as exemplified by a handful of media in the 1973 Watergate scandal or the earlier "Pentagon Papers" disclosure—may very well be a check on government, but the concept of the whole press as being a "fourth branch of government" is no more than a fine-sounding myth.

Let us assume for a moment that the "fourth branch of government" is valid, that it is more than a myth. Then we must ask: How are the branches of our government determined? In two cases they are elected by the people and in one case they are appointed by the executive who is an elected representative of the people. In other words, if our government is democratic, the people have a voice in its constitution or composition. How then is this "fourth" branch of government determined? Are its members elected or appointed by the people? The answer is, of course, that they are not. They get into business just as the owner of a hardware store gets into business. They sell their merchandise—news, advertising space, opinion and entertainment—to customers who want their type of information. But the people do not appoint nor elect the press to be part of their government. The idea is not only mythical, but almost farcical. It is highly presumptuous of journalists to call the press the fourth branch of government even if they really do not mean it.

Probably the answer to all of this is simply that the press likes to think of itself as a part of government—or a check on government, or a "watchdog" of some kind. In effect, the press (or portions of it) is a self-appointed governmental branch, check or watchdog. The U.S. Constitution certainly does not give the press such a status, although many persons claim they can "read into" the Constitution such responsibilities for the press.

Watchdog or Adversary?

The "watchdog" function of the press is a very powerful aspect of the fourth-branch-of-government concept; it is used regularly in journalistic speeches and literature. The press is a "watchdog", we are told. But just what does that mean? To whom does the watchdog belong? Whom is it watching, and for what reasons? If the press is a "watchdog," presumably it is protecting something. Just what is that? Is it the people's watchdog, watching the government, and keeping the government from doing harm or violence to the people? This must be the core of the concept. But the question arises: Who gave the watchdog this mission? Did the "people" buy the dog for this purpose? If so, then the press belongs to the people; they own it, and therefore they have a perfect right to expect it to protect them against their own government.

But, on even superficial analysis, we can see that this is not the case.

The "people" do not own the press; it cannot, therefore, be their watchdog. It has no specific duties—except those which the press people themselves want to accept. Why should the press "watch" the government any more than it should watch the people? The metaphoric myth of a "watchdog" is as meaningless as is its companion, the concept of the "fourth branch of government." Certainly *the press* does not recognize any such function. We see all around us newspapers and other media which like to consider themselves part of the "press" not serving as "watchdogs" on government, checks on government or critics of government. Some, in fact, tend to be apologists for government. They do not consider themselves "watchdogs" on anybody; or, if they do, they see themselves as dogs belonging to no master and having no leashes.

Related very closely to this concept, of course, is the idea that the press has an "adversary" relationship to government—that press and government are natural enemies. Many writers and speakers have stressed this adversary role of the press.[23] What is rather interesting is that it is usually journalism people who allude to this relationship and what they mean usually is that the press is to be an adversary to government—but not the other way around. The prospect of government being an adversary to the press is, of course, a natural part of a press-government adversary relationship, but it does not seem to occur to most journalists. They want it all one way. We fight you; but you don't fight us. We try to get information from you, but you don't have the right to try to withhold information from us. This is really not much of an "adversary" relationship. If the press values so highly this role of government adversary (a myth!), it should recognize that the government, then, has an equal right to be a press adversary. Otherwise there really is not any meaning to the concept, and journalists would do well to forget it.

Justice William O. Douglas once said that "secrecy in government is not fully eliminated by the First Amendment."[24] An understatement, but true; and if the press and the government are truly adversaries, then secrecy in government should not be eliminated. The press, in its adversary role, may try to get at the secrets, but the government, in its adversary role, will attempt to preserve its secrets. Douglas believes that the First Amendment "does not say that there is freedom of expression provided the talk is not 'dangerous'."[25] He might have gone further and said also that neither does the First Amendment say that the government cannot try to keep secrets.

[23] William Rivers, *The Adversaries* (Boston: Beacon Press, 1970) is a good example of the sizable literature existent stressing the adversary role of the press.
[24] William O. Douglas, *The Right of the People* (New York: Arena Books, 1972), p. 51.
[25] *Ibid.*, p. 11.

Conclusion

Out of all these fuzzy slogans and myths, there does seem to be a kind of general assumption emerging: that the Amercian press is at once *part of* the governmental apparatus of this country and also a kind of enemy or adversary of the governmental apparatus. James Reston even refers to "the artillery of the press" which he seems to think should be levelled at the government.[26] That is another strange metaphor, for why should the press try to bombard the government with artillery? Artillery is designed to subdue, destroy and kill. Why should the press want to do this to government—especially if the press itself is a "fourth branch" of such a government? But this is obviously just another mystical, meaningless and clever label, really meaning very little. For even James Reston ends his book, *The Artillery of the Press,* on a strange note which contradicts his "artillery fire" theme. "Clever officials," he concludes, "cannot 'manipulate' reporters, and clever reporters cannot really 'best' the government. From both sides, they have more to gain by cooperating with one another, and with the rising minority of thoughtful people, than by regarding one another as 'the enemy'." [27]

So, in the end, even Reston really recognizes the mythology implicit in his book's title, and in the whole concept of the adversary relationship of press and government. And, therefore, with the final sentence of his book, Reston wipes out the myth which he had been supporting all the way through. But unfortunately, many people do not read past book titles, and many others do not manage to read to the very last sentence of a book. So the effect of books like Reston's is that they perpetuate the myths rather than helping to dissolve them. Therefore, it is not difficult to understand why the three myths discussed in this chapter are becoming ever more entrenched in basic beliefs of Americans. Mythology is becoming Religion, and Religion is becoming Truth. Demythologization, especially in certain sacrosanct intellectual areas, is an unpopular and even dangerous exercise, and obviously it is in for much difficulty in the last half of the twentieth century.

[26] James Reston, *The Artillery of the Press* (New York: Harper & Row—Colophon Books, 1967).
[27] *Ibid.,* p. 108.

Part Two

THE JOURNALIST
AND HIS
JOURNALISM

6

Toward Professionalism

WHILE various influences outside journalism, dealt with in earlier chapters, are restricting press freedom and autonomy, other conforming forces are growing within journalism itself, instilling in its practitioners a readiness to accede to less and less editorial self-direction. As society becomes more complex and forceful and minorities get more active and powerful, these internal journalistic forces seem to become more seductive. The pressure to conform, to join, to cooperate, and submit to a hierarchical power-structure and to sublimate self to others has even infected journalists—traditionally among the most individualistic persons in the world.

As journalism becomes more institutionalized, causing it to perform in increasingly predictable ways, it appears to aspire for a "professional" status which would confer some sort of prestige on it which would substitute for the loss of personalism and autonomy which is fast disappearing. Journalists—at least growing numbers of them—like to feel that they belong to a group, an organization, a body of practitioners sharing similar skills, values and goals. Increasingly the single individual is pressured to join, to cooperate, to conform, and to accept as his guiding principles the social norms of his group, his organization, or his society. He is pulled closer together with others by the powerful magnet of collective thought and action for the public good.

Group allegiance is becoming the watchword of modern society and understandably it has become more important in journalism. Journalistic groups have grown into huge organizations and these have developed into potent social institutions. Mass media are now generally considered to be well-organized, highly structured social entities which presumably perform definite functional roles for the general and specialized publics. Journalists have already become institutionalized persons, fulfilling certain duties every day which are assigned them by their particular leaders. Even the journalistic leaders march to the tune of the "apparatus" or the institutionalized aggregate. This is why great editors, such as were common in the nineteenth century, are hard to find today. "Personal journalism" appears doomed, not because individual journalists have lost the ability to make independent decisions but because the pressures of the institution of journalism itself have forced them to abdicate much of their real autonomy to the Collective Will. Karl Jaspers writes of this situation when he takes note of the demise of the authentic person:

> He must work in an aggregate which, so far as he is concerned, exists in and by itself. Harnessed in an apparatus directed by an alien will, he obediently does the work that is assigned to him. If any sort of decision is demanded of him, it is taken haphazard within the limited province of his function, without his having to probe to the bottom of things.[1]

Editors are more and more willing to compromise their authenticity by making decisions on the basis of what their publishers say, what some of their colleagues say, or what some kind of "mass desire" their readers are presumed to have. The masses and "public opinion" are more important in journalism than ever before, with journalistic leadership eroding before the pervasive glorification of mass desires and "socially significant forces." Jaspers contends that such concern for the masses is nothing more than "a sophistical instrument for the maintenance of vain enterprises, for fleeing from oneself, for evading responsibility, and for renouncing the attempt to climb toward true humanhood." [2]

The Growth of "Mass-Mindedness"

As individualism declines, the collectivities that take over rationalize their depreciation of the person by calling forth the utilitarian argument of the most good to the most people. Such diverse writers as Ortega y Gasset, Erich Fromm and Eric Hoffer have, in recent years, warned about the loss of individualism and a drift to collectivism and robotization where giant entities or institutions—political, economic and social—guide the

[1] Karl Jaspers, *Man in the Modern Age* (Garden City, N.Y.: Doubleday Anchor Books, 1957), p. 54.
[2] *Ibid.*, p. 77.

destinies of individual persons with a firm but impersonal hand. In such a situation, smaller entities are gobbled up by larger ones, just as persons are swallowed by institutionalized collectivities. Journalists are consumed by newspapers and broadcasting networks, while newspapers and networks become prey to powerful political and economic powers. Listen again to Jaspers, writing specifically about the press:

> If the Press is to pay, it must enter more and more into the service of political and economic powers. Under such controls, pressmen cultivate the art of deliberate lying and indulge in propaganda on behalf of matters repugnant to their higher selves. They have to write to order.[3]

As negative and cynical as these words may be, Jaspers has hope for the journalists, believing that if they can become imbued with the spirit of Existentialism, they can redeem themselves and inject society with a saving serum of personalism and commitment. What must a journalist do, according to Jaspers, to break out of his institutionalized cage guarded by the "mass mind"?

Jaspers answers: He can "realize the ideal of the modern universalised man," and "merge himself in the tension and the reality of the day, adopting a reflective attitude toward these." And what is more, Jaspers maintains that a person (journalist) can rebel against being manipulated by others; and it is only through this rebellion that he becomes sincere. The journalist, Jaspers believes, "becomes insincere when he is content with that which brings satisfaction to the majority." [4]

These words have a strange similarity to those of Friedrich Nietzsche, who maintains in *Beyond Good and Evil*, that "the feelings of devotion, self-sacrifice for one's neighbor, the whole morality of self-denial must be questioned mercilessly" [5] and that the "noble human being honors himself as one who is powerful, also as one who has power over himself, who knows how to speak and be silent, who delights in being severe and hard with himself." [6] And, cutting right to the essence of the rebel against institutionalization, Nietzsche defines human nobility as "never thinking of degrading our duties into duties for everybody; not wanting to delegate, to share, one's own responsibility; counting one's privileges and their exercise among one's *duties*." [7]

Carl Jung, a psychologist, is just as frightened by what is happening

---

[3] *Ibid.*, p. 136.
[4] *Ibid.*, pp. 136–37.
[5] Friedrich Nietzsche, *Beyond Good and Evil* (New York: Random House Vintage Books, 1966), p. 45.
[6] *Ibid.*, p. 205.
[7] *Ibid.*, p. 221.

as are the Existentialist theologian and the philosopher-poet quoted above. This mass-mindedness which has obsessed the journalist along with the rest of us is, according to Jung, robbing him of "his foundations and his dignity" and causing him to become "a mere abstract number in the bureau of statistics." [8] Jung admits that there is much reason, in the face of giant collectivities, for man to lose confidence in himself and his own importance. "The man who looks only outside and quails before the big battalions has no resource with which to combat the evidence of his senses and his reason," says Jung. But this is exactly what Jung believes most people are doing; they are overawed by large numbers, giant enterprises, and are daily reminded of the futility and impotence of the individual personality, "since it is not represented and personified by any mass organization." [9] In the face of growing institutionalization and mass mindedness, it is little wonder that the indvidual shrinks and his faith in himself and his own judgment falters. The upshot, according to Jung, of this is that "responsibility is collectivized as much as possible, i.e., is shuffled off by the individual and delegated to a corporate body." [10]

Organization, of course, is necessary in a society of human beings. And life and work in any area is unthinkable without a certain amount of co-operation (voluntary, it is hoped) among individuals. But, as Aldous Huxley has pointed out, organization can also be fatal. "Too much organization," he writes, "transforms men and women into automata, suffocates the creative spirit and abolishes the very possibility of freedom." [11] Huxley contends that modern men have gone a long way toward becoming conformists and that their conformity "is developing into something like uniformity"; he quotes Erich Fromm as saying that "uniformity and freedom are incompatible" and that "man is not made to be an automaton, and if he becomes one, the basis for mental health is destroyed." [12]

Over-organization, institutionalization, mass-mindedness, and all the conformist pressures of the modern world are turning people into what Lewis Yablonsky has called "robopaths." These are dehumanized people-machines "whose pathology entails robot-like behavior and existence." [13] The term "robopaths" seems to exemplify what Jaspers, Nietzsche, Fromm, Huxley and others have discussed as mass-men, conformists and automata. Yablonsky defines robopaths as machine-like men who exhibit ritualistic

[8] C. G. Jung, The Undiscovered Self (New York: New American Library—Mentor Books, 1958), p. 24.
[9] Ibid., p. 25.
[10] Ibid., p. 26.
[11] Aldous Huxley, Brave New World Revisited (New York: Harper & Row—Perennial Library, 1965), p. 23.
[12] Ibid., p. 21.
[13] Lewis Yablonsky, Robopaths (Baltimore: Penguin Books, Inc., 1972), p. 7.

behavior patterns in the context of well-defined and accepted norms and rules, who are not spontaneous and creative, who are "other-directed" rather than "inner-directed" (to use David Riesman's terms), and who are alienated from *self* by being only a "component of a social machine." Yablonsky's robopaths are also alienated from *other people* (strange as it may seem) because "their interaction with others is usually in terms of 'others' as *objects*, not *human beings.*" [14]

George W. Morgan in his *The Human Predicament* is in agreement with Yablonsky about the growing robotization of persons. He believes that that "enormity of all organizations and institutions, the hugeness of the political apparatus, the apalling rush of events, and the unthinkable powers of extermination that constantly hover over us, all threaten to crush us into impotence." [15] And this situation, he implies, either leaves us foundering in frustration in life's turbulent seas, or it causes us to seek a haven in the enormous organizations or collectivities. (The Existentialist, however, might add that we could swim the best we can in spite of the turbulence and enjoy the challenge even if we finally sink beneath the giant waves.) Normally, according to Morgan, we choose to become institutionalized, not being able to handle the frustrations and anxieties that come with freedom. Sounding much like Yablonsky, Morgan writes:

> Man's every activity is more and more modeled after the machine—standardized, automatic, and repeatable. In all departments of life unceasing efforts are made to avoid, or render unnecessary, the judgments, decisions, and even the presence of the individual man.[16]

Conformity, it would seem, is indeed the haven for timid, herd-like men, and as societies become ever more complex, the haven appears increasingly attractive for those who would, in Fromm's words, "escape from freedom." Transcendentalists of the nineteenth century, like Existentialists of today, were concerned about the growing tendency of men to give up their liberty. Ralph Waldo Emerson, for one, reminded us that nothing is really sacred "but the integrity of your own mind" and that whoever would "be a man must be a nonconformist." [17] All of society, said Emerson, is conspiring against the manhood of each citizen. He compared society to a joint-stock company

> in which the members agree, for the better securing of his bread to each shareholder, to surrender the liberty and culture of the eater.

[14] *Ibid.*, p. 13.
[15] George W. Morgan, *The Human Predicament* (New York: Dell Publishing Co.—Delta Books, 1968), p. 66.
[16] *Ibid.*, p. 61.
[17] William H. Gilman (ed.), *Selected Writings of Ralph Waldo Emerson* (New York: New American Library—Signet Books, 1965), p. 260.

The virtue in most request is conformity. Self-reliance is its aversion. It loves not realities and creators, but names and customs.[18]

Numerous writers have not only pointed out the dangers to personal authenticity or human "nobility" inherent in mankind's drift toward mass-mindedness but have recognized the great appeal of such a drift. One of these, Nevitt Sanford, in his notable psychological work *Self & Society*, has noted the substantial material rewards of conformity: jobs, promotions, the liking and respect of colleagues and peers.[19] These rewards are, of course, in addition to the basic reward of peace and psychological comfort brought on by not having to make many decisions and suffer their consequences. Sanford maintains that those who do adapt to institutions suffer real damage, in spite of certain surface benefits mentioned above. Independent thinking declines with institutionalization, and fewer and fewer people are feeding original and creative thought into their societies. Journalists, in spite of their lip service to creativity and originality, are becoming extremely robotized, according to Sanford. He maintains, for instance, that "few correspondents or commentators show any independent thinking unless, like Walter Lippmann, they speak from positions of such dignity and status that they are virtually unassailable." [20]

There seems little doubt that there is a tendency toward institutionalization, and, as it takes place, the person increasingly loses his authenticity and individuality and becomes a mere cog in the social machine. He has, in a sense, been forced (at least, pressured) by social complexity to divest himself of more and more of his independence of thought and action in order to continue to exist and function in a mass-oriented and collectivized world. As he becomes ever more "other-directed," he progressively thinks less and less about his own autonomy and more and more about the "collective" in society and about the institutions which subsume him.[21]

The Institutional Concept

A discussion of institutions or the process of institutionalization immediately brings up the matter of concept or purpose. What is it that the institution is supposed to do? What is the objective, the philosophical goal, of the institution? What is its proper function in society? Every institu-

---

[18] *Ibid.*

[19] Nevitt Sanford, *Self & Society* (New York: Atherton Press, 1966), p. 211.

[20] *Ibid.*

[21] Many important works have dealt with the forces in man and in society which contribute to his collectivization and institutionalization: a few of these are Erich Fromm, *Escape from Freedom;* B. F. Skinner, *Walden II* and *Beyond Freedom and Dignity;* Eric Hoffer, *The True Believer;* William H. Whyte, Jr., *The Organization Man;* Bertrand Russell, *Power;* David Riesman, *The Lonely Crowd;* Friedrich Hayek, *The Road to Serfdom;* Gustave LeBon, *The Crowd,* and Victor C. Ferkiss, *Technological Man.*

tion, the sociologists tell us, has both a *concept* and a *structure*. The concept is the purpose, entailing all the proper functions, and the structure comprises the physical and human resources with which the institution tries to achieve the concept.

Journalism may well be considered such an "institution" in society; and further, within the institutionalized activity of journalism, its "units" —newspapers, magazines, and broadcasting stations—may also be considered institutions. When we talk about the purpose of journalism in the United States, for example, we are attempting to get at the overall broad *concept* of the activity. When we talk about the purpose of a particular medium (e.g., *Reader's Digest*), we are discussing an individual or specialized institutional *concept*. Thus, the press can be thought of as an institution and, at the same time, a certain newspaper can also be considered an institution. The *press*, theoretically, has a concept (general purpose—or purposes), and each individual medium also has a concept. And, of course, the press has a structure (all the media of the country including buildings, equipment and personnel of the total press system), and each medium has its structure (its own building, equipment and staff).

In a libertarian country the overall press concept is likely to be rather vague and undefined in the minds of the functionaries (journalistic workers) who tend its pluralistic structure. In an authoritarian country, on the other hand, the concept is better defined, and refined, and there is more of a common understanding of it among the journalistic functionaries. What seems to be happening in libertarian nations (at least in the U.S.A.) is that press functionaries are increasingly accepting the view that journalistic concepts and functions should be commonly shared by all *valid* or *responsible* journalists. There seems to be a growing desire for a more "shared" or monolithic concept and a concomitant suspicion of an individualistic or pluralistic splintering of press concept. This increased pull into the institutional "comfort" and security of conformity, adaptation and "group-think" is, of course, being developed and reinforced by the growing importance of press organizations, societies, groups, councils and associations.

Unionization (e.g., the American Newspaper Guild) of journalists is further depersonalizing American journalism. Associations of Big Establishment Journalism such as the American Newspaper Publishers Association (ANPA) and the American Society of Newspaper Editors (ASNE), representing the major publishers and editors of the country, are forces which provide additional impetus to the growing monolith which is American journalism. Journalism education, with its accrediting machinery for approving programs which meet "acceptable" standards, helps further to discourage non-conformity and journalistic individuality. Such internal institutionalizing forces, in addition to the external pressures from non-press social groups and from Government and the courts, all combine to present to the American press and to the individual journalist imposing barriers to their independent, authentic and autonomous development.

Journalistic institutionalization may be considered on three levels: (1) the total media system, (2) the individual medium, and (3) the individual journalist. It is the contention of this book that on each level (*see Figure* 6) the concepts are being eroded by the pressures and social forces discussed above. Theoretically, the concept of the *total media system* in the United States is libertarianism (no outside interference); the concept of the *individual medium* is editorial self-determinism, and the concept of the *individual journalist* is maximum personal freedom of expression and the freedom to work for any medium he chooses.

The above institutional concepts, of course, are ideal libertarian concepts on each level which evidently seem to many persons today to be outmoded, reactionary, unrealistic, selfish, and not in tune with the "social emphasis" which the press (and all social institutions) must put on their activities. So, in each case the ideal concept is being restricted, redefined, modified, refined and brought into line with what many believe to be "social reality." Government and other non-press forces interfere more and more with the total press system, interested in establishing for the press overall guiding principles; so the total press becomes increasingly monolithic—at least on a conceptual level. Editorial self-determinism of the individual medium is, at the same time, being shifted to the hands of associations of journalists, to the courts and to press councils of one kind or another.

As this happens, the individual journalist increasingly finds himself fitting neatly into the organization, writing to a formula, making fewer and fewer personal decisions, lost in the bureaucratic maze of the Journalistic Machine. Autonomy suffers in each instance, and a blandness spreads at each level: in the total journalistic system, in the particular medium and in the individual journalist. Journalists must fight against this pervasive loss of autonomy. Admittedly this is not easy, for the forces of social institutionalization, starting with the big organizations, creep steadily downward until the beleaguered journalist finds himself isolated, captured as it were, by impersonal and potent forces which threaten at every turn to affect his sense of values and his daily journalistic life.

Journalistic Roles and Duties

The main reasons (maybe the only reason) the press is criticized and offered a wide range of advice by those who feel they are qualified to

Figure 6

U.S. JOURNALISTIC "INSTITUTIONALIZATION":

THREE LEVELS

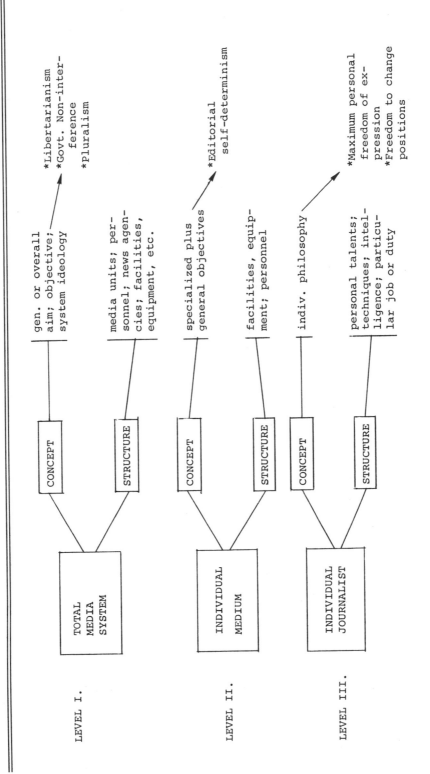

guide it are related to the belief that the press is failing in its proper functioning. This assumes that the functioning is "proper" if it will perform *certain* duties and perform *certain* roles in society. This criticism also assumes that *someone* other than the journalists themselves knows what the "proper" roles and duties are; and since the press is not (in all cases) in agreement with this role-definer and duty-prescriber, the press is therefore adjudged "bad," "irresponsible," "unjust," "prejudiced," *et cetera*. Most critics, fretting about the specific cases where portions of the press do not meet their expectations, indict *the press* (implying the whole press), not realizing that "the press" cannot be irresponsible or responsible or anything else. Even accepting the critics' criteria for judgment, only individual media can be "good" or "bad," "weak" or "strong."

Just what are the proper roles and duties for the American press? Nobody—not even the journalist—seems to know. Or, perhaps it would be more accurate to say that *everybody thinks he knows*. There are, of course, a few traditional or commonly expressed duties of the press which are held by some persons in certain quarters of the press; these are often taken for granted, taught in journalism schools and normally looked upon as "obvious" functions. For example, we hear that the press is supposed to present news, opinion, interpretation, entertainment and advertising. And, some say that it is the duty of the press to be objective, fair, balanced and complete in its news presentation. Some say the press must be a leader; others contend it must reflect what goes on in the society. On and on goes the list of press roles: to provide the community a forum, to interpret the news, to afflict the powerful and comfort the afflicted, to criticize the Government, to change the society or to perpetuate the *status quo*. Each person, it seems, has his own list of roles and duties for the press with certain of these roles considered more or less important than others.

What it all boils down to, really—or what it *should* boil down to—is that journalistic roles and duties are what the *individual media people* want them to be. Although this is perhaps changing rather rapidly, it is still substantially true; this can be seen not only in the conglomerations of duties suggested in literature and speeches but also in the actual content of the media themselves. A little bit of everything can be found in the diverse media system of the nation; different audiences are addressed; different topics are emphasized, and even similar ones are treated in different ways; different editorial positions are taken; different ways of presenting information (makeup, pictures, typography, etc.) are used. One medium says one thing about a certain subject; another says another thing. Commentators disagree (even within the same medium) and columnists propound different versions and interpretations of what happened. All this may not be the best for press credibility, but it is a hopeful sign for press freedom. This situation may also give rise to indictments of "press irresponsibility"; but as long as this variety of news and views persists, our free press has a chance. For shouts of "irresponsibility" indicate that the press is still free and signalize the continued existence of at least some autonomous segments in the media system.

In spite of what has just been said, it is true that, by and large, journalists pay lip service to a few institutionalized goals. The press, they say, should inform, alert people to dangers, interpret, educate, lead, persuade, provide a forum, inspire and entertain. The list could be extended, but really there is no need. Such lists are usually expressed in such generalized terms that each "duty" can be *interpreted* in innumerable ways by various journalists, thereby making the duties mean almost anything.

The press *should* do this or that; a particular newspaper or television station *should* perform this or that duty; an individual journalist *should* conduct himself thusly. These "shoulds" are being heard more and more as institutionalization of journalism progresses into professionalization, as the individual journalist accommodates himself to the comfortable bigness of the Organization and the media units of the press system recognize many advantages of Group-Think and collective activities. Press institutionalization systematizes ever-more-common ways of doing things and develops a certain exclusivity and eliteness about what is right and wrong, good and bad, for the *group* of journalists: this, of course, leads to a concern with professionalism.

The Road to Professionalism

Journalists—at least many of them—like to think of themselves as "professionals" and journalism as a "profession." They have seen that respectability, general esteem, even awe tends to surround any institutionalized activity which goes by the name of a "profession." They have also noted that medicine and law, for instance, in being accepted generally as professions, have not only been endowed with a kind of prestigious or elite image but have been able to regulate the numbers and functioning of their members and to have some semblance of common expectations and order in their routine activities. The journalists have also seen that, usually, with increased professionalization comes increased financial remuneration. It is little wonder that journalists, often intellectuals or pseudo-intellectuals, find the lure of professionalism very strong. Professionalism may give them an aura of respectability, of public acceptance, of dignity, and at least the collective psychological comfort which they fail to find as autonomous, individual tradesmen or craftsmen.

In spite of the fact that the idea of professionalism is growing in

American journalism, individual journalists do not really know what journalistic professionalism entails, what being a "professional" really means. Even two journalists with similar backgrounds may act in ways which each would consider "unprofessional" by the other. The term "professional," of course, can be used—and is used—in different ways; but when journalists talk about their "profession," they are limiting the meaning to something that can be dealt with. One of America's foremost sociologists of recent years, William J. Goode, has insisted that professionals comprise a homogeneous community whose members share identity, values, definition of role and interests. He says that members of a profession "are bound by a sense of identity" and "share values in common." [22] (The observer looking at American journalism can see very easily that journalists really do not have a single identity, nor do they share the same values, nor do they have a definition in common of their role.)

Just what is a profession? Originally a "profession" meant simply the act or fact of professing; it has developed from that base to mean the "occupation which one professes to be skilled in and to follow. . . . a vocation in which professed knowledge of some branch of learning is used in its application to the affairs of others, or in the practice of an art based upon it"—(Oxford Shorter Dictionary).

Professionals do profess—even now. They profess to know better than others the nature of certain matters, and to know better than their non-professionalized clients what they need to know and in what proportions they need to know it. Professionals claim the exclusive right to practice, as a vocation, the arts which they profess to know.

Other characteristics of a profession are given in the book *The Professions in America*, edited in 1965 by Kenneth S. Lynn and the editors of *Daedalus*.[23] Here are a few of them:

The professional is expected to think objectively and inquiringly about matters which may be, for the outsider, subject to "orthodoxy and sentiment which limit intellectual exploration."

The professional assumes that he can be trusted since he professes to have certain expertise which the layman does not have; therefore the professional journalist would say that a non-journalist is not a true judge of the value of the service he receives.

The professional asks protection from any unfortunate consequences

[22] William J. Goode, "Encroachment, Charlatanism, and the Emerging Profession: Psychology, Sociology, and Medicine," *American Sociological Review* 25 (1960), pp. 902–14.
[23] Kenneth S. Lynn (ed.), *The Professions in America* (Boston: Houghton Mifflin Co., 1965), pp. 2–3.

of his professional actions; the professional journalist would, therefore, collaborate with fellow journalists to make it very difficult for any one outside to pass judgment on the performance of one of their number. In other words, only the professional can say when he or his colleagues make a mistake. (The extreme sensitivity to criticism which has marked portions of the press in recent years attests to the growing enchantment with this aspect of professionalism by some press elitists.)

A professional believes in close solidarity with other members and thinks that it is a good thing to present a "solid front" to those outside the profession.

The professional would be a person who is able to meet various minimum "entrance" standards for the profession. This might be a particular academic degree as a qualification for practice; it might also be a special license which would identify him as a professional member in good standing.

And, finally, according to Lynn in his introductory section of the book, the true professional is never hired. He is retained, engaged, consulted by someone who needs his services. The professional has, or should have, almost complete control over what he does for his client.

Bernard Barber, writing also in *The Professions in America*, says that professional behavior may be defined in terms of four essential attributes: (1) a high degree of generalized and systematic knowledge; (2) a primary orientation to the community interest rather than to individual self-interest; (3) a high degree of group-control of behavior through codes of ethics and through associations organized and operated by the work specialists themselves; and (4) a system of rewards (monetary and honorary) for those who conduct themselves most notably within these codes of ethics.[24]

Having presented these basic characteristics of a "profession," it is well to look at journalism and ask the question: Is it a profession? Obviously it is not, although it has some of a profession's characteristics. There is no direct relationship between the journalist and his client. There is, in journalism, no minimum entrance requirement; anybody can be a journalist who can get himself hired—experience or no experience, degree or no degree. No journalist is expected (or required) to abide by any professional ethos or Code of Ethics. No journalist is licensed, thereby giving the "profession" some kind of control over him. There are no professional standards commonly agreed upon, and followed, by journalists. Journalists do not share in common a "high degree of generalized and systematic knowledge." Journalists do not claim for themselves the ex-

[24] *Ibid.*, pp. 17–18.

clusive right to practice the arts (all borrowed from other disciplines) of their trade. And finally, journalists in America do not "comprise a homogeneous community."

The same people who are hacking away at journalistic autonomy by extolling "social responsibility" of the press, access of the people to the media, the necessity for press councils and the like, are also the ones who are the advocates of journalistic professionalism. Even though they know that journalism is not *really* a profession, they seem to have their eyes on some great day in the future when journalistic professionalization will come about. Listen to William Rivers and Wilbur Schramm: "The slow, even painful way to promote change in mass communication requires a long process in which change takes place in people before it affects the system. This is professionalization." [25] While admitting that journalism is not really a profession, there is a kind of sadness about this fact which manifests itself in the expressions of many of the commentators on American journalism. There seems to be a hope that someday journalism will become a profession. Of course, most of the proponents of a profession of journalism would insist that professionalization should come about by journalists accepting an *individual* sense of responsibility.

Rivers and Schramm make the point of individual journalistic responsibility. But it is very difficult to imagine journalism becoming a *profession* without the individual having to sublimate his individual sense of responsibility to the profession with its elite leaders, its ethical codes, its licensing procedures and its minimum entrance requirements. As I see it, you cannot have both individual concepts of responsibility and a professional concept of responsibility. The latter would naturally tend to stamp out deviant and "eccentric" concepts and, ultimately, also the "professionals" who might embrace them.

Lewis H. Lapham, in a thoughtful article in *Harper's* (1973), writes of a kind of deep-rooted desire among press people to belong to a hierarchy ("hierarchical longing within the press"); he also observes in the press more and more talk about "legitimate" journalists, implying a willingness to accept some type of licensing or certification so that, presumably, a *bona fide* journalist can be identified. Lapham writes that the more the press becomes a profession, the more it will "discourage the membership of rowdy amateurs" and, as it is with other professions, "encourage the promotion of people diligently second-rate." [26] Lapham no doubt is right; professionalism will certainly restrict the ranks of journalism, eliminate

[25] William L. Rivers and Wilbur Schramm, *Responsibility in Mass Communication* (New York: Harper & Row, 1969), p. 240.
[26] Lewis H. Lapham, "The Temptation of a Sacred Cow," *Harper's* (Vol. 247, No. 1479, August 1973), p. 52.

the "non-professionals" from its practice, and make the press appear more respectable and responsible—at least from the perspective of the professional elitists.

Daniel P. Moynihan, in a significant article in *Commentary*,[27] notes that journalism lacks "an epistemology which is shared by all respected members of the profession"; he does not maintain that this epistemology be forced on journalism by some force such as a press council (he is anti-press council), but he does feel that if journalism in this country is to be a profession there must be basic knowledge agreed upon by all the "professionals." Presumably, this will only occur in a system where professionalism has progressed to the extent that all journalists will be products of a common education so that a standard body of knowledge and theory of ethics has been agreed upon. Of course, this millenium will likely never come, but education for journalism can, with sufficient professional motivation, go a long way in this direction.

Journalism, through increased emphasis on codes of conduct, press councils, peer pressure, entrance requirements checked by standard examinations and by more rigorous demand for professional journalism education, *can* become a true profession. There is no contention here that it is impossible; what is contended here is that it is undesirable, that what keeps our journalism vigorous and diversified (and to some, "irresponsible") is the very fact that it is not a profession. William Barrett, reflecting the Existentialist view of professions, states this case very well in these words:

> The price one pays for having a profession is a *déformation professionelle*, as the French put it—a professional deformation. Doctors and engineers tend to see things from the viewpoint of their own specialty, and usually show a very marked blind spot to whatever falls outside this particular province. The more specialized a vision the sharper its focus; but also the more nearly total the blind spot toward all things that lie on the periphery of this focus.[28]

[27] Daniel P. Moynihan, "The Presidency & the Press," *Commentary* (Vol. 51, No. 3, March 1971), p. 46.
[28] William Barrett, *Irrational Man: A Study in Existential Philosophy* (Garden City, N.Y.: Doubleday Anchor Books, 1962), pp. 4–5. Although certainly not in sympathy with existentialism generally, Ayn Rand reflects Barrett's opinion about the dangers of professionalism. Here is part of what she says: "If there is any one way to confess one's own mediocrity, it is the willingness to place one's work in the absolute power of a group, particularly a group of one's *professional colleagues*. Of any form of tyranny, this is the worst: it is directed against a single human attribute: the mind—and against a single enemy: the innovator. The innovator, by definition, is the man who challenges the established practices of his profession. To grant a professional monopoly to any group, is to sacrifice human ability and abolish progress; to advocate such a monopoly, is to confess that one has nothing to sacrifice." (Rand, *The New Left*, 46–47).

"Professional" Journalism Education

Barrett has put his Existentialist finger on the main weakness of professionalism: It narrows the focus and restricts the options and possibilities that lie beyond the confines of its values and concerns. This restriction of options and focus is especially dangerous in journalism, although it may well be helpful or even desirous—at least to a certain degree—in professions such as law or medicine. How a journalist is educated is, of course, at the very heart of any concept of professionalism. Although it is changing rather rapidly, training or education for journalism in the United States has been very much a piece-meal, spotty, uneven and diversified system. It has ranged from no formal schooling at all, through all levels and types of university and college work in the liberal arts and sciences, to the varied programs which have grown up in academic journalism departments, schools and colleges.

Editors and publishers, broadcast news directors, and advertising and public relations executives are every year hiring more and more of their new staffers from "professional" journalism education programs in our colleges and universities. It gets harder each year, happily attest the journalism educators, for the major in English or sociology or political science to get a job in the communications media. Usually this is said with great satisfaction as if this tendency in the direction of professionalization will assure the country of better journalism. Of course, there is absolutely no empirical evidence to confirm this, and there are still editors and other media executives who have their doubts about the journalism student's superiority over others. But their number is becoming smaller, it must be admitted, and presumably virtually all journalists hired by the year 2,000 will be products of formalized journalism education.

Journalism program accreditation is doing much to standardize the coursework in various universities across the country. Also the increase in the number and size of professional meetings, conventions, workshops for journalism educators, as well as the proliferation of literature dealing with journalism education, is having an impact on the development of a more coherent and unified program of education for journalism in the United States. Increasingly, journalism professors are reaching common objectives and understanding with their colleagues elsewhere, are moving more frequently from campus to campus, and are thereby spreading their educational philosophies and techniques nationwide—and even, in many cases, to other countries. All of this strengthens the growth of "professional" journalism education which, presumably, will in time weld the practicing journalists into a homogeneous professional society.

Emphasis more and more is on *professional* work in journalism. The

Columbia Journalism Review, for instance, has stated that if journalism is to be taught in any college or university, it should be taught as a "professional" course of study: "It has little more place in a liberal arts faculty than would education for law, medicine or business administration." [29] It must be said, however, that there is still considerable disagreement among journalism educators about what they are supposed to do; some would only teach journalism in a "liberal arts faculty"; others would have journalism education only on the graduate level; others would abolish all graduate work in journalism, and there are others who see no real need for formal journalism education at all. And there are shadings and degrees of all of these positions, and undoubtedly quite a few others.

Within every journalism faculty are the so-called "green eyeshades" teachers who emphasize techniques such as news reporting, newspaper makeup, headline writing and copyreading. Also—and usually in another camp—are the "Chi-square" professors, the faculty members (usually with Ph.D.'s in communication theory and methodologies of research) who mainly teach graduate level courses and apply their "scientific" skills to a variety of rather esoteric media studies. And last—and probably least —come the "hybrids": those faculty members who probably have some journalistic experience and also an academic eclecticism and liberal arts orientation which places them somewhere in limbo between the "trades" teachers and the researching theoreticians (or "communicologists" as they are sometimes called). These "hybrids" teach a variety of courses, but often they tend to be general courses such as "Mass Media and Society," "Law of Journalism," "Book Reviewing," "Journalistic Ethics," "History of American Journalism," and "Comparative Press Systems." [30] Thus far, these three main faculty types in journalism education have retained a diversity and tension which has delayed the "professionalization" of very many students.

Pressures, however, are building up against this tension created by disagreements among the three groups. Within journalism education itself there is increasing talk about the need to eliminate these disagreements and have more "cooperation" among the three groups. Also, more and more retired (or disgruntled) editors and journalists of one kind or

[29] John C. Merrill, "Answering the J-School Critics," *Seminar* (No. 5, Sept. 1967), p. 22.
[30] The present author discusses the three main types of journalism educators in the article, "The ABC's of a Journalism Faculty," *The Journalism Educator* (Spring, 1965). For a good look at varying roles of journalism education in the United States, as well as its history, see Ch. 19—"Mass Communications Education"—in Edwin Emery, Phillip Ault and Warren Agee, *Introduction to Mass Communications* (New York: Dodd, Mead & Co., 4th ed., 1973). For a good, although somewhat dated look at journalism education in other countries, see a special edition of *Gazette: International Journal for Mass Communications Studies* (Amsterdam: XII, 1, 1966).

another are entering journalism education to begin a "second career." This is causing the balance of faculty to begin a shift from the teacher who is mainly an academic to the teacher who is mainly a "professional" journalist. There is no doubt that as this trend increases—with even journalism school and department administrators coming freshly from the "profession" with little or no academic background—great impetus will be given to the aspects of journalism education which lead to professionalization. This situation is, of course, considered good by some and bad by others, depending on their philosophy of education and their feelings about the value of journalism as a profession.

One often wonders just what a "professional" school of journalism is, or how it differs from one which is not considered "professional." Obviously the term is used very loosely by the schools themselves, since nobody really seems to be able to explain just when a school (a new one, for instance) ceases being non-professional and becomes professional. Perhaps it might be well just to call them all professional—or, if you wish, call them all non-professional. The same basic courses are taught at all of them, even the small, struggling departments and programs with one or two faculty members; there is a sprinkling of reporting, feature writing, editorial writing, editing, journalism history, communication law, graphics and typography, advertising, public relations, radio and television news, and usually a basic introductory course dealing with the broad aspects of the mass media. In the larger schools, of course, these basics are supplemented by more specialized and esoteric coursework in cinematography, urban affairs and science reporting, information controls, ethics, literature of journalism, reviewing, international communication, information and communication theory, magazine production, film documentaries, and the like.

But the question persists: What is a professional journalism program? [31] Presumably it is one which will prepare a student to be a professional journalist, whatever that is. At least, it should prepare him somewhat to be a *practicing* journalist. The teachers of all journalism courses

[31] Increasing numbers of articles and portions of books are dealing with journalism education and are trying to define what is meant by "professional" education in journalism. A few of these from the early 1960's into the 1970's follow: B. R. Manago, "A Philosophy for a Liberal Journalism Education," *Add 1* (Spring 1962); Richard L. Tobin, "Journalism's Mounting Storms," *Saturday Review* (Dec. 4, 1965); J. C. Merrill, "The Modern Journalist: Soul of an Artist and Mind of a Scientist," *Vidura* (New Delhi, May 1967); John H. Colburn, "Journalism Education—At a Crossroads?" *The Quill* (April 1969); Joseph P. Lyford, "New Directions in Journalism Education?" *Seminar* (Dec. 1969); M. L. Stein, "Journalism Education—A Matter of Coexistence," *Saturday Review* (Oct. 9, 1971); John L. Hulteng, "The J-Graduate—How Well Prepared?" *The Quill* (April 1972); Harvey Saalberg, "J-Schools Search for Ways to Alleviate Overcrowding," *Editor & Publisher* (Jan. 27, 1973); LaRue Gilleland, "Educators Show Concern for Making Classrooms Relevant, Exciting," *Journalism Educator* (Oct. 1972); "The Ph.D. Debate," *Journalism Educator* (July 1973).

would contend that this is exactly what they are doing. There are many persons in American journalism who minimize the importance of the kind of journalism education a student gets and who believe that really all a journalist needs is native intelligence, curiosity, a desire to learn, imagination, basic literacy and energy. Higher education is not necessarily needed at all.

Louis Lyons, a veteran newspaperman who was curator of the Nieman Fellowships at Harvard for some twenty years, is one of those who would emphasize the capacity to learn—and not formal journalism education—for the practicing journalist. What Lyons would want to know is whether or not the journalist would grow on the job, because the editor or person doing the hiring can not really say what is needed from the journalist "since part of what we need is that he discover for us what is outside our reach and that he bring it within our ken." [32] Lyons concludes an *Atlantic* article with these words about a new journalist: "A capacity for discovery and interpretation is perhaps as close as we can come to what we need from him." Whether such a capacity can be taught in journalism school—or anywhere else in Academe—is a moot question. If, in truth, this is all that is expected of the journalist coming out of the university—this "capacity for discovery and interpretation"—then certainly journalism schools and departments are wasting tremendous time, effort, and money on a growing proliferation of *professional* courses.

I rather agree with Lyons, although there is no valid reason why journalism education cannot supplement a student's basic general education and make him better able to discover the world around him and to better interpret it to others. Certainly, all serious journalism teachers would claim this as an objective. It is quite likely, however, that journalism education generally, in its desire to be more "professional," is becoming more and more specialized, inward, parochial and conformist.

An increasing amount of journalism coursework is being required of the student, and fewer and fewer "electives" are left open for him; in some schools, the student cannot even "minor" in a non-journalism area or get a "double-major" in journalism and something else—for example, history. As journalism education grows, as it becomes more "professional" and more complex, as departments become schools and schools become colleges, and as additional years of graduate work in journalism are tacked on, it is understandable that the student's horizons get narrower and narrower. Often the student learns more and more *about* journalism as he goes along, but increasingly has less and less to communicate. And what is worse, graduate students in journalism seem to write worse than undergraduates.

Journalism education does increase and encourage conformist journal-

32 Louis Lyons, "What a Journalist Needs," *Atlantic* (Dec. 1957), p. 154.

ism. This, of course, is to some degree unavoidable, and, as Charles Siepmann rightly points out, it is not the aim of education to cultivate eccentrics—although "that society is richest, most flexible, and most humane that best uses and most tolerates eccentricity." For, as Siepmann says, "conformity, beyond a point, breeds sterile minds and, therefore, a sterile society." [33] Perhaps to far too great a degree journalism education does tend to turn journalism students into robots who can walk "surefootedly" into the world of Establishment journalism. It does discourage "unprofessional" practices and techniques, creativity and individuality, by instilling in all the students the "proper ways" of journalism.

Students who dare think for themselves, depart from the academic and journalistic conformist practices, are often punished by lower grades, poor letters of recommendation, and by a kind of silent but potent pressure from the institutionalized system which is engaged in producing standardized products. Admittedly, the above statement is a generalization; there are some students who are creative and who are not robotized by the journalism educational system. And, certainly, there are many professors who encourage individuality and creativity, but they are scattered rather thinly through journalism education, for the pressures of the system are also on them to conform.

Nevertheless, it is encouraging that some students, as well as some professors—brave souls, all—manage to fight the system, to develop and retain their authenticity and autonomy, and survive the educational treadmill in spite of its conforming and deadening aspects. But these are the exceptions, the ones who are proud of their own individual minds; these are the ones who have self-esteem and confidence that they can transcend the collectivizing influences of formal education and "professionalization" and inject into society their own sense of personality and authenticity. They are the committed ones; those who are certain that, with rational and skillful thought and action, they can succeed in institutionalized education and journalism without sacrificing themselves. These are the ones who form the "saving remnant" of libertarian journalism; it is they who will man the bulwarks in the fight against the forces of authoritarianism and conformity which are creeping in upon us from all sides.

[33] Charles A. Siepmann, *Radio, Television and Society* (New York: Oxford University Press, 1950), p. 225.

7

Journalistic Orientations

JOURNALISTS are extremely complex persons and it is difficult to generalize about certain orientations which they may have. Affecting their work is a wide variety of interest, ideologies, educational levels and cultural backgrounds, special talents, and so on. This is true even in societies where conformity and institutionalism have led to highly monolithic press systems. The journalist in any society—but especially in a libertarian or quasi-libertarian society—is a many-sided person with several strong traits and tendencies. But even though all this is true, there seems to be in all journalists a basic and dominant psycho-ideological orientation which tends to manifest itself in most of their thinking and journalistic action.

Before getting more specifically into the matter of journalistic ethics in the next two chapters, it would be well to consider some of these basic orientations which are closely related to the ethical principles embraced by a particular journalist. One's orientation, undoubtedly, has a great deal to do with the kind of ethical outlook one adopts as a journalist and even with the stylistic characteristics of his journalism. In fact, his orientation affects his total journalistic *Weltanschauung,* for it leads him to consider certain basic issues related to journalism in ways consistent with this orientation.

A journalist normally writes the way he thinks; he generally thinks according to his psycho-ideological orientation. A journalist, of course, may have a mixture of orientations, but one will usually dominate. The problem comes when we attempt to classify orientations, but it can be done. And, although there are innumerable ways to set up such classification systems, the tendency is for all such systems to gravitate into two journalistic orientational types: (1) the "scientific" journalist and (2) the "artistic" journalist. This dichotomy may not satisfy everybody, of course, but over the years while doing and teaching journalism, I have come to believe that these are the two main orientations. It is not a matter of "either-or"; rather it is a matter of dominant orientation, of a particular journalist being predominantly scientifically oriented or being predominantly artistically oriented. These two main tendencies will be taken up later in this chapter.

First, let us consider briefly several of the dualistic classifications into which basic orientations of journalists may fall.

Dualistic Orientations

One immediate problem with discussing orientations in dichotomies is that there are so many binary classifications which may be used. So we have the problem of selection. Then, of course, there is the more philosophical problem, emphasized in General Semantics, of the logical weakness of binary classifications: with such classifications we are certain to do injustice to reality for the "either-or" typology leads to distorted and simplistic thinking about the nature of the subject being classified. Naturally these are both formidable problems and each, in its own way, tends to distort reality. However, it must be noted that *any* system of classification (or of language usage in any form) distorts reality and is unsatisfactory in some sense. In spite of the weaknesses of typologies, failure to classify (even dualistically) might well lead to more problems of understanding. General Semanticists and other linguistic philosophers have not really helped much in this respect.

Therefore, in the absence of a better alternative to classification, let me discuss journalistic orientations by "types"—with considerable emphasis given to dualistic generalizations. For me, a larger problem than the *semantic* weakness inherent in a binary classification is the problem of *selection* of binary classifications. Journalists may be oriented primarily in dozens of ways which have approximate "opposites." What, then, are the most significant of these ways? This is the question I have had to contend with, and it is quite possible that better classifications (more useful for analysis) could be used, but these which follow should at least serve as catalysts for disagreement even if they do not provide for everyone a useful method for understanding journalistic orientations.

(1) *"Involved" and "Aloof"*. This is a very basic and common way of

considering journalists in binary fashion. The "involved" journalist is generally considered one who is oriented to participation, to activism, to being personally and emotionally involved in the events of the day. He does not believe in neutrality for the journalist; he thinks it desirable that he bring his own ideological beliefs, preferences and biases to bear on his journalism. He is the person many refer to as the "activist" journalist who, as J. K. Hvistendahl says, "looks at traditional reporting as being sterile and . . . considers reporters who refuse to commit themselves to a point of view as being cynical or hypocritical." [1] Hvistendahl goes on to say that "truth-as-I-see it" reporting might be a more accurate description of this new trend in journalism than "activist reporting" for these "new" journalists believe that the reporter who is seeking the truth should report the truth *as they see it*. The *involved* journalist, as I prefer to call him here, desires to bring himself, his intelligence, his sensitivities, his judgments to bear on the news of the day; he is not satisfied to be a bystander, an observer, a recorder or a neutralist.

The journalist with the *aloof orientation*, on the other hand, maintains that journalism is primarily a disinterested activity where audiences should not be incumbered by the journalists' biases, prejudices, judgments, feelings and opinions. The journalist with the *aloof* orientation is often called the "objective" journalist, although this is probably a misnomer. But he does subscribe to the Neutralist Position whereby the journalist keeps himself and his opinions and judgments out of his journalism. This is still a dominant orientation in the United States and is fostered in schools and departments of journalism—although it must be said that the subjectivists and activists of the 1960's made a deep impact on it and injected it with a new personalism which is easily discernible to this day.[2]

(2) *Dionysian and Apollonian.* Another interesting and useful dualistic way to describe journalistic orientation is to categorize principal ones as "Dionysian" and "Apollonian." These are the dichotomous tendencies toward emotion on one hand and toward reason on the other. This dualism was first highlighted in these terms by Nietzsche in *The Birth of Tragedy from the Spirit of Music*. He observed two opposite elements in Greek tragedies and believed them to be basic metaphysical principles in reality. Nietzsche named them for two Greek gods—Apollo, the god of light, and Dionysus, the god of wine.

Dionysus can be thought of as a symbol for emotion, mysticism, a free and unfettered spirit, intuition, irrationality and a kind of darkness.

1 "The Reporter as Activist: Fourth Revolution in Journalism," *The Quill* (Feb. 1970), p. 8.
2 The influence of such writers as Gay Talese, Gail Sheehy, Larry King, Willie Morris, Norman Mailer, Tom Wolfe, Truman Capote and Robert Daley were especially influential in the "New" journalism during the 1960's and into the 1970's.

Apollo, on the other hand, is symbolic of reason, beauty, order, wisdom, individuality, pragmatism and light.

Nietzsche considered Apollo (Reason) a necessary element, but unreliable and thus an inferior guide to existence; in other words, he believed that such an orientation provides man an inadequate view of reality. In many ways, therefore, Nietzsche might be considered the "Father of the New Journalism" which has burst onto the journalistic scene since the 1960's. For Nietzsche the symbol of Dionysus is superior to that of Apollo, for Dionysus is the free spirit that offers man, through some kind of mysterious sensitivity or intuition, a more valid and profound vision of reality.

This is an interesting, and perhaps valid, way to look at basic orientations, but as Ayn Rand has pointed out, it is not necessary for reason and emotion to be irreconcilable antagonists. Nor must emotions be a wild, unknowable element in men. She does state, however, that if people try to subordinate reason to emotions, this is what emotions are likely to become. Here is what she says:

> This much is true; reason *is* the faculty of an individual, to be exercised individually; and it is only dark, irrational emotions, obliterating his mind, that can enable a man to melt, merge and dissolve into a mob or a tribe. We may accept Nietzsche's symbols, but *not* his estimate of their respective values nor the metaphysical necessity of a reason-emotion dichotomy.[3]

Ayn Rand believes that the attempt on the part of many philosophers to divorce reason from reality (in line with the Dionysian emphasis on a "deeper" and more complete view of reality) has pushed much contemporary thinking to extremes of existentialism—to the abandoning of reason and the enthroning of intuition. Existentialists—or many of them, believes Rand, have looked at modern philosophy and have equated it with *reason* and have been alienated from, and disgusted with, rational philosophy. This is unfortunate, for what they are viewing is the modern philosophy of pragmatism-positivism, with its over-emphasis on scientism and linguistic analysis;[4] and the existentialists are equating these philosophical schools with reason. As Rand points out, however, this pragmatism-positivism should not be confused with rationalistic philosophy for these pragmatists and positivists have all but obliterated reason. Even so, the

---

[3] Ayn Rand, *The New Left: The Anti-Industrial Revolution* (New York: New American Library—Signet Books, 1971), p. 58.

[4] Pragmatism taught that truth is to be judged by consequences—by how well it "worked." Logical Positivism taught that ethical propositions have no cognitive meaning and are merely reports on our feelings. Linguistic Analysis is concerned with showing people what they really mean when they use language and with showing that knowledge consists in nothing more than linguistic manipulation.

existentialists have generally held them up as examples of rationality, rebelled against them, and have proceeded to all but reject reason.

The consequence of all this, according to Rand, is that the main thrust of existentialist thought has lost all faith in rationalism and has embraced a kind of relativism which has resulted in "a chaos of subjective whims setting the criteria of logic, of communication, demonstrations, evidence, proof, which differ from class to class from teacher to teacher." [5]

(3) *Poetic and Prosaic.* A third dualistic classification of journalists might be constructed on the basis of their stylistic proclivities. Some journalists, of the Dionysian type discussed above, tend to subjectivize their journalism in an attempt to get beneath the surface of reality and present a fuller and more authentic picture. These are the *poetic* journalists. Other journalists, largely Apollonian, are content with the more traditional style of expression common among journalists who have adopted what might be termed "the wire-service" style.

This basic difference in communicative expression stems from the dominant orientation accepted by the journalists: poetic (a kind of "open" or flexible style) or prosaic (a kind of "closed" or mechanistic style). The Poetic Journalist is more personal or individual and less dogmatic in his style than is his counterpart. He is willing to experiment with his journalism, especially in matters of story form and style. He is not as "hemmed in" by normal or traditional practices as is the more disciplined Prosaic Journalist. He is not very concerned about keeping himself out of his story; in fact he delights in giving his journalism the stamp of his own individual personality. He places great importance on his own ability to adapt his style to the story, and has great respect for self-expression, freedom, and autonomy.[6]

The Prosaic Journalist, on the other hand, is a believer in facts. He stresses literalness and explicit statements; he is interested in the accuracy of his stories—at least in the accuracy of what he selects to be in his stories. He praises what he calls "objectivity," considering it the same as reliability and truthfulness. The prosaic mind, according to George W. Morgan, considers the objective as identical with the factual. "In addition, and most important," Morgan writes, "it is believed that to be objective means to withhold the feelings and to be detached and impersonal." [7]

As Morgan rightly points out, facts are important to a person (and

[5] Rand, *The New Left*, p. 31.
[6] For a discussion of "psychic openness" and other characteristics in communication style of the Poetic Journalist, see Ch. 6 ("Style: The Dimension of Self") in A. Donald Bell and J. C. Merrill, *Dimensions of Christian Writing* (Grand Rapids, Mich.: Zondervan Publishing House, 1970).
[7] George W. Morgan, *The Human Predicament* (New York: Dell Publishing Co.—a Delta Book, 1970), p. 83.

certainly to a journalist), but they can be overstressed to the detriment of other things which are equally important. For example, Morgan says that persons with "prosaic minds" tend to have little respect for interpretation "because it appears incompatible with fact: fact is what *is*, they think, while interpretation is whatever one makes it; facts are believed to be objective, and interpretation, subjective." Morgan notes that for prosaic persons, knowledge of facts—no matter how isolated, irrelevant or minuscule—becomes genuine knowledge and interpretation becomes prejudice; for the journalist with this orientation, "sticking to the facts" is the height of responsibility—anything else is "irresponsible fancy." [8]

(4) *Personalists and Factualists.* These orientations are quite similar to the poetic and prosaic discussed above except that they relate to the total outlook on journalism and its purpose, going beyond the simple *style* of the journalism. The Personalist is the "people-oriented" journalist who makes most decisions on the basis of the way he thinks they will affect *people*—including himself. His main concern is with people, and he takes their feelings and sensitivity into consideration before he writes a story or gives it a certain emphasis in the news. People are always at the center of his jounralism, and in an important way he is a utilitarian for he is thinking of consequences. In other words, the Personalist will be largely controlled by his sensitivity to people connected with the story; this is very much an "involved" or "subjective" stance and is at variance with what might be called *factualism*—or the orientation of dispassionate neutralism which focuses on *what* was said or done.[9]

The Factualist is one who is oriented toward journalistic aloofness or neutralism, taking a kind of prosaic position in his communication style. He concentrates on the facts, the events themselves, on what happened, on what people say, and the like. The *what* of the story is more important than the why—even if the *what* is simply an accurate accounting of somebody else's version of what happened, or somebody else's opinion. Although the Factualist recognizes that people are important in news stories, he is little concerned about the *consequences to people* involved, letting his facts fall where they will with consequences taking care of themselves.

The Factualist is usually considered the "objective" journalist, having varying degrees of suspicion of, or hostility to, what he sees as involved, evaluative or subjective journalism. He tries diligently not to become involved in his story—or with the people of his story. His is the orientation of detachment, at least from personal opinions, attitudes or biases for

8 *Ibid.*, p. 88.
9 For a more extended discussion of people-oriented and fact-oriented journalists, see Merrill and Lowenstein, *Media, Messages, and Men* (New York: David McKay, 1971), pp. 244–46.

self or for others so that his subjective feelings will not determine what he considers news or how he presents it. Facts to the Factualist are sacred; they are to be presented dispassionately and accurately, and if they are, the audience member should get the best possible picture of the total event, unadorned by the ideological and psychological biases of the reporter and editor.

(5) *Existentialists and Rationalists.* The last of the dualistic classifications which will be mentioned here shifts the emphasis slightly to epistemological questions. How do we best know what we want to know? How involved and committed should we be? What is reality and how should we get at it? And, finally, how should we pass on such "reality-information"? Earlier, the existential orientation was related to the Dionysian, and the rational orientation to the Apollonian. Just as easily, we might refer to the existential orientation as Romantic and the rational orientation as Platonic. It is basically the old conflict between Emotion (Intuition) and Reason (Logic). Also, we might connect the Artistic orientation with the Existential orientation, and the Prosaic (or Scientific) orientation with the Rationalist.

At the risk of confusing the issue, we could further postulate that an *intellectual* orientation is closely related to Existentialism and a *pragmatic* orientation shares many characteristics with Rationalism. The term "intellectual," however, is enshrouded in more semantic fog than almost any term we could use, and it is difficult to speak of a journalist with an "intellectual" orientation or even one with a "pragmatic" one. The intellectual journalist, as C. Wright Mills sees him, is somewhat akin to the Existentialist because he has a tragic sense of life.[10] He realizes that grassroots democratic controls have become practically nonexistent—at least minimized—and that seemingly irresponsible actions by persons at the top are permitted—even encouraged—by The System. Others are dependent on the Leaders and must suffer the consequences of their ignorance and mistakes, their self-deceptions and their biased motives. It is the recognition of this that gives the Intellectual a sense of tragedy.

The intellectual journalist easily becomes frustrated, for too often he has gained the illusion that his thinking and concerns make a real difference in the affairs of society; he slowly wakes up to the fact that this is not really the case. But even though the Intellectual may have some characteristics in common with the Existentialist, he is often quite different. For instance, the Existentialist would fight harder than the Intellectual

---

[10] See C. Wright Mills, "The Social Role of the Intellectual," Ch. 3 in *Power, Politics and People* (New York: Ballentine Books, 1962). For another excellent discussion of this subject in relation to journalism, see Leo Rosten, "The Intellectual and the Mass Media," *Daedalus* (Spring, 1960), pp. 333–46.

for freedom and autonomy; he would not "give up" as quickly. According to Mills, the intellectual person is a slave to somebody or to some policy; and, although he may exercise a limited amount of freedom in his actions, he knows he must not go beyond these limits. He must ever watch his step. He must pull his punches to keep from offending his editor, his publisher, or some powerful person or group in his community. In many cases the intellectual journalist has adapted to these pressures, to these restricting forces, and has tried to confine his "creativity" and "individuality" to compiling rationales for comformity and to formulating schemes for better (therefore more "responsible") collective action.

The Intellectual, of course, does not have to escape into a private or unauthentic world of his own; he can become existential; he can be committed; he can keep pushing, learning, discussing, writing and acting—tuning in to important dialogue everywhere. He does not need to cease caring, thinking, agitating, taking serious things seriously; but it is a temptation, for being a "thinker" he realizes the growing insignificance of the individual person and the deterministic tendencies of a mass society.

The Existentialist position insists that the journalist involve himself, commit himself, keep moving, continue changing—in short, he must continue to make or create himself. "Man is nothing else but what he makes of himself," Sartre has said, calling this the first principle of Existentialism.[11] Certainly the existential journalist, in the serious business of making himself, would not be devoid of rationality, nor would he be a complete foe of Reason. Again, it is a matter of emphasis: the existential journalist would stress intuition, feeling and any other aspects of subjectivism which might help him acquire a more complete and realistic picture of the event or personality he is describing.

Existentialism does not exclude rationalism, but it does give significant emphasis to mystical, emotional and intuitive concerns. It also gives extraordinary attention to personal freedom—including the freedom to react emotionally or instinctively to one's environment. As Hazel Barnes says, the Existentialist's "one certainty is his own freedom." [12] The Existentialist believes that one cannot be ethical in his actions unless he is free; ethics implies freedom. I *ought* implies I *can*—that I have a choice. Therefore, it is easy to see why Existentialists believe that B. F. Skinner and other determinists are "beyond ethics" since they believe that people are enslaved to forces over which they have no control, forces which cause them to act in certain ways regardless of their desires.

The Rationalist, in contrast to the Existentialist, has a tendency to be

11 Jean-Paul Sartre, *Existentialism and Human Emotions* (New York: Philosophical Library, 1957), p. 15.
12 *An Existentialist Ethics* (New York: Random House—Vintage Books, 1971), p. 51.

more the scientist than the artist, the prosaic man than the poet, the Platonist than the Romantic, the Apollonian than the Dionysian. William Barrett has compared him to Jonathan Swift's "Laputans" in *Gulliver's Travels*.[13] He would be one of the cerebral people, powerful but dreary, and scientifically oriented. And, as Barrett says, the whole Romantic movement was an attempt to escape from Laputa—a protest of feeling against reason. This Romantic protest was furthered by the early Existentialists such as Kierkegaard, who maintained that "it was intelligence and nothing else that had to be opposed." But Kierkegaard did not disparage intelligence; in fact he speaks of it with great respect. But he did believe it needed opposition with all the resources and intelligence at his disposal. It is significant that Kierkegaard called himself the subjective thinker." [14] It is this "subjective thinking"—a sort of harmonious marriage of emotion and intelligence—that marks the Existentialist in journalism and differentiates him from the Rationalist in journalism who is determined to exclude emotion from his work and make his every decision—ethical and otherwise—on the basis of Reason, and Reason alone.

Four Basic Allegiances

Another way to think of journalistic orientations is to consider the main allegiances or loyalties which a journalist may have. Four principal allegiances suggest themselves: (1) to people, (2) to institutions, (3) to ideologies, and (4) to events or facts. Again, as is true with all classification systems or typologies, there is often an overlap among these allegiances, but at any time there is the tendency for one of them to dominate. And, of course, the basic journalistic allegiance ties in with the general orientation a person has, and has a direct bearing on the journalistic philosophy (especially in the area of ethics) which he embraces. The four allegiances suggested above may be referred to as the allegiances or loyalties of personalism, institutionalism, ideologism, and neutralism.

The Personalists. These have been mentioned earlier in the dichotomous classifications; they are the "people-oriented" journalists, those who have strong loyalties to people—either themselves or others. They are egoists or altruists, sensitive to the consequences of their journalism to themselves or to others. They have, therefore, mainly a utilitarian motivation in their activities. Because of this basic allegiance to people, they tend to be more personal, polemical, opionated, subjective and humanistic in their journalism.

13 William Barrett, *Irrational Man* (New York: A Doubleday Anchor Book, 1962), pp. 122–23.
14 *Ibid.*, p. 150.

The Institutionalists. These journalists have their main allegiance to their journalistic organization or to some other group or institution. They differ from the Personalists in that they are directed mainly, not by their own self-interests or the interests of outside persons, but by an institutional loyalty. Theirs is more of a collectivist orientation than an individualist one. Loyalty to an institution, to their body of colleagues: this is the motivating factor of importance. These Institutionalists are either oriented toward their own journalistic media or to some other entity, such as a political party or a religious group. It is quite obvious that if their prime allegiance is to some institution, their overall philosophical stance in journalism will be quite different from the Personalists who shape their activities to persons and their needs—either themselves or other individuals.

The Ideologists. These journalists are mainly loyal to a cause or to a social "idea" or to a particular philosophical or political concept. Often these journalists are tied rather closely with institutionalism though not always, but their espoused ideology is often reflected in some institution or organization. These journalists enthrone philosophies, causes, programs, movements and concepts, and find their loyalties tied to potent ideas rather than to persons or organizations. A journalist oriented in this way may have his chief allegiance to a political or nationalistic philosophy or movement (e.g., Marxism or Zionism), or a special ideological movement (e.g., Women's Liberation or the Peace Movement). In any case, it is the ideology or the philosophical idea that is the dominant catalyst for journalistic action.

The Neutralists. These are "fact-lovers"—the "event-oriented" journalists or the "objectivists," as they are often called. They enthrone events-and-situations "out there" and deemphasize persons, ideologies and groups. The Neutralist is mainly a reportive journalist, not a judgmental or polemical one; his main allegiance is to the objective event or to the facts surrounding the event. He is little concerned with consequences either to himself or to others connected with the story, nor is he directed by any sense of loyalty to his journalistic group or to any other group such as party or government or religious group. His dedication or loyalty is to the story—and the event—and nothing more.

Two Basic Journalistic Tendencies

Out of all the dichotomous orientations and the four allegiances already discussed, two basic journalistic tendencies emerge. One of these is what might be referred to as a "subjective" orientation or tendency and the other as an "objective" tendency. The first is a tendency toward involvement and the second is a tendency toward aloofness. The first is more "sense-oriented" and the second is more "fact-oriented." The journalist with the so-called "objective" tendency might be said to be more scientific than the so-called "subjectivist," who could be called more artistic.

Although every journalist is, indeed, schizophrenic to some degree in respect to these two tendencies, my experience with journalism students and practicing journalists for more than twenty years convinces me that every person in journalism evidences significantly more of one of these tendencies than of the other. An interesting hypothesis presents itself— a hypothesis which I believe is valid, but which has never really been tested: that journalists with the aloof, scientific or disinterested orientation are those whose pre-journalism education and interests were more "prosaic" than "poetic," more "scientific" than "artistic." And, on the other hand, the so-called "subjective" or involved journalists are persons with a pre-journalism background showing an inclination toward imaginative literature, philosophy and the humanities generally. It is also probable that the "subjectivists" are more emotional, more sensitive, more convinced of their own rightness, more desirous to proselytize and propagandize, and more dogmatic than are the so-called "objectivists" or uninvolved journalists.

If the two orientations were to be summarized in terms of the various dichotomous tendencies discussed earlier, here is the way each would look:

• *The Involved or Artistic Orientation*—existentialist, romantic, poetic, Dionysian, mystical, intuitive, emotional, subjective, personal, informal, directive, persuasive, propagandistic, humanistic, judgmental, liberal.

• *The Aloof or Scientific Orientation*—rationalist, neutralist, Platonist and Apollonian, prosaic, objectivist, impersonal, formal, reportive, disinterested, non-judgmental, calm, unemotional, conservative.

Institutionalized journalism, or what might be called "Establishment" journalism in the United States, has championed the second of these basic tendencies. Journalism schools and departments give significantly more emphasis to it than to the more subjective Artistic orientation. The underground journalistic movement of the 1960's, coupled with the resurrection of subjective "New" journalism by such writers as Tom Wolfe, Norman Mailer and Truman Capote, made a noticeable dent (at least temporarily) in the Aloof or Scientific Orientation, but news media and programs in journalism education still give short shrift to judgmental, involved, intuitive journalistic subjectivism. There is still an overriding conviction in journalism that reporters should keep their opinions and biases out of their stories and that subjective pieces and commentary be separated from news stories and be clearly identified. Those who are in favor of "integrated" journalism—in the sense of combining the reporter's judgments and opinions with the verifiable facts—are very much in the minority and are felt to be the eccentrics of modern American journalism.

This basic segregation of "news" from "reportorial judgment" in journalism may well change, however, in the next decade. There are increasing numbers of faculty members who are beginning to recognize that there is no real demarcation between journalistic subjectivity and the actual "facts" of an event—that reportorial impressions and subjective insights blend into reality in such a way that it is impossible, and even unnatural, to try to segregate them from one's journalism.

One such faculty member is William Stephenson, a distinguished professor at the University of Missouri's School of Journalism, a man trained in both psychology and physics. Dr. Stephenson has been insisting for years that the separation of "news" and reportorial "views" is unnatural and that what is needed is a synthesis which will make possible a fuller and deeper journalistic account. He has insisted that *fact* is not enough; what is needed is what he calls "factuality"—something that goes beyond the surface and verifiable splinters of information and statements by this source or that; something that brings the intelligence and insights and sensitivities of the reporter to bear on the story; something that fills in the gaps; something that puts flesh on the dry bones of fact and makes the story live in greater and more realistic dimensions. Although there are others who are saying what Dr. Stephenson has been proclaiming, they are generally—as is Dr. Stephenson—written off by journalism teachers and Establishment journalists as impractical, unprofessional and unrealistic persons who would turn American journalism into a bedlam of opinion with no credible base.

Stephenson, like C. P. Snow, believes that the scientist and the artist cannot only coexist; each can go further and develop characteristics and tendencies normally found in the other. Moreover, there is no valid reason why the scientifically oriented journalist cannot produce better journalism by injecting it with heavy doses of subjective insight. The Artistic journalist, on the other hand, might do a much better job if he were to employ the more systematic and dispassionate methods of the scientist. What might very well bring a new vigor and more *factuality* to journalism would be a synthesis orientation where the fact-oriented concept were merged with the sense-oriented concept: a kind of journalistic Artistic Scientism. Journalism, like everything else, must change, and it is unrealistic to think that old ways of looking at it can prevail effectively in every age.

Journalism has been largely one-dimensional for some years. Even in more advanced countries journalism has been thought to be pretty simple: just give the facts in order of their importance. Oversimplification is, to a great extent, still the rule. The journalist has, at least in the United States, been conceived of as somebody who, either because of an ability or desire to write or a penchant for prying open doors of secrecy, gravitated to a journalistic position. Or, he was a political agitator who landed in journalism instead of politics. Generally, the journalist has been an uninvolved, reportorial type who has been nurtured in an atmosphere of the "objective" school of neutralism. When he did find himself in the role of the opinionated and outspoken journalist, it was off in the segregated corners of journalism—in a column or in an editorial.

In today's highly specialized and complex world, journalism is not something anyone should stumble into. Well-turned phrases are not enough; neither can strongly held political or ideological positions and articulate dogmatism nor "straight" facts strung together suffice. Blunt editorializing of a purely personal or emotional kind—either in a news story or in a well-identified opinion piece—is inadequate. Readers react quite differently—and unpredictably—to stories; the impact of the press is not as significant (or obvious) as previously thought; and the press is only one small link in a complex communications system through which opinions are formed and reinforced.

A journalist today must have deep respect for national processes— the surface activities of institutions and persons—yet be sensitive to the psychological and poetic impulses which motivate these institutions and stir the depths of these persons. And these two aspects of journalism must be integrated or synthesized, not segregated. The modern journalist—if he is to be rational, sensitive and committed—must submit himself to a program of reading, conversing, thinking and meditating to keep intellectually alive and emotionally atune to his times, community and country. He must be intellectually aloof but sensitively and emotionally involved. He must love his own people but be cosmopolitan, understanding that what affects others thousands of miles away also affects him. He must, in short, have the soul of an artist and the mind of a scientist.

Within the context of all national press systems there are men and women ready to step into journalistic positions requiring the artist-scientist orientation. Admittedly, not all countries are equally prepared for this new synthesized journalism, but the potential and challenge is there. That the political environment of a nation determines the kind of journalist needed is true to a degree. But there is no reason to believe that Spaniards cannot think like scientists (they already think like artists) in their journalism. Russians do not necessarily have to produce empty, propagandistic journalism devoid of preciseness and sensitivity. Within all journalists in whatever political environment there is tremendous latitude for expression and freedom if they will determine to have a love for, and dedication to, personal authenticity. A wide area exists in every political system in which the journalist with self-esteem can increase his creativity, flexibility and freedom.

The synthesis journalist who aspires to produce Dr. Stephenson's *factuality* journalism will integrate the scientific (aloof) orientation with the artistic (involved) orientation. He will aspire to be nothing less than the artist-scientist, looking at his world through heightened senses and analyzing his world with keen intellect. It is only in this way that the modern journalist can serve both himself and his fellow men, thus achieving the balance and fullness which his calling demands.

Quest for Objectivity

Regardless of which of the tendencies and orientations described above might be embraced, most journalists claim to have a high regard for "objectivity" in journalism and believe that they are trying to reach it, albeit by different roads. One of the main problems with any discussion of objectivity is that there are so many ways of viewing it, so many definitions of it. William Stephenson's concepts of "fact" and "factuality" (mentioned earlier) get pretty close to the heart of the matter; people generally think of objective journalism either as being "factual" and accurate, composed of verifiable bits of information, or as being something far more complex and sophisticated—something that goes beyond the mere reporting of acts and statements and brings to the story another dimension which might be called reportorial discernment and sensitivity.

Undoubtedly there are many other views of "objectivity" in journalism than the fact-factuality ones just mentioned, but they are probably closely related to these two. As has been pointed out already, the first view ("fact") dominates today and insists on reportorial detachment and neutralism and glorifies the separation of fact and reportorial opinion. This concept is well described by Senator Barry Goldwater who writes:

> I am a great believer in the device, practiced by most responsible American newspapers, of separating the news developments and the newspapers' editorial opinion. The first should be a flat, unembroidered account of the facts surrounding the item of news. It should be, so far as is humanly possible, free from the writer's or the commentator's personal interpretation or views.[15]

[15] Barry Goldwater, *The Conscience of a Majority* (New York: Simon & Schuster, Inc.—Pocket Books, 1971), p. 157. Much literature and many speeches have dealt with journalistic objectivity in recent years; one of the best articles is Donald McDonald's "Is Objectivity Possible?" in *The Center Magazine* (Santa Barbara, Cal.), Sept.–Oct. (Vol. IV, No. 5) 1971, pp. 29–43.

Just as Goldwater catches the essence of one main view (the "fact"- concept) of objectivity and expresses it briefly and succinctly, Erich Fromm points out the opposing view (the "factuality" concept) just as cogently. Objectivity, as Fromm discusses it in *Man for Himself*, requires more than simply seeing an event or object dispassionately and neutrally; it requires the observer to become related in some way to that which is being reported. The nature of the object and the nature of the observer (or subject) must be merged and considered equally important if we are to get at what constitutes objectivity.[16] Fromm goes on to say that

> objectivity is not, as it is often implied in a false idea of "scientific" objectivity, synonymous with detachment, with absence of interest and care. How can one penetrate the veiling surface of things to their causes and relationships if one does not have an interest that is vital and sufficiently impelling for so laborious a task?

Fromm stresses that objectivity does not mean detachment; rather, he says, it has more to do with "respect" than detachment. And he points out that the idea that lack of interest is a condition for recognizing the truth is fallacious.[17] All productive thinking and observing and communicating is stimulated by the interest of the observer, according to Fromm. And it would seem that productive journalism, or journalism that reaches furthest toward objectivity, would also be that which involves the interest of the reporter. It is impossible for a journalist to detach himself from his story if he is to give an honest and full account. As Fromm says, "To be able to listen to oneself is a prerequisite for the ability to listen to others; to be at home with oneself is the necessary condition for relating oneself to others." [18]

[16] Erich Fromm, *Man for Himself: An Inquiry into the Psychology of Ethics* (New York: Holt, Rinehart & Winston—Fawcett Premier Books, 1966), p. 111.
  For a very good discussion of objectivity and the importance of the observer and his personality in an observation, see Harold R. Isaacs, *American Jews in Israel* (New York: The John Day Co., 1966). He says in part (p. 38): "In most sciences nowadays, it is recognized that every observation includes the observer as well as the observed. If this be largely true for the natural sciences, it is wholly true for the so-called social sciences. It has always seemed quite plain to me that virtually all inquiry into the affairs of man is, like all art, in some way autobiographical. Every inquirer who concerns himself with something important in human experience is trying to capture the elusive truth about himself and wants at least to leave some mark to show others where the pursuit led him and how far he got."
[17] For an excellent discussion of this contention, see Karl Mannheim's *Ideology and Utopia* (New York: Harcourt, Brace & Co., 1936).
[18] Fromm, *Man for Himself*, p. 113. This idea is reinforced by Michael Novak in his *Belief and Unbelief: A Philosophy of Self-Knowledge* (New York: Mentor-Omega Books, 1965). Understanding, he points out, assumes intelligent subjectivity. "Subjectivity," he says, "is the ground of objectivity" and "nothing is known objectively except through a knower."

Now someone may object, "But what about facts? Are not facts un-distorted and objective reflections of reality?" In another book, *The Revolution of Hope,* Fromm deals with this subject, too, and makes some interesting observations about "facts." Not only can facts be meaningless, he says, but they can be untrue by their very selection, "taking attention away from what is relevant, or scattering and fragmenting one's thinking so much that one is less capable of making meaningful decisions the more 'information' one has received." [19] Why is this? Because, says Fromm, the selection of facts implies evaluation and choice. *So even the presentation of facts* (however they might be defined) *is subjective.* Fromm makes the point, not often heard in journalism schools, that a person (journalist) objectively reporting on the activities of a certain individual must know the individual "in his individuality and suchness, his character—including the elements he himself may not be aware of" so that his act might be evaluated properly.[20] But, the reader may ask, why not just *present* it and not evaluate it? Because, Fromm would say, the evaluation of the act—the motive for doing it, etc.—is part of the story of the act, is part of the objectivity of the act. In addition, according to Fromm, the reporter would have to know himself, his own value system, his ideology, his in-terests—selfish and otherwise—if he wished to improve his objective reporting.

Facts in themselves have little correspondence to objectivity. Often they distort and mislead. A fact, says Fromm, presented "merely descrip-tively" may make the audience member more or less informed, and "it is well known that there is no more effective way of distortion than to offer nothing but a series of 'facts'." [21] Pictures—in a sense visual "facts," too, can distort, whether they are "still" shots in the print media or filmed or live shots on television. Philip Wylie has expressed well, in spite of his cynical tone, this point in *The Magic Animal.*[22] He writes

> . . . it is claimed that TV has made a greater number of Americans better acquainted with more truth than they were in pre-TV days. Nothing could be less correct. More people doubtless have a slanted half-glimpse of more events, ideas, so-called scientific marvels, the faces and voices of prominent people and so on, than they had before. But fewer than ever have any background for appraising these un-related, unevaluated, and random bits. Time was when a Vanderbilt caused public outrage by allegedly exclaiming, "The public be

[19] Erich Fromm, *The Revolution of Hope* (New York: Bantam Books, 1971), pp. 54–55.
[20] *Ibid.*, p. 55.
[21] *Ibid.*, p. 56.
[22] Philip Wylie, *The Magic Animal* (New York: Simon & Schuster—Pocket Books, 1969), p. 205.

damned!" Today, damnation is universal and the public either does not know it or, if it knows, takes damnation for granted.

Most citizens, concerned with getting the "truth" and most journalists, concerned with providing the "truth," have a deep respect for objectivity. They simply have various theories about how it is achieved. The "Goldwater-perspective" presented earlier seems to dominate today, although the "Fromm-perspective" appears on the rise as people generally —and journalists especially—get more sophisticated and better educated. The search for journalistic objectivity goes on; but there is no agreement on its nature or on when it has been achieved. This is good, really, in a free society where pluralistic journalism is produced largely by autonomous journalists. It is certainly unrealistic to expect a common definition of objectivity to develop or a monolithic journalistic objectivity to emerge in the United States as long as journalists are willing and able to fight against all manner of subtle and insidious authoritarian influences which would happily define for us all the "nature" of objective journalism.

Objectivity's Two Faces

Another interesting way to analyze objectivity or objective reporting in journalism is to consider two epistemological perspectives: realism and idealism. The *realistic* view of objectivity would consider objective reporting—or the objective report—as a relational concept involving the event (object) and the report-of-the-event (another object). It would put little or no emphasis on the audience member who perceives the report. On the other hand, the *idealistic* position on objective reporting is primarily a relational concept involving the audience member and the report-of-the-event. It has little or nothing to do with the actual event-out-there, for the only "event of any importance" is the one in the mind of the audience member.

Let us look a little more closely at each of these two views of objectivity. First, the Realist. As applied to "news" the Realist would postulate that (1) a news event is a news event even though it is not reported; (2) a newsstory is an *object*-in-itself even though an audience member does not ever see or hear it; and (3) even if an audience member does see or hear the report, his perception of the report has nothing really to do with the "objectivity" of the report. A newsstory, for example, is a newsstory even though nobody reads it in the press, just as the original event existed in reality even though no reporter reported it. (A story in a newsroom wastebasket it just as much a newsstory as one on the newspaper's page.) News, to the Realist, is not a "report of what happened";

rather it is *what happened*, and a newsstory is not what is *read* (perceived)
by an audience member but what is *written* (or otherwise transmitted)
by a reporter. The Realist places the relational focus on the *event-reported*
and on the *report* itself. The question of importance so far as objectivity
is concerned is: How closely does the report approximate the actual event.
The Realist focuses on *objects*, not on subjects perceiving these objects.
He sees objectivity having to do mainly with events and reports-of-events
and reportorial objectivity as referring to the correspondence (relationship) between the actual event and the report of the actual event.

Next, let us consider the Idealist. As applied to "news" the Idealist
would postulate that (1) a news event is basically what happens in the
mind of the audience member; (2) a newsstory is the device which "trig-
gers" a perception (image) in the audience member's mind; and (3) there
is no "news" except that which is perceived by the audience member. For
the Idealist, news is not news until it is reported, i.e. "perceived" by an
audience member via a report. Therefore, we cannot talk about objectivity
in a news report without taking the audience into consideration. A report
cannot be objective until (and unless) the report is perceived by the audience member. Here the relational focus is on the report and audience
member—with major stress on the latter. The Idealist says, in effect, that
"objectivity" is a personal thing with the audience member; it is the individual perception of the report that really counts; therefore there may
be as many *objectivities* as there are perceivers or audience members. The
main question for the Idealist is this: How do the audience members perceive the report?

In conclusion, let us consider a few inferences which can be made
from the above analysis. The Realist is more object-and-event-minded than
the Idealist. He is also more concerned with keeping himself out of the
story than is the Idealist, more concerned with "reportorial neutrality."
The Realist is less concerned with audience perceptions than is the Idealist, and more concerned with factual and tonal correspondence between
the report and the event-reported. How various audience members perceive
the event via his report is of secondary interest to the Realist; certainly he
does not think these perceptions in any real way affect the objectivity of
his report.

The Idealist, on the other hand, tends to be a "subjectivist" when it
comes to objective reporting—feeling that the reporter's own feelings,
reactions, conclusions, judgments (as well as those of the audience members) are necessary for the production of objectivity. He is concerned
primarily with the perceptions in the minds of the subjects. The Idealist
is more likely to be a "New Journalist" or one dedicated to involvement
and advocacy. The Idealist is also more concerned with how an audience

member *perceives* the event than he is in the actual event itself. In a sense, the only event that is important to him is the perception in the mind of the audience member. Therefore, he would be more prone to have an interest in audience analysis than in content analysis, making him considerably more "psychologically oriented" than would be the Realistic Journalist. Being interested in what is lodged in the mind of the audience member, of course, also forces him to have some concern for the related perception in the mind of reporter. He would find it meaningful and interesting to try to compare the audience perceptions with those of the journalist who did the reporting.

These, then, are the two ways (or at least two important ways) of considering journalistic "objectivity." And they are related to other orientations discussed earlier in this chapter; specifically the Realist is akin to the journalist who has been identified with neutralism, event-orientation, dispassion, impersonalism, and uninvolvement, whereas the Idealist tends to be more closely related with subjectivity, advocacy, personalism, people-orientation and involvement. All of these orientational factors are important to the individual journalist; they affect his general journalistic philosophy and play a large part in evolving his specific ethical concepts.

8

Ethics and Journalism

W HEN we leave the subject of basic orientations and allegiances and enter the area of journalistic ethics, we pass from the more solid ground of socio-psychological empiricism into a swampland of philosophical speculation where eerie mists of judgment hang low over a boggy terrain. In spite of the unsure footing and poor visibility, there is no reason not to make the journey. In fact, it is a journey well worth taking for it brings the matter of morality to the individual person; it forces the journalist, among others, to consider his basic principles, his values, his obligations to himself and to others. It forces him to decide for himself how he will live, how he will conduct his journalistic affairs, how he will think of himself and of others, how he will think, act and react to the people and issues surrounding him.

Ethics has to do with duty—duty to self and/or duty to others. It is primarily individual or personal even when it relates to obligations and duties to others. The quality of human life has to do with both solitude and sociability. We do right or wrong by ourselves in that part of our lives lived inwardly or introvertedly and also in that part of our lives where we are reacting and responding to other persons. This duality of individual and social morality is implicit in the very concept of ethics. The journalist, for example, is not simply writing for the consumption of others; he is writing as *self*-expression, and he puts himself and his very being into his journalism. What he communicates is in a very real way what he himself *is.* He pleases or displeases himself—not just those in his audience. What he does to live up to some standard within him not only affects the activities and beliefs of others, but in a very real way, the very essence of his own life.

A concern for ethics is important. The journalist who has this concern obviously cares about good or right actions; such a concern indicates an attitude which embraces both freedom and personal responsibility. It indicates also that the journalist desires to discover norms for action that will serve him as guiding principles or specific directives in achieving the kind of life which he thinks most meaningful and satisfying. Ethical concern is important also for it forces the journalist to commitment, to thoughtful decision among alternatives. It leads him to seek the *summum bonum*, the highest good in journalism, thereby heightening his authenticity as a person and journalist.

What characterizes most journalists today is a lack of commitment and consistency, a lack of a coherent life plan. Before any journalist chooses any particular ethics he must decide whether or not to be ethical: this is the first and most important choice facing him. However, it may well be, as Sartre and other Existentialists have believed, that "not to choose is already to have chosen"; that the "refusal to choose the ethical is inevitably a choice for the nonethical." [1] There is a tendency today to identify as "ethics" any personal decision to act; anything I want to do, I do—therefore, it is ethical for me to do it. Hazel Barnes points out that this is exactly parallel to what has happened to "religion." She says that "an age which is willing to apply the term 'religion' to communism, aesthetic awe, devotion to one's fellow man, and allegiance to impartial demands of pure science has no difficulty in labeling any guiding motif or choice a personal ethics." [2] If one accepts this position he is really saying that nobody is really nonreligious or nonethical; all meaning will have been drained from the concepts "religious" and "ethical" if nobody can be non-religious or non-ethical.

Ethics is that branch of philosophy that helps journalists determine what is right to do in their journalism; it is very much a normative science of conduct, with conduct considered primarily as self-determined, voluntary conduct. Ethics has to do with "self-legislation" and "self-enforcement"; although it is, of course, related to *law*, it is of a different nature.[3] Although law quite often stems from the ethical values of a society at a certain time (i.e., law is often reflective of ethics), law is something that is socially determined and socially enforced. Ethics, on the other hand, is

[1] Hazel Barnes, *An Existentialist Ethics*, p. 7.
[2] *Ibid.*, p. 5.
[3] For a good discussion of law, taking the position that "a sentiment of respect for law is a rational one," see Bertrand Russell, *Human Society in Ethics and Politics* (New York: Mentor Books, 1962), p. 28 f.

personally determined and personally enforced—or should be. Ethics should provide the journalist certain basic principles or standards by which he can judge actions to be right or wrong, good or bad, responsible or irresponsible.

It has always been difficult to discuss ethics; law is much easier, for what is legal is a matter of law. What is ethical transcends law, for many actions are legal, but not ethical. And there are no "ethical codebooks" to consult in order to settle ethical disputes. Ethics is primarily personal; law is primarily social. Even though the area of journalistic ethics is swampy and firm footing is difficult, as was mentioned earlier, there are solid spots which the person may use in his trek across the difficult landscape of life.

First of all, it is well to establish that ethics deals with *voluntary* actions. If a journalist has no control over his decisions or his actions, then there is no need to talk of ethics. What are voluntary actions? Those which a journalist could have done differently had he wished. Sometimes journalists, like others, try to excuse their wrong actions by saying that these actions were not personally chosen but *assigned* to them—or otherwise forced on them—by editors or other superiors. Such coercion may indeed occur in some situations (such as a dictatorial press system) where the consequences to the journalist going against an order may be dire. But for an American journalist not to be able to "will" his journalistic actions —at least at the present time—is unthinkable; if he says that he is not so able and that he "has to" do this-or-that, he is only exhibiting his ethical weakness and inauthenticity.

The journalist who is concerned with ethics—with the quality of his actions—is, of course, one who wishes to be virtuous. Just what a virtuous person is, however, is somewhat circular and gets us back to the question: What is a moral or ethical person? However, the nature of virtue is not really so relative or vague if we have any respect for the great thinkers of history; there has been considerable commonality of meaning among philosophers generally, even though "virtue" has been conceptualized in terms containing considerable semantic noise.

The "Virtuous" Journalist

The virtuous journalist is one who has respect for, and tries to live by, the cardinal virtues which Plato discusses in *The Republic*.[4] First is *wisdom*, which gives "direction" to the moral life and is the rational, intellectual base for any system of ethics. Wisdom is part natural and part acquired, combining knowledge and native abilities; it largely comes from

[4] Cf. Josef Pieper, *The Four Cardinal Virtues* (Notre Dame University Press, 1966). Pieper uses the term "prudence" for "wisdom" and the term "fortitude" for "courage," but retains the terms "justice" and "temperance" as used by Plato.

maturing, from life experiences, from contemplation, reading, conversing and study. Second, there is *courage*, which keeps one constantly pursuing his goal, the goal which wisdom has helped him set for himself. Courage is needed to help the journalist resist the many temptations which would lead him away from the path which wisdom shows.

The third virtue is *temperance*, the virtue that demands reasonable moderation or a blending of the domination of reason with other tendencies of human nature. It is this virtue, giving harmony and proportion to moral life, which helps us avoid fanaticism in pursuit of any goal. And, last, there is *justice*, distinguished from the other cardinal virtues in that it refers more specifically to man's social relations. Justice involves considering a man's "deservingness"; each man must be considered, but this does not mean that each man has to be treated like every other—for example, justice would not require that every person elected to a city, state or national office receive equal attention on television or the same amount of space in a newspaper. Equal treatment simply does not satisfy deservingness—does not imply "just" coverage.

One sign of virtue in journalism may well be a deep loyalty to truth. At least the pursuit of truth by the journalist surely takes wisdom, courage, temperance and justice. John Whale, an editorial writer for the *Sunday Times* of London, contends that at the base of journalistic ethics is an allegiance to truth. It is the authenticity of the information contained in the story that is the journalist's chief ethical concern, according to Whale. What methods should a journalist use in trying to get at this "truth"? Whale answers: *Only those methods which the journalist would be willing to publish as part of the story*. This is one reason why Whale and many others (including me) are opposed to the passage of "shield laws." What is far more important than keeping a source's name secret, Whale maintains, is whether what he said is true. It is hard to verify truth if the source's name is hidden from the public. This allegiance to truth, not to some person (source) who reveals information, is what is important. Too often those who reveal information and elicit the journalist's promise not to identify them have motives other than a desire to let the truth come out. Virtue in journalism, believes Whale, has to do with getting as much truth as possible into the story—and, of course, the source of the information is *part of* the "truth" of the story.[5]

The desire to search out and present the truth does, indeed, seem to be one of the moral foundations of libertarian journalism.[6] Most journal-

[5] John Whale, in a lecture, Journalism School, University of Missouri, July 19, 1973.
[6] See a good discussion of journalistic truth in Ch. 13 ("Ethics for Newsmen") in Gene Gilmore and Robert Root, *Modern Newspaper Editing* (Berkeley, Calif.: The Glendessary Press, 1971), pp. 242–43.

ists think of truth as they do of objectivity—as temporary, splintered and incomplete. Accuracy, fairness, balance, comprehensiveness are generally related to objectivity by the journalist—and, therefore, have to do with truth.

Naturally, the main problem with such truth is that it must be considered in context with editorial determinism. *What* truth—or what parts of what truth—will a journalistic medium choose to present? "All the news that's fit to print," replies *The New York Times*, proclaiming to all that certain matters (even if *truthful* or contributing to the truth) which are not considered "fit" will not be printed. Therefore, *The Times* is explicitly saying what all journalists believe and practice: truth is what journalists consider fit to call truth, just as news is what they decide is news—nothing more and nothing less.

Moral philosophers have at least given us a wide variety of alternative standards for determining virtuous actions. In general, these ethical standards boil down to two main ones: *teleological* theories and *deontological* theories. The first consider the moral rightness or wrongness of an action as the good that is produced. The second, on the other hand, hold that something other than (but sometimes, perhaps, in addition to) consequences determine which actions are morally right or good.

Teleological theories. Teleologists look at the consequences of an act; they consider consequences and only consequences as determining the moral rightness or wrongness of actions. Teleologists differ among themselves only as to whose good it is that one ought to try to promote. Egoists, for example, hold that one should always do what will promote his own greatest good; this view was held by Epicurus, Hobbes and Nietzsche, among others. Utilitarians—or ethical socialists—take the position that an act or rule of action is right or good if and only if it is, or probably is, conducive to the greatest possible balance of good over evil everywhere. Some utilitarians (e.g., Jeremy Bentham and J. S. Mill) have been hedonists in their view of good being connected with the greatest happiness (pleasure) to the greatest number.

Ethical egoism, one of the teleological theories, holds that it is the duty of the individual to seek his own good. This stance has a great deal to say for itself; for if we regard the moral end as perfection, it is likely that we can do very little to achieve the perfection of anybody other than ourselves. A man may influence to some degree the activities of others, but he can *control* only his own activities. This is somewhat related to Kant's "duty ethics" whereby man is urged to seek his own perfection by being obligated to a rationally accepted principle or maxim. Self-perfection is the goal of a moral life.

The universal or social ethics of utilitarianism, on the other hand, holds that every person should seek the good of his group, community, na-tion—or world—as a whole. It claims, in a way, to combine the true ele-ments of egoism and altruism—as the good of the group or community will include, of course, the agent's own good. Its appeal is that it sets no narrow limits on the range of moral obligations. One form of utilitarian-ism, the extreme *altruistic* stance, emphasizes the seeking the good of other individuals with no regard for the agent's own good; this is the stance of self-sacrifice, with the emphasis being entirely on *others*.

The social (utilitarian) ethical theory enthrones others—the group, the collective or society generally—and sees the good as that which benefits the life of the group or the society. This is usually the ethics of collective altruism, and has been expressed generally in terms of the utilitarian principle that good conduct is that which results in the greatest good to the greatest number. There are two practical problems with this theory: (1) the problem of determining what is really good for most people, and (2) the problem posed by equating "good" with majority opinion or ac-tion. The journalist, for instance, in deciding whether or not to present a story, has no sound way of knowing which action will result in the greatest good to the greatest number of people. He can only guess—and hope. The second problem above leads the journalist to a kind of "give them what they want" ethical stance, abdicating personal commitment (and personal reason) for the social determinism of "vote-morality."

Deontological theories. These theories are quite different from the teleological ones just discussed for they hold that something other than consequences determine which actions are morally right. Some deontolo-gists say the important thing is the motive of the agent; Kant, for ex-ample, contends that an action is justified if the intentions of the doer are good, regardless of the consequences that might ensue from the action. A deontologist believes that producing the greatest possible happiness to the greatest possible number has nothing (or may have nothing) to do with the morality of the action. He also believes that personal satisfaction or gain is irrelevant to ethical action. He sees an action being right or obligatory simply because of some fact about it or because of its own nature.

Probably the best example of a deontologist is Immanuel Kant, and his basic principle or rule—the Categorical Imperative—lies at the base of his ethical system: "Act only on that maxim which you can at the same time will to be a universal law." Kant is here offering this "imperative" as the necessary principle for determining what more specific and concrete ethical rules we should adopt to guide our behavior. He is saying, in effect, that a person is acting ethically only if he is—or would be—willing to have everyone act on his maxim. Or, said another way, a person is acting ethically if he would be willing to see his rule applied by everyone who is in a similar situation.

If we ask "Which actions are right" we are really asking for some way to identify right actions. Utilitarians (teleologists) would reply: Those which maximize utility or which do the greatest service for the greatest number, or something like that. Kant and other deontologists would claim that those actions are right which pass the test of some personal and rationally accepted imperative. For Kant, for example, virtue has nothing to do with pleasure or with any other "consequences." Bertrand Russell has written of Kant:

> Kant was never tired of pouring scorn on the view that the good consists of pleasure, or of anything else except virtue. And virtue consists in acting as the moral law enjoins, *because* that is what the moral law enjoins. A right action done from any other motive cannot count as virtuous. If you are kind to your brother because you are fond of him, you have no merit; but if you can hardly stand him and are nevertheless kind to him because the moral law says you should be, then you are the sort of person that Kant thinks you ought to be.[7]

The reader can tell from the tone of Russell's quotation that he was not in sympathy with Kant's absolutist ethics; and Russell's view tends to be the generally accepted one in the modern world. Kant's ethics is far too "cold" and rigid for most "scientifically inclined" persons in our increasingly relativistic society.

If consequences and states such as happiness are not important in determining ethical actions, then what is relevant must be something to do with basic maxims or principles. For the deontologists what is important is the principle from which the action has been performed; and the test applied to the maxim must be something independent of consequence. The Categorical Imperative is not really a specific maxim from which one acts—rather it is a principle or general rule which will allow a journalist (or anyone else) to test all maxims from which he acts. It is a kind of "super-maxim" which serves to guide thinking about specific rules to be applied in specific cases. If a journalist accepts the Categorical Imperative, then it is unnecessary for him to carry around in his head (or on a printed Code or Creed) specific rules or guidelines to follow. These he formulates on the basis of his "super-maxim" as the various occasions arise. If these guidelines for each case pass the test of the Categorical Imperative, then his action based on that "super-maxim" is ethically sound, and the journalist may be considered virtuous.

[7] Russell, *Human Society in Ethics and Politics*, p. 39.

Although Kant's philosophy has profoundly influenced Western thought, it is obvious that at least among modern intellectuals his strict and absolutist "duty ethics" has lost considerable appeal and force. A kind of relativism or situationism is in ascendency, an ethics which has a great appeal to those who like to think of themselves as "rational." This new situationism is a kind of synthesis emerging from the clash of ethical legalism, on one hand, and ethical antinomianism on the other. It will be discussed in the following section.

The Appeal of Relativism

The ethics of "law," of "duty" and "absolute obligation" is a little strong for most thinkers. So this *legalistic* stance in ethical thinking has been confronted by its opposite: what has been called *antinomianism*. The rebel against Kantianism and other legalistic ethics has accepted what might actually be considered by some as a "non-ethics"—a completely open kind of morality which is against any rules. The antinomian has, in effect, tossed out all basic principles, precepts, codes, standards and laws which might guide his conduct. Just as the legalist tends toward absolutist or universal ethics, the antinomian tends toward anarchy or nihilism in ethics. He is against standards; he thinks he needs no *a priori* guidelines, directions or moral rules. He is satisfied to "play it by ear," making ethical judgments and decisions intuitively, spontaneously, emotionally, and often irrationally. He is a kind of Existentialist—or very closely related—in that he has great faith that personal, existential instincts will give the ethical direction needed.

The antinomian in journalism is usually found in the free-wheeling ranks of rebellious journalism where an anti-Establishment stance is considered healthy. The antinomian journalist affronts mainstream journalism, making his ethical decisions as he goes—almost subconsciously— about his daily activities. His ethical (or nonethical) system might be called "whim ethics," and his confrontation with mainstream journalism is not very potent or successful because it is weakened considerably by a lack of rational force.

From the clash of these two ethical "extremes"—legalism and anti-nomianism—a kind of synthesis has developed which has a potent impact on ethical thinking. It is usually known as *situation ethics*.[8] Although it is related to code or legalistic ethics more closely than it is to antinomian ethics in most of its characteristics, it does synthesize certain strains of both orientations. Like code ethics, it is basically rational, and like anti-

---

[8] See John Merrill and Ralph Lowenstein, *Media, Messages, and Men*, pp. 251–55— section on the "Ethical Dialectic".

nomian ethics it is relativistic and is not tied securely to absolute principles. Situation ethics begins with traditional legalistic ethics but is willing to deviate from these basic principles when rationality and the situation call for it.

The journalistic situationist may well be the one who believes that he should tell the truth *as a basic principle*, or that he should not generally distort his story, but who will, after due consideration of the situation in which he finds himself, conclude that it is all right to distort *this particular story*, or even to lie. Do the circumstances in this case warrant a departure from basic—generally held—moral guidelines: this is the rational question which always confronts the situationist. He is one, then, who takes special situations into consideration in making his ethical decisions; he is a relativist to be sure, but a rational relativist, one who *thinks* before breaking a basic ethical rule.

One who subscribes to what may be called "Machiavellian ethics" is one type of situationist. Maurice Cranston has pointed out that Machiavelli believed that persons (statesmen, at least) should not allow their relationships with other states always to be governed by the same ethical scruples that govern their dealings with private persons. His ethics, however, were really absolutist, says Cranston; he accepted one true morality, but he believed the ruler should sometimes disregard it. As Machiavelli says in *The Prince*, the ruler "should not depart from what is morally right if he can observe it, but should know how to adopt what is bad when he is obliged to." [9] Machiavelli does not contend that the bad is anything other than bad; he only contends that bad things are to be done only sparingly—and then only in a concealed manner, if possible.

Journalists like to point out Machiavellianism in others (especially in government officials), but they themselves very often operate under this variant of situation ethics. They usually contend they believe in absolutes (such as giving their audiences all the pertinent facts or not changing or distorting quotes from a source), yet they depart from these principles when they think that "in this special case" it is reasonable to do so. They normally talk about their belief in "letting the people know" but they determine innumerable exceptions to this principle—times when they will not (because of the circumstances of the special situation) let the people know. And, of course, they are not very interested in letting the people know that they are not knowing.

The press is much more interested, of course, in pointing out Machiavellian situationism in government officials. This is natural and it is very healthy for the press to do this, for certainly our government is filled

[9] Maurice Cranston, "Ethics and Politics," *Encounter* (London), Vol. 38, No. 6, June, 1972.

with myriads of Machiavellian functionaries busy justifying to themselves (and sometimes to others) their departure from basic moral principles. It is interesting to note how closely members of the Nixon Administration—especially some of his closest "advisers"—followed Machiavellian situationism in rationalizing the many unethical practices connected with the Watergate Affair which got world-wide airing in 1973. Not only did these officials seem to know that what they had done was wrong or unethical, but they felt that it would be best if they kept these things secret. Certainly they were not inclined to reveal them until the press and the Congress (and the courts) forced their disclosure.

Very little has been written about journalistic ethics beyond certain repetitious phrases appearing in "codes" and "creeds" designed largely for framing and hanging as wall trappings. Perhaps one reason for this is that most editors, publishers, news directors and other journalists simply write the whole subject of ethics off as "relative," giving little or no importance to absolute or universal journalistic principles. A newspaper friend put it succinctly recently when he said that he looked at ethics as "just the individual journalist's way of doing things." Certainly a free journalist has the right to consider ethics in this way, but such a relativistic concept relegates ethics to a kind of "nothingness limbo" where anything any journalist does can be considered ethical. Or, said another way, what one journalist does can be considered just as ethical as what any other journalist does.

If we throw out absolute theories of ethics (exemplified by Kant), then a discussion of morality becomes merely a discussion of preferences, arbitrary choices, detached judgments—none of which establishes obligation. The statement "this was the right journalistic decision" means no more than "I liked this decision"—just as one might say "I liked the view of the ocean." One form of relativism in ethics contends that a journalistic practice in Context A may be quite good—ethical—while if practiced in Context B it might be bad or unethical. In other words, it would be all right to submit to government censorship without objection in the Soviet Union but not all right to submit to government censorship in the United States. Or, taking this further, it would be all right to submit to censorship in the United States "under certain conditions" but wrong to do this under other conditions. Circumstances dictate the ethics; contexts determine "rightness" or "wrongness," say the relativists.

Often I have heard, for instance, that in Mexico journalists often accept bribes to supplement their meagre incomes; I am also informed that many journalists also work for a newspaper part-time and for some politician as a sort of private "press agent"—therefore having a conflict of interest. And, I am told, that this is all right in Mexico—maybe not in the United States—but quite "acceptable" (therefore ethical?) in Mexico where the conditions are different. The relativist's position here is: If it's good in a particular society, it's good, and if it's bad, it's bad—there is really no objective or universal principle. Also I hear from Soviet journalists that close party-government control of what goes into the press and over the air-waves is quite "ethical" in the Soviet Union; it is not only "all right" that this happens—it is actually the best situation, the most moral.

The situationist positions mentioned above can be considered a part of "subjectivist" ethics for what one does in a certain situation is determined *subjectively* by the individual at the time when an ethical decision is demanded. The temper of the times has thrust the subjectivist into a dominant moral position—at least from the point of being in the majority. And for many persons today if the majority believe something ethical, then it is ethical. These are the days of the subjectivist—the relativist and situationist. These are the days when it is considered unenlightened to make a value judgment, to take a stand, to feel a sense of "duty" or have a commitment. These are the days of the person who believes one opinion is as good as another and that one man's moral standards are as good as his neighbor's. These are the days of the "we-are-probably-both-right" school of thinking, the days of the tolerant men—the "adapters"—who feel no impulse to speak out loudly and clearly on moral standards.

Although the relativistic position is indeed intriguing due to its aura of individualism (and therefore seeming to enhance the theme of this book), I must reject it. In fact, at the risk of making a value judgment, I will even say that it is not really an ethical position at all; rather it is a "non-ethics" or an "anti-ethics." When the matter of ethics is watered down to subjectivism, to situations or contexts, it loses all meaning as ethics. If every case is different, if every situation demands a different standard, if there are no absolutes in ethics, then we should scrap the whole subject of moral philosophy and simply be satisfied that each person run his life by his whims or "considerations" which may change from situation to situation.

Without a doubt there is rationality involved in situation ethics; this is surely not denied. It is quite possible to take situations into account *rationally*; of course, it is also possible to take them into account emotionally. Subjectivist and relativist ethics is, understandably, attractive and satisfying to many highly intelligent persons—especially to pragmatists and utilitarians. In the following section, let us consider the thoughts of two relativistic philosophers concerning the nature of ethical values. This should point out the intellectual appeal of relativism and perhaps even take note of some of its inherent weaknesses.

Dewey, Russell and the Issue of Values

What is "good" journalism? What is "right" journalistic action? What is socially responsible journalism? What ethical system should a journalist subscribe to—if any? What values should be embraced by the journalist and how should these values be determined? What should the journalist do in regard to this or that story or picture? Should he conceal part of the story (or all of it) to assure national security? What is the value to society (or to anyone) of printing the names of rape victims? Why should the impending invasion of a certain country be publicized by the journalist if he manages to get the information? Should he print the names of young people if they commit criminal acts? All such specific ethical questions as these must be faced at some time by the modern journalist and are related to the system of values which he has accepted as his own.

A broader question for the journalist is this: Should his ethics be "individualistic" or should the concern be with a "group-approved" (social) morality—with codes, creeds, standards and other collectively determined "arrangements" being the norm? Should the journalist, in short, determine his own ethical code or should he adopt the group values? These are all questions being discussed here and there in the journalistic world today, and from this dialogue various "proposals" are proliferating and new organizations, such as press councils and courts of honor, along with ombudsmen of one sort or another, are being born. These organizations and arbiters, despite sincere motives, all have the tendency to shift the emphasis away from personal or autonomous ethics and toward socially pressured-or-enforced ethics.

At the heart of any discussion of values or of journalistic ethics generally is the clash between the traditional absolutist position and the more modern, more "scientific" and dynamic school of thought which espouses "relativistic" values. It is very easy to assume that absolutist or "duty" ethics is not individualistic or autonomous, but this assumption does not necessarily follow; all that is necessary is that the "duty" ethics be personal or freely accepted. On the other hand, relativistic ethics is easily thought to be individualistic in the sense of being freely willed or authentically personal. This may or may not follow, for it is quite possible for the relativist (as it is for the absolutist) to permit his standards to be imposed on him from some outside source—person, group or total society. So it is very difficult to generalize about the *autonomy* or *personalism* of the individual who accepts either the absolutist or the relativistic value system.

In spite of what has just been said, it does seem—especially at first glance—that an emphasis on subjectivity and situationism would help in repelling a kind of monolithic or standardized journalism that is anathema to those who cherish press freedom. Such an emphasis does indeed have individualistic propensities, but it may well lead—while ostensibly emphasizing the individual—to a kind of conformity that prizes pragmatism and utility (workability and other-directedness) at the expense of a personally determined and rationally accepted journalistic morality.

This pragmatic or instrumental morality, which is undoubtedly the dominant one today, has probably found its best recent advocates in America's John Dewey and Britain's Bertrand Russell. Although these two philosophers do not deal specifically with values or ethics *for journalists*, what they have to say can very easily be projected to those working in the mass media. Both men are proponents of a kind of utilitarianism; Russell has summed it up in these extremely clear words:

> I will repeat once more that I mean by "right" conduct that conduct which will probably produce the greatest balance of satisfaction over dissatisfaction, or the smallest balance of dissatisfaction over satisfaction, and that, in making this estimate, the question as to who enjoys the satisfaction, or suffers the dissatisfaction, is to be considered irrelevant.[10]

Although Dewey and Russell may stand rather far part in many ways and have had many disagreements in philosophical discourse, largely arising from the former's "pragmatism" as opposed to the latter's more mystical "intellectualism," their ideas pertaining to *values* appear quite similar and form the foundation of their ethical system. Even though Russell has philosophized about such "impractical" (to Dewey) things as the existence of an external world, he does have a great respect for Science, and in this respect is often classed with Dewey as a "non-Aristotelian" (to use a term prized by the General Semanticists).

It may well be that philosophers deal more specifically with "values" in other of their works, but it is undeniable that Dewey's *Reconstruction in Philosophy* and Russell's *Religion and Science* [11] afford a very clear insight into their attitudes on the subject, and these two books serve as the primary sources for the discussion which follows. In these books we can note the emergence of a kind of "individualistic" (or "relativistic") ethics

---

10 Russell, *Human Society in Ethics and Politics,* p. 119.
11 See Russell, *Religion and Science* (London: Oxford University Press, 1935), and Dewey, *Reconstruction in Philosophy* (New York: Henry Holt, 1920). Russell's *Human Society in Ethics and Politics* and Dewey's *Theory of the Moral Life* (New York: Holt, Rinehart and Winston, 1960) are also useful in considering the two philosophers' concept of values and ethics in general.

shared by the two philosophers, while noting certain important and interesting differences.

Relativity of Values. It is quite true that Dewey had some kind of conception of social values connected with the scientific method, a conception which, of course, would not separate "values" from "Science" as would be the case with Russell. This is the point of greatest difference in the concepts of "values" of the two men, a difference which would appear to be more significant at first glance than it really is. Basically, when each of these concepts of value is shorn of all extraneous issues, it is left with a core of "relativistic" meaning. Therefore, it might be well to point out that while Russell seems *more* individualistic in respect to his value concept than Dewey, both men are firm relativists as to values.

Being "non-Aristotelians" in the sense that they both rebel against the rigidity of the older classical or "unscientific" philosophy, Dewey and Russell must therefore naturally shy away from anything which might tend to be absolutist or fixed.[12] They represent the *dynamic* school of thought, which sees everything—even morality—as in constant flux; there are no statics, no absolutes, no universals. Both philosophers would condemn anything that might make for sterile minds—inflexible, reactionary and resistant to change.

Both men place great emphasis on the individual but see him as basically a "social" person who needs to adapt to the collective in order to maximize his pragmatic value; but they do seemingly have great faith in every man's ability to fathom the complex world in his "own way" and to come up with his own workable (thus moral) set of values. To Dewey and Russell there is no absolute good—no *summum bonum*—unless it would possibly be "change" (for Dewey) and "mystical emotionalizing" (for Russell). While Russell contends that he finds happiness in a sort of mystical personal religion, Dewey, who is far too practical for such things, seems to find his happiness in the more pragmatic (though equally vague) idea of "experimental intelligence."

The two men appear to share the belief that values must vary with person, time and place, and that only the individual intelligence (or mystical insight) can determine them. Dewey, especially, finds one thing alone that seems universally good—*growth* or change. Russell, who appears to have especially strong faith in personal "feelings," believes that mysticism will lead to a state of mind "out of which right conduct will come." Like Dewey, he would consider "rules" as insufficient to guide individuals in

---

[12] Both Dewey and Russell are claimed by proponents of General Semantics, a scientifically oriented psycholinguistic school of "non-Aristotelians" founded by Alfred Korzybski and carried on by his disciples, including S. I. Hayakawa, Irving J. Lee, Wendell Johnson and Stuart Chase.

varying circumstances. Only from within the person—not from any outside source—can "guides" of living be imposed. Since both men believe that there are no absolute values, that they are all relative or conditional, they view all value judgment as purely subjective and beyond proof or disproof. Dewey might stress the "conditional" more than the "relative" and say that *ultimately* (after some sort of trial and error), one value or value system might evolve "scientifically" correct or incorrect. Here he, too, manifests his utilitarianism.

No "Fixed" Values. Values as they are commonly understood, according to Dewey, only tend to frustrate a person who looks on them as "fixed ends to be attained." Concepts such as "honesty," "justice" and "temperance" are only vague generalizations; they should be looked on as "directions of change in the quality of experience." Dewey adds: "Growth itself is the only moral 'end'." This, to Dewey, would scrap the idea of values as a terminus or limit to be reached, and would make values nothing more than active processes which bring about a change. Perfection, as Dewey sees it, is not the final goal—rather the final goal or aim in living is the process of "perfecting and maturing and refining." Dewey bemoans the idea of "fixed values," believing that men who accept them "have chosen for the most part the way of prejudices and sanctioned ideas." To both Dewey and Russell what is needed in the modern world is a sort of "relativistic" philosophy which avoids all generalizations. This would be a "specific-cases" type of philosophy which, as Dewey says, would teach that "institutions are made for man and not man for institutions."

Russell sees values as lying beyond the domain of knowledge, and believes that when people try to define "Good" they are only appealing to their own emotions and are employing "such rhetorical devices as shall rouse similar emotions in others." Without such "fixed" values, says Russell, individuals would cease having all types of guilt feelings and frustrations. Or, as Dewey would put it, with "fixed values" a person can lose the feeling of "resignation and submission" brought on him by the old two-valued philosophical orientation. Mistakes, says Dewey, are not to be mourned; they are not sinful; they are "lessons in wrong methods of using intelligence." For Dewey mistakes are simply indications that a revision is needed or that a readjustment must be made. This is certainly a satisfying way to look at actions which go awry in some way—simply as "mistakes."

Dewey sees morals as "not a catalogue of acts, not a set of rules to be applied like drugstore prescriptions or cookbook recipes," and he calls for the pragmatic "logic" of situationism which finds in every case its own "irreplaceable good and principle." Likewise, Russell insists that "values" are really meaningless in the common "Aristotelian" sense; he observes in a somewhat trite way that "even the best moral rules have some exceptions." So it can be seen that both Dewey and Russell consider *situation* ethics really the only logical or rational moral stance. It is surely a stance which has tremendous appeal—more appeal, actually, to the *intellect* than it has to a kind of deeper *moral sense* which is in some way part of a human being.

Anti-Authoritarianism. Russell indicates throughout *Religion and Science* (as does Dewey in *Reconstruction in Philosophy*) that he is against authoritarianism.[13] He especially relates this stance to the Church. Strangely he puts Science and Religion in two "camps," thereby painting a this-and-that picture, although he advocates a "non-Aristotelian" position and claims to be a foe of those who categorize. It might be well here to mention another paradox: Russell's insistence that the individual should have primacy over society and centralism is everywhere to be avoided, while at the same time Russell was embracing a socialistic political philosophy.

In his case against authoritarianism, Russell shatters the idea of a "soul." He, like Dewey, believes that this conception (like many others which cling on in this "scientific" age) results from inadequacies in the language. The syntactical concept of "persons" and "things" has led to the idea of "body" and "soul," he says, and he (like Dewey) stresses that the new scientific philosophy considers everything as constantly changing and merging. Nothing is what it was; therefore, the idea of "body" cannot be valid. He carries this reasoning to the "mind." Minds or souls are nonexistent when a person is *alive*, he says, so a soul could not exist when a person is *dead*. (One is tempted to speculate as to how Russell would determine if a person were *dead* if there is no *body*.)

According to Russell, values contain nothing scientific—nothing in the way of fact or knowledge. Only "desires" are relevant; therefore Science cannot deal with values since it is concerned with what is true or false. This leads Russell into a discussion of the "subjectivity" of values, which parallels almost exactly the value concept of Dewey in this respect. According to Russell, when persons disagree about values, there is really no disagreement "as to any kind of truth." There is only a difference of "taste." So, Russell's subjective or relative values arise from desires, which he says are "personal." A desire, he says, cannot be rational or irrational; it is merely personal and unproveable. Systems of ethics or values, he concludes, are simply embodiments of the desires of those who propose them.

---

[13] This aspect of the philosophy of both Dewey and Russell—the antagonism to outside controllers or authoritarians—is perfectly harmonious with the libertarian thrust of this book. It is simply their emphasis on relativistic values which causes a part of their thought to be somewhat at odds with the Kantian strain of the present volume.

Dewey, like Russell, scorns authoritarianism and reacts strongly against authoritarian methods in most every realm, especially looking on the classical approach in philosophy as the basis for most authoritarian beliefs and practices. A person, while he is considered by Dewey to be an individual and quite "different" from others, must be growing and thinking in a context of inter-actions and relations. Although this idea seems to minimize certain individualistic characteristics of the person, Dewey sees it as extending the limits of his possible development and therefore in the long run being more "individualistic."

As is also the case with Russell, Dewey contends that there are no degrees of goodness or value. He says that anything that is "good in a given situation is of equal worth, rank, and dignity with every good of any other situation." In knocking down the idea of "fixed values," Dewey notes that more should be expected of some people than of others, a rejection of "fixed" or absolute expectations. Actually the important consideration for Dewey is that there be *movement*. He says in *Reconstruction in Philosophy* that no person or group should be "judged by result, but by the direction in which they are moving." He does not explain how the judge would know which direction is good and which is bad; if he would contend that it does not really matter or that it is simply a "personal" thing, then it would seem that Dewey's theory expressed in the last quotation is meaningless.

Dewey proceeds to give the example of the man "who no matter how morally unworthy he *has* been" moves to become better. He calls him the "good" man. Likewise, he says the "bad" man is the person, no matter how good he *has* been, is beginning to deteriorate. Two questions arise concerning these two statements. First, how would Dewey define the state of *goodness* from which his bad man is falling? Secondly, how would he define the state of *badness* from which his good man is struggling? It seems unlikely that such definitions could be given if there were no absolute values somewhere or if there were no "degrees" of goodness or badness which could be used as reference points. Of course, Dewey does say that the real value in the world is improvement and progress, rather than the "outcome and result." It still seems a necessary consideration that there must be some method of knowing in which direction is improvement and progress. It would appear that Dewey's basic concept implies a "starting point" or some kind of fixed value. It would also seem to demand a judgment by *somebody* as to what "direction" it would be valuable (or good) to progress in; but Dewey, of course, tends to scorn value judgments, thinking them somehow tendencies in the direction of authoritarianism.

Both Dewey and Russell would reject any authoritarian system which would tend to impose values upon them. They would not completely disavow the existence of some sort of Supreme Being (by whatever name), but they would insist that this Being be within each person a varying and changing Being, different in every case and adapting Itself to individual needs. They would consider "individuality" as something always changing, developing and being "wrought out." They would not completely set the individual into chaotic and standardless motion, but would conceive of *authority* as an orchestra leader "who makes no music himself but who harmonizes the activities" of those who really make the music.

Finally, in their insistence on "individual" worth and potential, Dewey and Russell would break up all stereotypes, classifications, groups and other linguistic techniques by which the individual is "lost." Each person being different from every other person, he should in a manner of speaking, go about seeking his own salvation—finding his own values—in his own way. In this, of course, they are very close to the Existentialists and also to a central premise of this book.

A Few Reactions. The philosophy of Dewey and Russell discussed briefly above, one of "individualistic values" as opposed to generalized or absolute values, makes for a comfortable philosophical attitude which endows with importance those personal "feelings" and "insights" which slip into our consciousness and adapt themselves to the particular need at the particular hour in the individual situation. This is somewhat similar to both "situation ethics" and its first cousin "antinomian ethics" discussed earlier. There is the common relativism and personalism that permeates this whole area of "individualistic" ethics.

Being relativists, both Dewey and Russell condemn fixed standards and stable values and would replace them with what is dynamic morality —a constantly changing and varying set of amorphous and individualistic "feelings" or a groping, always-moving "experimental intelligence." To them there is no real "goal"; there is no ultimate aim; there is no Ultimate Truth. There is no "this," no "that," only a sea of constantly shifting moral sands washing about in the swirling waters of change.

While insisting that generalizations should not be made and that people should not be put in categories, Dewey and Russell waste no time in dividing the world (or at least the world's philosophers) into two classes: the reactionary or "static" metaphysical philosophers of the classical "Aristotelian" school, and the new liberal philosophers of the dynamic, "multi-valued" scientific school. But since they seem to have little love for classical logic, this obvious contradiction should not greatly disturb them. Both philosophers seem to dislike the "prescientific" philosophies because these would propose "guides" or "values" which not only are static or absolute, but which are also "general." Since, as both these gentlemen apparently feel, individuals behave or react in specific or particular ways and not in general ways to their problems, they cannot be guided in "general."

If this philosophical world of Dewey and Russell—reinforced and modified by a growing number of general semanticists (it is strange that the new "category" of semanticists prefaces its title with the adjective "general")—comes to pass, I have the feeling (and I am sure I am on solid ground in having a "feeling") we shall find ourselves surrounded by increasing numbers of maladjusted, frustrated persons who, because they are without firm ethical standards to guide them, will be floundering (in the "right" or the "wrong" direction, I would not know) in this helpless world of unstructured and relativistic values.

This "new" philosophy may well be the push that will aid our world to deteriorate into a social bedlam (or our journalism into a communication bedlam) which characterized the "little societies" of the classroom when Dewey's philosophy was related to the American school system. Gone would be (and they seem to be going fast) all standards and absolute values in education, in journalism—and in other areas of endeavor. It is important to stress at this point that absolute ethics does not imply commonality of norms or the imposition from *outside* the person of a standard; it simply means that there are absolutes for the individual person which *he has freely accepted and freely feels "duty-bound" to follow.*

It is my wish that we re-inculcate into our thinking—and into our journalistic education and journalism itself—through our total educational system a respect for the older classical philosophy away from which the "progressive" Dynamic School of scientifically oriented philosophers are leading us. For the past half century, at least, the world has veered in the direction of the new, un-rooted, relativistic philosophy, and resulting social and moral chaos—and individual uncertainty—on a world-wide scale would seem to indicate a need to reconsider basic premises of relativism.

These doubts about the value of situationism and utilitarianism do not even mean that I am trying to escape from a scientific orientation into the "heavenly courts" of the humanities. It does not mean that I would want to retreat into a hundred or so "great" books (although I insist that some books have more absolute "value" than others) or that I would have everyone sitting around philosophizing with no thought to worldly pragmatism. I am simply not that unpragmatic. Retreating too far into the lofty halls of the humanities will certainly make for a sterile and unreal existence and frustrate a person's communication with the real and dynamic world. Being in the field of "mass" communication, I certainly would not propose that this be done.

However, I would like to repulse the new "non-value" or "multi-value" philosophy that is sweeping upon us and filling us with an arrogant (or is it timid?) attitude that "all ethical values are equal." Although I respect Dewey and Russell's faith in the individual person, I would repel the idea that nothing is fixed and that one person is as "right" or "just" as the next, and that it is all dependent on the specific person in the specific contest. I also insist that there is a difference between "good" and "best," and that the difference (contrary to the beliefs of Dewey and Russell) is not merely a "linguistic" one.

The brief comments above have been "value judgments" on my part. And I would be a fool if I disagreed with Russell and said they could be proved or disproved. Since "truth" lies outside the realm of proof, as Russell says, my value judgments may well be true, totally independent of proof. (I, of course, do not *really* believe this.) So I shall conclude by saying that these are my opinions and judgments, my "feelings" if you prefer, and that they are unprovable. I shall let it rest with future disciples of Dewey, armed with their "experimental intelligence," to find the ultimate truth (if such, indeed, exists).

9

The "Apollonysian" Journalist

THE THESIS of this book is not only that the journalist should recognize the imperative of freedom, but that he should incorporate into his journalistic philosophy the two other emphases of tremendous importance: rationality and commitment. At the same time he must—and *will* with these philosophical dimensions—become a kind of journalistic scientist-artist, part Apollo and part Dionysus, a person who merges the perspectives of objective reason and existential subjectivity.

Such a synthesis will produce a journalist who may well be called the "Apollonysian": a person who thinks *and* feels, who is both rational *and* sensitive, who is both concerned with facts *and* with feelings, who is dedicated to the objective world "out there" *and* to his subjective world "in here." He is, in essence, the rational synthesizer—the journalist who is able to *intentionally* develop a journalistic philosophy which merges the strains (or stances) of freedom, rationality and duty. As has been stated earlier, "responsibility" (noticeably missing in the above lists) is considered implicit in each of these orientations: the free journalist who tempers his journalism with reason, sensitivity and commitment *is a responsible journalist.*

edom, Rationality and Commitment

In a very real sense these three terms form the philosophical frame-work of this entire book; they certainly converge to describe the proposed journalistic philosophy. In them are found the strains of existentialism, rational humanism and Kantianism which flow throughout these pages; implicit in these terms, also, are found the orientations—the *intellectual* (rational) and the *mystical* (emotional)—designated by Nietzsche as "Apollonian" and "Dionysian." Let us look briefly at the three strains of freedom, rationality and commitment before considering each of them in more detail.

First, *freedom*. As the French writer and journalist, Albert Camus, has said: "When the press is free it may be good and bad—but certainly without freedom it can never be anything but bad. . . . For the press, as for man, freedom is the opportunity to become better: servitude is the certainty of becoming worse." [1] The whole idea of ethics depends on personal freedom—freedom to make choices. Ethics is, as Hazel Barnes says, "an inner control which the individual exercises over himself," [2] and certainly freedom to exercise this control is basic to any moral concept. Existentialism puts supreme value on freedom, contending that if "one accepts freedom as a fact, then no act is ethical which acts as if men were not free." [3] Not only Existentialists, but rationalists and Kantians place great importance on freedom.

Second, *rationality*. This is one of the cornerstones, along with free-dom, of a journalistic philosophy. Objectivists such as Ayn Rand and hu-manists such as Erich Fromm pay homage to it. Even the Existentialists agree that it is important, although they would certainly accord the emo-tions and the senses equal status. What the Existentialists want to do is to reunite the "irrational parts of the psyche" with the rational parts. It is a shift of emphasis only, a shift to the thinker who has the idea and away from the idea itself. Existentialism accepts as valid and important man's thought—but goes further and stresses the validity of other aspects of man: his body, blood, bones, his frailty, contingency and fallibility.[4]

Hazel Barnes stresses the importance placed on rationality by the Existentialist:

[1] Lee Hills, *Don Mellett's Unfinished Story* (booklet containing the 31st Mellett lecture at the University of Oklahoma, March 29, 1960), p. 15.
[2] Hazel Barnes, *An Existentialist Ethics* (New York: Random House Vintage Books, 1971), p. 8.
[3] *Ibid.*, p. 26.
[4] Gordon E. Bigelow, "A Primer of Existentialism," *College English* (Dec. 1961), p 173.

> An ethics must introduce rationality as one of its criteria even though it may at the same time insist that its goal is happiness or satisfaction or some other state which is closer to emotion than to reason. Fidelity to the truth of man and the Universe is essential. . . . Rationality involves more than intellectual honesty. It requires as one of its corollary values a respect for consistency.[5]

Any philosophy which does not admit rationality to the field of ethics would, undoubtedly, be cooperating with anarchistic or autocratic forces which would tend to regulate man's affairs or would inject chaos into them.[6] If there is not a large dose of reason in one's ethical determinations, there can really be little or no consistency and predictability to ethical actions. And, of course, one of the main purposes of ethics is to serve as a reliable and helpful guide to right actions. Such a guide cannot be provided simply by whim or instinct; otherwise we could talk of dogs and cats as being ethically motivated.

Now, lastly, *commitment* or *duty*. The existential commitment is very similar to Kantian duty; both actually imply a rational choice and a determination to be loyal to that choice. The concept of "either/or" is important to the Existentialist; one should commit himself either to this or to that. A choice is forced upon him. Karl Jaspers says that when, in any matter, a man is truly himself he will recognize that there are alternatives and that his action will not be a compromise. "He will want to force a decision between the alternatives he has recognized," Jaspers writes.[7] This choosing between alternatives is actually the basis of ethics; in choice there is a rational commitment. Kant, too, insists on personal commitment; for each man must rationally come up with his own standards and values, and he must *obey* them. Ethics, to Kant, is as personal as it is to the Existentialists. It is actually one's duty to obey the laws of logic, of reason, and to have very high (and strict) personal standards of conduct—not to be rationalized away by thoughts of consequences.

Acting morally, for Kant, is acting on the basis of duty or on principle itself and not on any outcome (supposed or otherwise) of the action. Thus the principle is *a priori*—prior to the action—and when we take a principle as an inner rule for ourselves, it is a maxim which we have a commitment to. For example, in journalism, if a newspaper accepts the maxim that villainy ought to be exposed, then it has a *duty* to that principle; it should not consider consequences or try to rationalize it in any

---

[5] Barnes, *op. cit.*, p. 26.
[6] For a detailed treatise on the importance of rationality in ethics, see Stephen Toulmin, *Reason in Ethics* (Cambridge: Cambridge University Press, 1968).
[7] Karl Jaspers, *Man in the Modern Age* (New York: Doubleday Anchor Books, 1957), p. 81.

way—it should simply proceed to expose villainy. The British journalist, Arnold Goodman, makes this specific point in the *New Statesman*, when he writes:

> A great newspaper—if it believes that villainy ought to be exposed—should expose it without hesitation and without regard to the law of libel. If the editor, his reporters and his advisers are men of judgment and sense, they are unlikely to go wrong; but if they do go wrong the principle to publish and be damned is a valiant and sensible one for the newspaper and it should bear the responsibility.[8]

The authentic journalist—the truly moral one—would not act to please somebody or to gain some advantage or to secure some reward. If he acted on the basis of consequences, his journalism would fall to the level of expediency. The act should be done because the journalist is convinced that it is right. The Kantian journalist, like the Existential journalist, is not one who looks around for reasons to justify his action; he is unimpressed with the consequences of his journalism (honor, self-preservation, comfort, status, love, happiness for self or others, etc.). The basis of duty, according to Kant, is conformity to principle, and principle is a rule that can apply to all men; thus man makes his actions moral by bringing them up to the level of universality.

Now, a word on the synthesis of these three strains. Connected with the strain of *freedom* (with its existential emphasis) is the journalistic orientation which has been referred to earlier as "Dionysian." And, connected with the philosophical strains of *rational humanism* and Kantian *obligationism* is the orientation which has been called "Apollonian." These strains merge to result in a journalistic philosophy which I am calling "Apollonysian"—an orientation which makes for a kind of rationalistic commitment to humanistic existentialism. It is this philosophy that the *Apollonysian* journalist embraces. His main dedication is to *freedom*; but he recognizes that freedom is empty unless merged with commitment, rationality, and other residual concepts stemming from Kantianism and Objectivistic Humanism. (*See Figure 9 for the three strains and their philosophical origins and their merging into Apollonysian journalism.*) Let us now look more closely at these three strains.

Freedom: The Existentialist Strain

What a journalist does in specific cases does not matter as much as the fact that he *does* something. The supreme virtue for the Existentialist is probably the most old-fashioned of all: *integrity*. And a person cannot

[8] "As it is Writ," *New Statesman* (March 31, 1972), p. 426.

Figure 9

THE "APOLLONYSIAN" SYNTHESIS

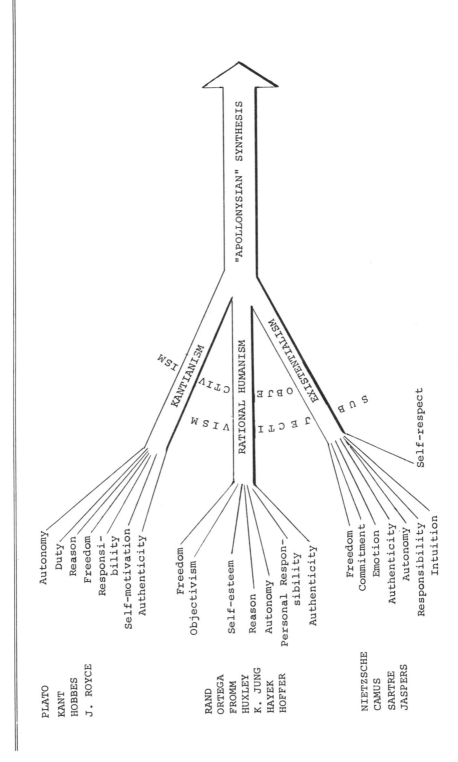

have integrity unless he utilizes his capacity to choose, to act, to make decisions. Basic to man is this act of choosing; the Existentialist sees man's very nature consisting of choosing. And this choosing is an outgrowth of freedom; or, said another way, it can have real meaning only in an atmosphere of freedom. To the question, "What good is life?" comes the answer: Life in the abstract is worthless. As a person lives his life, its value can be judged by what he puts into it. Values are a projection of man's personal freedom. For the Existentialist, man *is* freedom; he does not *possess* freedom. Freedom, for the Existentialist, comes as close as possible to constituting man's very essence. Man's most basic desire is for independent, free choice.

The Existentialist sees responsibility as freedom's anchorage. Man is responsible for himself, of course, but also for each act, and for the consequences of each act. Nobody else can be responsible for what a person is; each person must act freely and accept the responsibility for his action. And to choose for oneself is to choose for others. What would others do in my place? Strangely, perhaps, Existentialists view this universalized personal choice in much the same way as the coldly formal Kant did: You must never will what you cannot consistently will should be willed by other rational (i.e., free and responsible) beings. This heavy sense of personal responsibility the Existentialists call "anguish." Sartre has said that man is "condemned" to be free, and Kierkegaard wrote of the necessity to choose only "in fear and trembling." But choose we must—for ourselves and for all others, with no final assurance that our choice is the "right" one.[9]

Naturally we attempt to escape the implications of this existential situation. Often we try to deny that we are responsible for our actions by denying that we are free. The journalist, for example, may often say that *he* would not have written the story in such a way—or would not have written it at all—but that he "had to do it" because he was told to by his editor. He is thereby denying his freedom and refusing to accept personal responsibility for his actions. In practical terms, this embrace of "determinism" in various of its forms, amounts to denying that we are to blame for our actions—or for our morality. Existentialists, enthroning freedom, have no sympathy for these deterministic philosophies. And people who accept them, who try to escape from the human condition of freedom and personal responsibility, are seen as cowards. The Existentialist realizes that man must accept unquestioned responsibility for his ethical choices and actions. Man is an individualist: he is the end-all and be-all of values.

Self-deception, for the Existentialist, is the greatest vice, for it robs

[9] Abraham Kaplan, *The New World of Philosophy* (New York: Vintage Books, 1961), pp. 97–128.

man of his personhood, his integrity; it deludes him into thinking that he is nothing more than a robot having an essence pushed upon him by *outside* forces. Man *makes himself*, says the Existentialist, or defines what he is in the course of choosing, acting and existing.

The philosophical strain of freedom is basic to a sound and authentic journalistic orientation. Existentialism stresses this strain; so does Kant, but there is a difference. Sartre agrees with Kant in conceiving of freedom as desiring "both itself and the freedom of others." But, Sartre notes, Kant believes that "the formal and universal are enough to constitute an ethics"; Existentialists, on the other hand, "think that principles which are too abstract run aground in trying to decide action." [10] Sartre emphasizes personal responsibility—absolute responsibility for actions taken in specific cases and considering specific circumstances. So we see that the Existentialist, though prizing freedom, is basically a situationist while Kant is a universalist.

Action implies freedom. Since Existentialists advocate action, they would, of course, place freedom near to the heart of their philosophy. They have a passion for freedom; this is true of all varieties of Existentialists. Freedom for the Existentialist (as for Kant) is a basic postulate for action; it is already present as a condition for human existence. Freedom, of course, is dangerous; it even tends to contain in itself the seed of its own destruction. Nikolai Berdyaev, an Existentialist who has written articulately on the subject of freedom, puts it thusly: "The tragedy of the world process is that of freedom; it is born of the inner dynamic of freedom, of its capacity of changing into its opposite." [11] In striking this note, Berdyaev is consistent with many of his fellow Existentialists. Plato, of course, in his classic "Paradox of Freedom," had pre-dated the Existentialists in pointing out this danger centuries earlier when he noted that free men could freely decide to become enslaved.

Freedom may indeed be dangerous. And for many it is uncomfortable; they constantly try to "escape" from it. Nevertheless, freedom is absolutely necessary to an open society, to a democracy, to a libertarian people —and certainly to a pluralistic and diversified journalism. And, as Existentialists contend, there is no human dignity without freedom—and "the risk of increasing freedom must constantly be taken," as John Macquarrie puts it.[12] Existentialists generally link freedom with creativity. Without freedom *from* restraints, man cannot have freedom *for* creative activity. Berdyaev and other Existentialists reveal a certain elitist or aristocratic

---

[10] Jean-Paul Sartre, *Existentialism and Human Emotions* (New York: Philosophical Library—The Wisdom Library, 1957), p. 47.
[11] John Macquarrie, *Existentialism* (Baltimore: Penguin Books, 1973), p. 140.
[12] *Ibid.*, p. 141.

tendency: the masses, they say, do not really value freedom and are satisfied with the routine daily existence. For this reason the masses "are
peculiarly exposed to the dangers of dictatorship, founded on demagogy." [13]
This is perhaps true, for it is the rebel against the tyrannizing and con-
formizing influences of the masses who cherishes freedom; it is he who
protests against every attempt to diminish freedom. It is he who realizes,
as did Albert Camus, that "freedom preserves the power to protest and
guarantees human communication." [14]

The freedom-loving journalist can find perhaps his greatest support
from the Existentialists, for here is a philosophy which rebels against any
social control system which tends to enslave the individual human being
and to lead to his depersonalization. Frederick Patka writes that Existentialists "protest against this total subjection of the individual by the organized many" and that they "demand a bold revolt against this state of
affairs with a view to the emancipation and autonomy of the individual
person." [15] Existentialists, however, often draw attention to the danger
inherent in mass communication. The following words reflect existentialist
thought on this subject:

> The existentialists rightly point out that mass-communication, or sys-
> tematic manipulation of human beings, does not and can not achieve
> the goal of self-transcendence. On the contrary, it becomes the re-
> sponsible cause of the complete depersonalization, disintegration,
> and self-estrangement of the individual human being. This situation
> imposes the need to reject the assumptions of mass-conditioning
> and to bring human communication back and up to the personal
> form of an "I-Thou" relationship, which will eventually lead to the
> satisfaction of man's higher aspirations for the immaterial, cultural,
> moral, and religious ideals of existence.[16]

The modern journalist, within whom the strain of existentialist freedom is strong, will recognize the potential danger of manipulating and
enslaving others. If he desires freedom for himself, he will desire freedom
for others and he will cherish their authenticity and autonomy as he
cherishes his own. The real freedom-lover, in other words, will defend
freedom for others as well as for himself. He knows full well that when
only *some* have freedom, they are tyrants and autocrats—or at least they
have the potential within them. When *all* have freedom, at least everyone has the power to counteract tyranny and autocracy—or to escape from

---

[13] *Ibid.*
[14] Albert Camus, *The Rebel* (New York: Alfred Knopf, Inc. and Random House—
Vintage Books, 1954), p. 291.
[15] Frederick Patka in F. Patka (ed.), *Existentialist Thinkers and Thought* (New York:
The Citadel Press, 1966), pp. 42–43.
[16] *Ibid.*, pp. 57–58.

it through his own freedom. The existential journalist is certainly free to exercise his freedom in ways considered irresponsible to others, but the rationalist, the humanist and the Kantian in him will temper his activities with moderation, concern and reason and will keep him from falling into the abyss of nihilism.

The existential strain is especially important for the journalist for it provides the fundamental foundation of freedom. It gives him the spirit of creativity, of action, of commitment, the desire to launch out into new journalistic regions and the willingness to take the consequences for his actions. What he *does* makes him authentic, real, human. How he reacts to his world through his journalism defines him as a journalist. *"Respondeo, ergo sum."* [17]

Journalists must respond to their environment—to their own journalistic situation. They are more than neutral observers; if they are not, say the Existentialists, then they are *nothing*. The true Existentialist in journalism gets *into* the story, becomes part of the story. His sensitiveness to the stimuli of the story infiltrates the story; in short, the existential journalist is part of the story and the story is part of him. This, of course, affects the journalistic Self and disrupts any demeanor of "objective neutrality"; it brings subjectivity to bear on the Event-Reporter-Report nexus, and it is what largely injects journalism with Dionysian ingredients of artistry, sensitivity, emotionalism, personalism, mysticism and opinionism.

Reason: The Objectivist-Humanist Strain

The importance of reason is not to be denied in any kind of viable system, journalistic or otherwise. It is really the link that connects Existentialism, with its freedom, and Kantianism, with its duty. Reason is especially strong in the Objectivist-Humanist strain. This is true even among such diverse thinkers as Erich Fromm, Ayn Rand, Aldous Huxley, Ortega y Gasset, Eric Hoffer and Max Eastman—all of whom embrace some form of objectivism or rational humanism. These are, in general, the thinkers who reject the subjectivist notion that value judgments have no objective validity; Fromm and his philosophical kin believe that some values are better than others and that not all opinions, notions or people are equal— that there are objective differences.

Ayn Rand, expressing her "objectivist" philosophy, places special importance on reason. Her "New Intellectual" is a person "who lives up to the exact meaning of his title: a man who is guided by his *intellect*—not a zombie guided by feelings, instincts, urges, wishes, whims or revelations.

---

[17] See Ch. 12 ("Respondeo ergo Sum") in F. H. Heinemann, *Existentialism and the Modern Predicament* (New York: Harper Torchbooks, 1958), pp. 190–204.

. . . an *integrated* man, that is: a thinker who is a man of action." [18] And, like the Existentialist, Rand sees the strong connection between reason and freedom. She writes:

> Reason requires freedom, self-confidence and self-esteem. It requires the right to think and to act on the guidance of one's thinking— the right to live by one's own independent judgment. *Intellectual* freedom cannot exist without *political* freedom; political freedom cannot exist without *economic* freedom.[19]

Objectivists and rational humanists also make much of self-esteem, and Ayn Rand, of course, has built a whole philosophy on rational self-interest. Erich Fromm points out that there is nothing wrong with selfishness, and that the self must be affirmed; in fact, he says that if a person "can only 'love' others, he cannot love at all." [20] Eric Hoffer stresses the importance of self-esteem and self-confidence throughout his writings; he even sees a lack of self-esteem as a chief cause for persons willingly submitting to "holy causes" and other forms of collectivism where they lose themselves in "spectacular doings of a leader or some collective body—be it a nation, a congregation, a party, or a mass movement." [21] And Bertrand Russell maintains that rational men always consider their own self-interest of great importance. "If all men acted from enlightened self-interest the world would be a paradise in comparison with what it is," he writes, and goes on to stress the "enlightened" aspect of this self-interest, saying that it is "very rarely to a man's interest to do anything which is very harmful to others." [22]

Rationality, for Ayn Rand, is man's basic virtue and the fountain of all his other virtues. This virtue means, she says, "the recognition and acceptance of reason as one's only source of knowledge, one's only judge of values and one's guide to action." [23] The emphasis here is on the "focused" mind, a person's "full, conscious awareness" and a "commitment to the fullest perception of reality within one's power." [24]

---

[18] Ayn Rand, *For the New Intellectual* (New York: New American Library Signet Book, 1961), p. 51. Rand also thinks true happiness is derived from using reason. A. N. Whitehead agrees, saying that "the function of Reason is to promote the art of life." *The Function of Reason* (Boston: Beacon Press, 1958), p. 4.

[19] Rand, *For the New Intellectual*, p. 25.

[20] Erich Fromm, *Escape from Freedom* (New York: Avon Books, Discus ed., 1968), p. 136.

[21] Eric Hoffer, *The Ordeal of Change* (New York: Harper Colophon Books, 1964), p. 9.

[22] Bertrand Russell, *The Will to Doubt* (New York: Philosophical Library, 1958), pp. 15–16.

[23] Ayn Rand, *The Virtue of Selfishness* (New York: New American Library Signet Books, 1964), p. 25.

[24] *Ibid.*

Such a position on selfishness is not inconsistent with humanism, although it may seem so at first glance. Ayn Rand's thought is quite humanistic and also shows a great affinity with that of Kant when she insists that the basic *social* principle of her Objectivist ethics is that *life is an end in itself*. She maintains that "every living human being is an end in himself, not the means to the ends or the welfare of others—and therefore, that man must live for his own sake, nether sacrificing himself to others nor sacrificing others to himself." [25] So we can see that in such a philosophy as has been sketched above, rationality is connected with freedom, with consideration of others, and also with man's self-esteem and self-interest.

Intertwined in such a philosophy is the existential emphasis of commitment and personal responsibility. Hazel Barnes writes that Randian Objectivists and also Existentialists "argue that every person is responsible for what he has made of his life" and goes on to relate humanism to this aspect of Objectivism and Existentialism: "In so far as they claim that man himself is his own end and purpose, both may properly be called humanistic." [26] One also hears in these words the reverberations, again, of Kant.

All people have the power to respond to reason and truth, says Aldous Huxley, but so, unfortunately, do they have the tendency to respond to "unreason and falsehood." [27] It seems that our minds generally are filled only with bits and pieces of information and we have not been really educated to *think*—to use Reason, to use our minds creatively. Erich Fromm lays much of the blame for this state of affairs at the door of our educational system, and proceeds to describe ways education discourages thinking.[28] One barrier to thinking is the emphasis placed by education on knowledge as facts—or as information. Fromm maintains that the superstition persists that by knowing more and more facts one arrives at a knowledge of reality. (It is amazing how prevalent this idea is in journalism.) Another way thinking is discouraged, says Fromm, is the practice of regarding all truth as relative. "Truth is declared to be an entirely subjective matter, almost a matter of taste," declares Fromm.[29] Fromm, of course, disagrees with this contention.

A person is also discouraged in his thinking by the general assumption that problems are too complicated for the average person to under-

---

[25] *Ibid.*, p. 27.
[26] Barnes, *An Existentialist Ethics*, p. 125.
[27] Aldous Huxley, *Brave New World Revisted* (New York: Harper & Row—Perennial Library, 1965), p. 33.
[28] Fromm, *Escape from Freedom*, pp. 247–77. Compare with very similar comments of Ayn Rand about education in *The New Left: The Anti-Industrial Revolution* (New York: New American Library Signet Books, 1971), pp. 152–204.
[29] Fromm, *Escape from Freedom*, p. 274.

stand. The journalist, for example, is often led to feel that a particular event or subject is too complex for adequate explication or discussion; this feeling of inadequacy leads to the journalistic technique of "simply giving the facts" without any reportorial judgment or perspective being included. It is Fromm's belief that many of the basic individual and social issues are really very simple and can be communicated so that everyone can understand them. Another way, according to Fromm, of paralyzing critical thought is the "destruction of any kind of structuralized picture of the world." He blames the mass media largely for this—pointing to the fact that "the announcement of the bombing of a city and the death of hundreds of people is shamelessly followed or interrupted by an advertisement for soap or wine." [30]

Fromm believes that newspapers too often "tell us the trite thoughts or breakfast habits of a debutante with the same space and seriousness they use for reporting events of scientific or artistic importance." And what is the result? We cease to be related to what we read or hear; we cease to be excited—and says Fromm, eventually "our attitude to what is going on in the world assumes a quality of flatness and indifference." Life loses all structure, he insists, and is "composed of many little pieces, each separate from the other and lacking any sense as a whole." [31]

A respect for Reason, a determination to mentally "focus" on journalistic problems will bring new form to the reality-linguistic problem, will eliminate much of the fuzziness in journalism, and will develop in the journalist a preciseness based on rationality. The worst thing that can happen to a journalist is for him to get to the point where he loses faith in Reason. Socrates warned against what happens to a person when he becomes a *misologist*—one who has lost respect for human reason: he is, in a very real sense, dead.

Journalists, like everyone else, generally pay lip service to Reason, but in the daily routine of their work it is very easy for them to perform their tasks and make their decisions with little mental focusing; it becomes ever easier to simply turn loose and float on the smooth waters of instinct and intuition. Mental focusing is difficult; seriously thinking about alternatives is hard work. It is easy to become a misologist almost without realizing it, as we increasingly do routine tasks, take orders and directions on more and more things, and give in to our "feelings" in more instances. We are all threatened by our irrational and emotional tendencies, although we may not ever become complete misologists. The worst thing that can happen to any man is to cease to think. And the worst thing that can happen to a journalist is to give up his autonomy, his authenticity; for

[30] *Ibid.*, p. 276.
[31] *Ibid.*, p. 277.

then he becomes nothing more than a puppet, a robot which moves and has his being as forces or persons beyond himself dictate. Reason is undoubtedly the key philosophical *force* in authentic journalism, and, operating in conjunction with personal freedom, it provides a motivating power source for the development of a meaningful, self-satisfying journalistic philosophy.

Duty: The Kantian Strain

A commitment to reason and a duty to follow basic principles rationally adopted: this is the gist of Kant's moral philosophy. Kant is close to the objectivistic humanists in his respect for reason—and for freedom. In fact, Kant contended that "morality makes sense only if men are free; freedom is just the ability to act from reasons; thus morality will make sense only if it is grounded on rationality." [32] A person, then, for Kant has a duty to rationality and to freedom. At first glance Kantian "duty" seems very similar to the Marxist-Leninist concept; but there is a big difference. For Marx, duty was the "moral necessity or obligation to subordinate one's individual interests and conduct to the interests and demands of the social units." [33] It was always social in nature. For Kant, duty was to one's *own* principles, freely determined. Moral law, to which a person has a duty, is derived from reason and results in universal or "ultimate principles" which Kant considered "the metaphysics of morals."

A *good will*, for Kant, is indispensable and basic; actually his oft-quoted remark is the key to his ethics: "It is impossible to conceive of anything in the world, or indeed out of it, which can be called good without qualification save only a good will." [34] The term "good" takes on meaning not as one considers a consequence (for Kant was a consumate foe of utilitarianism), but as one takes up what Kant thought to be the definitive characteristic of moral consciousness—*duty*. A will which acts for the sake of duty is a good will.

This may be clearer if "for the sake of duty" is contrasted with "in accordance with duty." The latter could include honest reporting in journalism because it is prudent; it would be hypothetical and not binding. Certainly, it would not be universal (since *dishonesty* in journalism is viewed by some as the best, i.e., most prudent, policy). But "duty," according to Kant, "is the necessity of acting out of reverence for the

[32] Jeffrie G. Murphy, *Kant: The Philosophy of Right* (New York: St. Martin's Press, 1970), p. 42.
[33] Richard T. DeGeorge, *Soviet Ethics and Morality* (Ann Arbor: University of Michigan Press—Ann Arbor Paperbacks, 1969), p. 74.
[34] T. K. Abbott (trans.), *Kant's Critique of Practical Reason and Other Works on the Theory of Ethics* (London, 1909, 6th ed.), p. 9.

law." [35] And the law he refers to is a standard or test in terms of which worldly decisions must be made if they are to be of moral (i.e., non-utilitarian) value: "I am never to act according to any maxim which I would not want to be a universal law." It will be noted that this negatively paraphrased version of Kant's famous Categorical Imperative is absolutely binding on everyone, everywhere, forever.

Kant's Categorical Imperative also includes the concept that people should always be treated as ends and never merely as means; the result of following such a principle is very similar to the Existentialist's "authenticity." Sartre, for example, saw the authentic man as one who related to others as individuals ("persons as ends")—persons who were not to be used, or changed, but to be related to as autonomous persons with every right to be themselves and not mirror-images of others.[36] Another implication of Kant's Categorical Imperative is that any concept of the "end justifying the means" is basically immoral; from the purely moral viewpoint, Kant would say, not even the loftiest end can justify evil or harmful means; evil remains evil, whatever its purpose or result.

Kant's emphasis is on acting out of duty and duty alone. Consequences are not to be considered. A good act done to please somebody or to gain an advantage or to secure a reward would cease to be good; it would fall to the level of expediency. An act should be done because the actor sees for himself that it is right, that it is his duty to perform it. The moral imperative is here categorical, not hypothetical—in other words, it is unconditional obedience.[37] Actually Kant contends that morality is not contingent on changing institutions or varying situations; his is really an *a priori*, prescriptive ethics. We do not get these "guides" to morality from social sanctions or from "feelings" as to rightness or wrongness of actions, but from reason alone. This reason is regulative; when we accept a principle by reason, it then regulates our activities.

Acting ethically for Kant would mean acting on the basis of duty—or acting for the sake of some principle. Thus the justification of an action is not in the action itself but in something outside it. The moral value of an action, likewise, must not be in the consequences of the action, but rather in the *principle* of the action. Since the principle is prior to the action, it is *a priori*, and when we internalize a principle or make it our own private rule, then it becomes a maxim. Conformity to principle is the core of the Kantian concept of duty. An ethical action means that I act in such a way that it is possible for me to will that the maxim of my action be-

[35] *Ibid.*, p. 16.
[36] Anthony Manser, *Sartre: A Philosophical Study* (New York: Oxford University Press, 1967), p. 158.
[37] E. L. Allen, *From Plato to Nietzsche* (Greenwich, Conn.: Fawcett Publications, Inc.—a Premier Book, 1964), p. 126.

come law for everyone at all times. The journalist of Kantian persuasion would make the journalistic decision that he would like to see all journalists make. He would not tell the truth because he sees a good reason for telling it, some benefit accruing to him or to others if he does it. He would not consider the consequences; he would do it simply because he felt duty-bound to do it. He would let his journalistic act be an end in itself.

The Kantian journalist, for example, might well feel a duty to reveal the sources of his information, to let his audience know who provided the particular facts. He would not provide the source because it might prove useful to do so or for any specific reason; he would provide it simply because he felt it was his *duty* to give it. His dedication would be to the rationally derived *a priori* principle (or maxim) of providing the reader with important related information necessary for validating the story and appraising the reliability of the attributed information. The reporter's rationalization that he will sometimes *withhold* the source's name so as not to "dry up" that source in the future is a utilitarian concern and one which the Kantian would not consider; it would be beside the point of true morality. Providing the reader the news source is an end in itself; it is ethical *in principle*, and that is all there is to it. The Kantian journalist feels he has an obligation to act in a certain way (e.g. to present as much of the "truth" of the story as he has); he does not "rationalize" his action *a posteriori*; rather he rationally accepts the principle (that exists prior to the act) which he then feels duty-bound to follow.

Bertrand Russell points out that the only moralists who have seriously attempted to "be consistent in regarding virtue as an end in itself are the Stoics and Kant." [38] Russell proceeds to summarize the spirit of Kant's ethics (as he sees it) of non-utilitarianism in these words:

> Kant was never tired of pouring scorn on the view that the good consists of pleasure, or of anything else except virtue. And virtue consists in acting as the moral law enjoins, *because* that is what the moral law enjoins. A right action done from any other motive cannot count as virtuous. If you are kind to your brother because you are fond of him, you have no merit; but if you can hardly stand him and are nevertheless kind to him because the moral law says you should be, then you are the sort of person Kant thinks you ought to be.[39]

Russell, of course, is being somewhat subtly critical of the Kantian position in this passage. He is pointing out one of the oft-mentioned weaknesses (or suspected weaknesses) of Kant's morality of duty: that it is a

[38] Bertrand Russell, *Human Society in Ethics and Politics* (New York: New American Library—Mentor Books, 1962), p. 39.
[39] *Ibid.*

very mechanical—and perhaps weak—rationale for ethical action. This criticism of Kantian ethics is often combined with another: that Kant's universalizing of an ethical maxim is nothing more than a person projecting his *subjective* opinion on everyone. A contemporary philosopher, R. M. Hare, has argued that Kant's notion (implied in his Categorical Imperative) is "really quite radically subjective in character" and that "no matter how evil or unworkable the state of affairs, if the agent is willing that he and everyone else labour under it, then the judgment is moral." [40]

Kant, of course, would consider such arguments as nonsense. He would say that *merely subjective ends* have no place in determining the nature of rational morality; he would point out that *objective* ends are those which a rational being *must*, in so far as he is rational, desire or promote. "Kant assumes that there is only one such end and thinks it quite obvious what this end is—*rational nature* itself." [41] Kant appears to believe that the rational person will insure that he is attempting to reach his own ends (whatever they may be), and he is quite willing to let every other rational being have the *freedom* to pursue his own ends. This stance points up the *personalism* in Kant, the respect for the individual's autonomy, and the faith in the rational process itself. In other words, Kant trusts others as ends in themselves, not because he thinks it is a good policy, but because they *are* ends in themselves. Kant is really saying: "I treat other rational beings as ends in themselves by respecting in them that same value which I find and seek to defend in myself—freedom." [42]

This concept is very important to the rational and free journalist. If he really respects libertarianism, for example, he will respect it (have a duty to it) in *principle* and will defend it everywhere, in all persons, at all times. If he really respects libertarianism, for example, he is going to respect the *freedom* with which other journalists perform their acts even though he might not respect their *acts*. He is really concerned only with his own actions; regardless of what others use as their ethical guides, he wills to act in a way which he would like to see become a universal journalistic principle. As Jeffrie Murphy has put it: "The essence of morality is revealed in maxims which respect the value as an end in itself of each rational being, i.e. maxims which would, if acted on, leave each rational being free to pursue his own ends in acting." [43] It would be difficult to find a better statement of the stance of a libertarian journalist.

Kant would see the rational man adopting his Categorical Impera-

[40] Murphy, *op. cit.*, p. 66.
[41] *Ibid.*, p. 73.
[42] *Ibid.*, pp. 74–75.
[43] *Ibid.*, p. 87.

tive;[44] only when we are not fully rational would we feel an inclination to adopt a contrary morality of subjective situationism or utilitarianism. This is why, according to Kant, the will must be commanded to a considerable extent. "Journalists shall not lie" is better than "It is wrong for a journalist to lie." The first is an imperative which demands allegiance; the second is stated as a value judgment which a journalist might feel inclined to ignore or to depart from. If the journalist accepts a principle such as "I will tell the truth in my journalism," then he will not lie. He will not simply refrain from lying in *certain circumstances*; he will refrain from lying in all circumstances. If he always tells the truth, he will not even have to worry about when he will lie and when he will not. Regardless of the surface "narrowness" of such a position, Kant maintains that it is necessary for true morality. A journalist—or any person—cannot be ethical if he applies certain rules of morality only when he feels inclined to apply them.

The concept of duty to principle, then, is the third strain of the journalistic philosophy advocated in this chapter. It anchors freedom and fulfills rationality. It keeps the journalist from being blown back and forth by the winds of social pressure and personal expediency. It protects him against the morality of utilitarianism. The journalist pursues truth because he would will that all journalists pursue truth; he has an obligation to pursue and present truth, not out of some conviction that "truth will make for better government" or out of some other hoped-for benefit, but simply because he has a duty to the maxim that *journalists must present the truth*. This non-utilitarian emphasis of morality provided by Kant is very important in giving the journalist philosophical stability which is largely lacking in other strains of ethical theory.

The Kantian strain, along with Existentialism and Rational Humanism, contributes ingredients of freedom, personal responsibility and rationalism to the "Apollonysian" synthesis being proposed in this chapter. But it stresses the aspect of *duty* which is considered peripheral in the other strains that merge into the Apollonysian stance. Kantianism also joins in with Rational Humanism in providing an objectivist or rational (Apollonian) side of the synthesis. It is the Existential strain that contributes a strong dose of Dionysian sensitivity and subjectivism into the scientist-artist synthesis.

The Existential strain also emphasizes the main concept of this book —*freedom*, along with its natural corollaries of commitment and personal

---

[44] See H. J. Paton, *The Categorical Imperative: A Study in Kant's Moral Philosophy* (New York: Harper Torchbooks, 1967) for a detailed discussion of the implications of Kantian ethics.

responsibility. All three of these strains which have been discussed are important; all have valuable contributions to make to the "Apollonysian" journalist. Certainly duty and reason and freedom are all extremely important to this kind of meaningful, authentic journalistic philosophy. But the most important of these is *freedom* since it is the very ground of being for the other two; for without freedom there is really no authentic (human) sense of duty, nor is there a rationale for the creative use of reason.

IO

Postscript: The
Imperative of Freedom

IN SPITE of the philosophical synthesis just discussed, the theoretical
focus of this book should not be blurred. Freedom is the central issue;
journalistic autonomy is the highest value, and the person who submits to
extra-self determinism gives away himself, forfeits his very essence and
authenticity. This, of course, is fundamentally an existential stance; and in
emphasizing the importance of freedom it is quite valid to say that this
book advocates an *existentialist journalism*. For the journalist there is,
indeed, an imperative of freedom. Freedom is the very source of personhood; it is the wellspring of ethics; it is the foundation that supports the
related concepts of rationality, commitment, integrity and responsibility.

The free journalist who cherishes his authenticity and his integrity
has one dedication: a dedication to his freedom and the viability of his
freedom. This whole book has attempted to stress the importance of
freedom or journalistic autonomy—not only for the individual journalist,
but also for the individual media and the press systems themselves. With
the potent pressures that are exerted on media systems and journalists, it
is a wonder that we have as much journalistic freedom as we do. Certainly
we have seen that escaping from freedom is a very strong human desire;
and regardless of how important freedom and autonomy are to some
people, not everyone considers such states desirous or even necessary.

Freedom, of course, is not an imperative for everybody; this certainly must be conceded. As Erich Fromm has pointed out, freedom can even be a burden and a person can have a very basic "instinctive wish" for submission to the dictates of someone else or to some group.

But the journalist is in a special position. If he abdicates his pursuit of autonomy and freedom, he largely projects his stance on his whole audience; in a sense he expresses his disdain for individualism and selfhood and joins in tacit support of collective mentality, institutionalized morality, and personal and political slavery. He certainly has the "right" (stemming from freedom) to give up his freedom and accept slavery, but this really gets him nowhere except in a position where *further* free choices become extremely difficult if not impossible. For the free man who *wishes to remain free* can never will that restrictions be placed on his freedom. But even the freedom-loving journalist is in danger of losing his freedom to the forces which surround him.

The journalist works under the persistent pressures which often cause him to adapt to the "social good" and to institutional expediency. Being a member of a group and accepting institutional responsibility tend to suppress conscience and true existential consciousness. It is not easy for the institutional and professional journalist to retain his authenticity. A journalist, Robert Stein, has written that "journalists are going to have to rely on their own values more rather than less, not only in interpreting the news but in deciding what it is." [1] Stein is appealing to the journalist to express his real authenticity to a greater degree and indicating how easy it is for the journalist to be swallowed up by his group. He puts it this way:

> As publishers, broadcasters, editors and reporters work under the constant demands of deadlines and competition, their private values tend to be pushed further and further into the background until, in some cases, particularly at the executive level, they disappear completely. For years I have been fascinated by what happens to individuals (including myself) when they gather around a corporate table. Institutional responsibility seems to act simultaneously as a narcotic that suppresses conscience and a stimulant that brings out every bit of low cunning that can be used to profit the organization. [2]

The freedom-loving journalist will, of course, fight constantly against such depersonalizing submission to groupism. He will promote in himself the basic Nietzschean theme of saying "yes to life" thereby becoming

[1] Robert Stein, *Media Power: Who is Shaping Your Picture of the World?* (Boston: Houghton Mifflin Co., 1972), p. 265.
[2] *Ibid.*, p. 244.

more noble and heroic—and more authentic.[3] The ideal journalist would be something of a Nietzschean Superman—a person who has learned to transcend himself, to rise to, and beyond, his highest potential. He would be a "higher man"—a law unto himself, a center of virtue, and a powerful, happy person of exuberant self-expression and self-confidence.[4] A key concept of Nietzsche, consistent with his existentialist orientation, is his passionate belief in the worth of the individual and his view of the hero as the person who does not submit to authority—or at least fights constantly against it.[5] Karl Jaspers reinforces this position. The true existential person, he writes, is the one who on his own initiative gains "possession of the mechanism of his life"; if he does not, Jaspers sees him as "degraded to become a machine" that surrenders to "the apparatus." [6]

To stay free is the primary imperative of the authentic journalist. Only the free journalist can be a truth-seeker. As Luka Brajnovic says, "Defending and divulging the truth is the first postulate of press freedom." [7] The Yugoslav philosopher, now teaching in Spain, stresses the importance of truth—not "artistic" truth, but truth based on evidence, on exactness which comes close to objective reality. Of course, the free journalist *may* lie, may not be willing to correct errors, may distort, and may intentionally provide misconceptions, says Brajnovic; but the *unfree* journalist cannot be dedicated to the truth; the truth is not in his journalism because the importance of truth is not part of his national philosophy.[8] This is perhaps a little strong—and unfair—to the existentially "free" journalist working in a controlled society (and this could apply to Brajnovic himself), but as a basic generalization, it is undoubtedly valid. And surely Brajnovic is right when he says that to seek the maximum truth, the journalist must seek the maximum freedom—for himself and for his own medium and media system.

Brajnovic strikes the Kantian note when he writes of "human dignity" being a check on the use of freedom. "We are the owners of our own destiny because we possess freedom," he says. He also contends that this dignity places just limits on freedom for the simple reason that man does

[3] Karl Jaspers, *Nietzsche: An Introduction to the Understanding of His Philosophical Activity* (Chicago: Henry Regnery Co.—a Gateway Edition, 1969), p. 167 ff.
[4] See E. L. Allen, "The Superman" (Ch. 5) in *From Plato to Nietzsche* (Greenwich, Conn.: Fawcett Publications—a Premier Book, 1964), pp. 180–82.
[5] Bertrand Russell, *The Will to Doubt* (New York: Philosophical Library—the Wisdom Library, 1958), p. 101.
[6] Karl Jaspers, *Man for Himself* (Greenwich, Conn.: Fawcett Publications—a Premier Book, 1966), p. 195.
[7] Luka Brajnovic, *Deontología Periodística* (Pamplona: Ediciones Universidad de Navarra, S.A., 1969), p. 218.
[8] *Ibid.*, pp. 196–97.

not live isolated in society; all members have this same human dignity.[9] And this human dignity he refers to, just what is it? We are told that the "moral man" has it. And who is this moral man? The man who does not succumb to his instincts or to his passions; who does not change his opinion without justification; is not a flatterer or renegade. Brajnovic calls all of these characteristics "monstrosities" which negate dignity, as well as the rights and the liberty of man.[10]

This freedom is not only checked by human dignity of the moral man but also by a sense of journalistic responsibility. No good will be served here by exhaustively going back over what has been said about responsibility and freedom in earlier chapters. But it is probably worth reemphasizing the view that responsibility for the journalist should be *personal* responsibility. The concept of "social responsibility," however good it may sound, is one which the libertarian journalist should approach with great care. The current emphasis on "social responsibility" in journalism may well be nothing more than a subterfuge under which elite groups or persons go about trying to make the press system over in their own image. Self-realization demands a rejection of the whole concept of social responsibility—except that sense in which it might be taken to mean that *personal* responsibility which a free and rational journalist determines for himself. The existential responsibility to one's self and for one's own actions is the responsibility of a free person and a free society.

These words are not meant to imply a criticism of "responsible" journalism or a "responsible" press system. They are meant only to warn against any attempt or pressure from outside journalism to provide some kind of "common" or standard definition of journalistic responsibility to society. This is simply the libertarian position, but of late it is increasingly being considered "outdated" and unrealistic. From all points on the political spectrum we see pressure increasing for programs to guide the press to more responsible actions. We get it from the various branches of government—branches which have it in their power to restrict the freedom of the journalist.

The Judiciary, especially, is poking its nose into the activities of the press and is using its power to interpret laws (and the Constitution) in ways unacceptable to the libertarian journalist who treasures the principles of Jefferson and the First Amendment. Journalists who accept the imperative of freedom must insist on non-interference from outside powers, must ever fight against the pressures which are mounting against journalistic autonomy by persons and groups who claim they have the "social

[9] *Ibid.*, p. 151.
[10] *Ibid.*, p. 224.

interest" at heart and who contsantly attempt to relegate the concept of press freedom to a subordinate position—or to redefine it out of existence.

Being a libertarian today is not easy. Current philosophy—social, political, religious and personal—is rigged against libertarianism. The emphasis is on collectives and their "rights" and not on individuals and their "rights." Naturally this results in a depreciation of libertarianism, a suspicion of autonomy, and a growing praise for cooperation and social harmony. The individual person tends to get lost and the individual journalistic media blend together into "the press system."

Individual responsibility is giving way to social responsibility—meaning that responsibility to self is being replaced by responsibility to the collective. And who is it that defines what this responsibility is? Not the individual persons, freely regulating their own journalistic actions, but some elite group—some arrogant collectivity whose members feel they can inject *their* sense of responsibility into each of us.

The libertarian journalist rebels against such responsibility-definers. He wants to determine his own responsibility and desires that each medium act according to a self-determined sense of responsibility. *Autonomy*, of course, is the key word, but it is a concept heard less and less. The word today is "adjustment" and we generally advance in our jobs in relation to our ability to adjust or conform to *group* norms and expectations. How can a journalist be autonomous? Of course, if he is working for someone else—and with others—he cannot be completely autonomous, but he can certainly be *more* or *less* autonomous. The degree of autonomy he has is determined largely by his personal philosophy, his basic attitudes and personality. If his "Freedom Quotient" is high—if he is a persistent freedom-seeker—then he will see to it that he exercises a great amount of personal freedom. If his "FQ" is low, he will succumb rather easily to all attempts to restrict his autonomy, and will adjust comfortably in a predetermined role in a conformist situation.

The freedom-lover, on the other hand, will always manage to operate with considerable freedom. Even in authoritarian or closely controlled environments he will maintain his freedom and retain his autonomy. Actually it is wrong to say that because the United States has a free press system all the journalists operating in the country are free; likewise it is erroneous to assume that all journalists in a controlled country (like Spain) are without freedom. A freedom-lover in *any* society will make a great many autonomous decisions; he simply recognizes his difficulties and problems, but he does not admit his inability to act with considerable freedom. In fact, the journalist in a tyrannical society often develops greater sophistication and cunning than are found in his free-society counterpart. He *must* be more subtle in the exercise of his freedom for he cannot afford the luxury of the direct "sledge hammer" use of his freedom which is possible in open societies.

Freedom may be harder to exercise for the freedom-lover in a controlled society, but it is more exciting because it is a challenge; there is a system to circumvent, censors to elude and perceptive readers to satisfy. When there is opposition to freedom, freedom-lovers operate best; where freedom comes easy, freedom-lovers take it for granted, are likely to settle into complacency and hardly notice the erosion of freedom. It may be said with considerable truth that some of the most authentic, the most skillful, autonomous and persistent journalists in their personal fight for freedom are found today in closed or authoritarian societies. Their numbers may not be great, but their "FQ's" are extremely high and their freedom-seeking activities are ingenious.

The point being made is that the autonomous journalist exists everywhere and one cannot assume too much about his dedication to freedom by simply noting his country of operation. Personal authenticity and the capacity to push back the limits of journalistic control are found everywhere in the world. Some of the freest journalists to be found today are in Taiwan, Spain, Mexico and Eastern Europe, although they might not be expected to be there. Free journalism means nothing if it is not *used*. Having a "free press" is meaningless unless the *journalists* exercise their freedom through it, unless they constantly defend it through using it to the maximum. The libertarian journalist, therefore, can be found everywhere; he is really the existential person, committed to freedom and to action. If he is not so committed and active, he is a slave—regardless of the society in which he lives and works.

The journalist who is committed to freedom is a free journalist. His authentic commitment in a real sense defines his very essence. He will be free because he *wills* that he be free, and this freedom is not contingent on outside control systems or on press laws, or government secrecy, or over-classification of documents, or closed meetings. Freedom does not mean that he can *get* access to everything he wants or that someone will tell him everything he wants to know; freedom (at least in the existentialist sense) simply means he can *try* to acquire what he wants. He likewise does not have the freedom to write or broadcast everything he wants to, but to *strive* to do it.

Always the truly libertarian journalist will find a way to accomplish a great deal of what he seriously desires to accomplish. This is the authentic meaning of freedom, the core of its personalized existential essence. Freedom thus lies *within* a person; it is not stationed "out there" somewhere in a society as some kind of commodity which a person or group can decide to give or withhold.

Returning to the rather pessimistic thesis presented at the beginning of this book, it is well to note that libertarian journalism is, indeed, in danger. Many factors are contributing to this, of course, but a central cause for the erosion of freedom is the failure of journalists to *will* that it not be eroded. At the root of the problem is the individual journalist who has, in large degree, abdicated his loyalty to the concept of libertarianism. Obligations to society (or supposed obligations) have begun to be his main concern—or, in the case of many, a kind of passive drifting through his journalistic days with *no* real philosophical concern at all—social *or* individual.

The imperative of freedom, therefore, is really an imperative for the *individual journalist*, although its spirit may be injected into the total fabric of his press system. Actually, there is no imperative of freedom for any journalist who does not care to be authentic or fully human. Likewise, no country or press system need feel an urgent need for press freedom unless it (the leadership generally) wants it to achieve its greatest or highest human potential and political authenticity. Just as a country can never reach its full development without considerable autonomy, the press system and the individual journalist can never reach their potentials without autonomy.

So we close on the individualistic notes of autonomy and freedom. Autonomy breeds self-reliance and self-esteem; it also forces a journalist to choose, to commit himself—to *use* his freedom. There is no way to escape freedom for the autonomous journalist or independent newspaper. Therefore the person or press unit that really desires freedom will fight for maximum autonomy. This is the key to authentic journalism; it is the imperative of freedom.

Bibliography

Abelson, Raziel. *Ethics and Metaethics: Readings in Ethical Philosophy*. New York: St. Martin's Press, 1963.

Allen, E. L. *From Plato to Nietzsche*. Greenwich, Conn.: Fawcett Publications, Inc., a Premier Book, 1964.

Aronson, James. *Deadline for the Media: Today's Challenges to Press, TV and Radio*. Indianapolis: Bobbs-Merrill, 1972.

Arora, Satish K., and Harold D. Lasswell. *Political Communication: The Public Language of Political Elites in India and the United States*. New York: Holt, Rinehart and Winston, 1969.

Banfield, Edward C. *The Moral Basis of a Backward Society*. New York: The Macmillan Co., a Free Press Paperback, 1958.

Banner, William A. *Ethics: An Introduction to Moral Philosophy*. New York: Scribners, 1968.

Barnes, Hazel. *An Existentialist Ethics*. New York: Random House, Vintage Books, 1971.

Barney, Ralph D. *The Mass Media, Their Environment and Prospects in Western Polynesia*. Columbia: University of Missouri (Unpublished Ph.D. Dissertation, 1971).

Barrett, William. *Irrational Man: A Study in Existential Philosophy*. Garden City, N.Y.: Doubleday Anchor Books, 1958.

Barron, Jerome A. *Freedom of the Press for Whom?* Bloomington: Indiana University Press, 1971.

Becker, Carl L. *Freedom and Responsibility in the American Way of Life.* New York: Vintage Books, 1960.

Bell, A. Donald and J. C. Merrill. *Dimensions of Christian Writing.* Grand Rapids: Zondervan Publishing House, 1970.

Benge, Ronald C. *Communication and Identity.* London: Clive Bingley Ltd., 1972.

Berkeley, George. *The Principles of Human Knowledge.* Cleveland: World Publishing Company, Meridian Books, 1963.

Berlin, Isaiah. *Two Concepts of Liberty.* Oxford: Clarendon Press, 1958.

Berns, Walter. *Freedom, Virtue, and the First Amendment.* Baton Rouge: Louisiana State University Press, 1957.

Blanchard, Robert O. (ed.). *Congress and the News Media.* New York: Hastings House, Publishers, 1974.

Brajnovic, Luka. *Deontología Periodística.* Pamplona: Ediciones Universidad de Navarra, S.A., 1969.

Branden, Nathaniel. *The Psychology of Self-Esteem.* Los Angeles: Nash Publishing Corp./ New York: Bantam Books, 1971.

——. *Who is Ayn Rand?* New York: Paperback Books, 1969.

Brinton, Crane. *Nietzsche.* New York: Harper & Row, Torchbooks, 1965.

Brucker, Herbert. *Freedom of Information.* New York: The Macmillan Co., 1949.

Camus, Albert. *The Rebel.* New York: Alfred Knopf, Inc. and Random House —Vintage Books, 1954.

Capaldi, Nicholas. *Clear and Present Danger.* New York: Pegasus, 1969.

Commission on Freedom of the Press. *A Free and Responsible Press.* Chicago: University of Chicago Press, 1947.

Cooper, Kent. *The Right to Know.* New York: Farrar, Strauss and Cudahy, 1956.

Davison, W. Phillips. *International Political Communication.* New York: Frederick A. Praeger, 1965.

DeGeorge, Richard T. *Soviet Ethics and Morality.* Ann Arbor: University of Michigan Press—Ann Arbor Paperbacks, 1969.

Dennis, Everette E. and William Rivers. *Other Voices: The New Journalism in America.* San Francisco: Canfield Press, 1974.

Deutsch, Karl W. *Nationalism and Social Communication.* Cambridge: The M.I.T. Press, Paperback, 1967.

Dewey, John. *Human Nature and Conduct.* New York: The Modern Library, 1957.

——. *Reconstruction in Philosophy.* New York: Henry Holt, 1920.

——. *Theory of the Moral Life.* New York: Holt, Rinehart and Winston, 1960.

Dostoevskii, Fedor Mikhailovich. *Brothers Karamazov.* Garden City, N.Y.: Literary Guild of America, 1953.

Douglas, William O. *The Right of the People.* New York: Arena Books, 1972.

Eastman, Max. *Reflections on the Failure of Socialism.* San Diego: Viewpoint Books, 1955.

Edel, Abraham. *Ethical Judgment*. Glencoe, Ill.: Free Press, 1955.

Ellul, Jacques. *Propaganda: The Formation of Men's Attitudes*. New York: Random House Vintage Books, 1973.

Emery, Edwin, Phillip Ault, and Warren Agee. *Introduction to Mass Communications*. New York: Dodd, Mead & Co., 1973.

Emmet, E. R. *Learning to Philosophize*. Middlesex, England: Penguin Books, Ltd., 1968.

Ewing, A. C. *Ethics*. New York: The Macmillan Co., Free Press Paperbacks, 1953.

Ferkiss, Victor C. *Technological Man*. New York: New American Library, Mentor Books, 1970.

Fletcher, Joseph. *Situation Ethics: The New Morality*. Philadelphia: The Westminster Press, 1966.

Frankena, William K. *Ethics*. Englewood Cliffs, N.J.: Prentice-Hall, Inc., 1963.

Friedrich, Carl J. and Zbigniew K. Brzezinski. *Totalitarian Dictatorship and Autocracy*. New York: Frederick A. Praeger, 1965.

Frings, Manfred S. (ed.). *Heidegger and the Quest for Truth*. Chicago: Quadrangle Books, 1968.

Fromm, Erich. *Man for Himself: An Inquiry into the Psychology of Ethics*. New York: Fawcett Premier Books, 1966.

——. *May Man Prevail?* Garden City, N.Y.: Doubleday and Co., Inc., Anchor Books, 1961.

——. *The Revolution of Hope*. New York: Bantam Books, 1971.

García Labrado, Francisco. *Criterios de Independencia en la Prensa*. Madrid: Tesina de fin de carrera (Escuela de Periodismo), 1968.

Garner, Richard T. and Bernard Rosen. *Moral Philosophy*. New York: The Macmillan Co., 1967.

Gilman, William H. (ed.). *Selected Writings of Ralph Waldo Emerson*. New York: New American Library, Signet Books, 1965.

Gilmore, Gene, and Robert Root. *Modern Newspaper Editing*. Glendessary Press, Inc., 1971.

Gilmore, Myron P. (ed.). *Machiavelli: The History of Florence and Other Selections*. New York: Washington Square, 1970.

Goldwater, Barry. *The Conscience of a Majority*. New York: Simon & Schuster, Inc., Pocket Books, 1971.

Gross, Gerald (ed.). *The Responsibility of the Press*. New York: Simon and Schuster, Clarion Books, 1969.

Hare, R. N. *Freedom and Reason*. Oxford: Oxford University Press Paperback, 1965.

Harris, Sydney J. *The Authentic Person: Dealing with Dilemma*. Miles, Ill.: Argus Communications, 1972.

Haselden, Kyle. *Morality and the Mass Media*. Nashville: Broadman Press, 1968.

Hayek, Friedrich A. *The Road to Serfdom*. Chicago: University of Chicago Press, Phoenix Books, 1944.

Heinemann, F. H. *Existentialism and the Modern Predicament.* New York: Harper Torchbooks, 1958.

Hobbes, Thomas. *Leviathan.* New York: Collier-Macmillan, Collier Books, 1962.

Hocking, William E. *Freedom of the Press: A Framework of Principle.* Chicago: University of Chicago Press, 1947.

Hoffer, Eric. *The Ordeal of Change.* New York: Harper Colophon Books, 1964.

——. *The True Believer.* New York: Mentor Books, 1958.

Hofstadter, Richard. *Social Darwinism in American Thought.* Boston: Beacon Press Paperback, 1955.

Hohenberg, John. *Free Press, Free People: The Best Cause.* New York: The Free Press, 1973.

Hook, Sidney. *The Paradoxes of Freedom.* Berkeley: University of California Press, 1967.

Hudson, William D. *Ethical Intuitionism.* New York: St. Martin's Press, 1967.

Hughes, Frank. *Prejudice and the Press.* New York: Devin-Adair Co., 1950.

Huntford, Roland. *The New Totalitarians.* New York: Stein and Day, 1972.

Huxley, Aldous. *Brave New World Revisited.* New York: Harper & Row, Perennial Library, 1965.

Isaacs, Harold R. *American Jews in Israel.* New York: The John Day Co., 1966.

Jaspers, Karl. *Man in the Modern Age.* Garden City, N.Y.: Doubleday & Co., Anchor Books, 1957.

——. *Nietzsche: An Introduction to the Understanding of His Philosophical Activity.* Chicago: Henry Regnery Co., Gateway Editions, 1969.

Johannesen, Richard L. *Ethics and Persuasion.* New York: Random House, 1967.

Jung, Carl G. *The Undiscovered Self.* New York: New American Library, Mentor Books, 1958.

Kaplan, Abraham. *The New World of Philosophy.* New York: Vintage Books, 1961.

Kiefer, Howard E. and Milton K. Munitz (eds.). *Ethics and Social Justice.* Albany: State University of New York Press, 1970.

Konvitz, Milton and Gail Kennedy (eds.). *The American Pragmatists.* New York: Meridian Books, Inc., 1960.

Kovesi, Julius. *Moral Notions.* New York: Humanities Press, 1967.

Krieghbaum, Hillier. *Pressures on the Press.* New York: Thomas Y. Crowell Co., 1972.

Landis, Benson Y. (ed.). *Ethical Standards and Professional Conduct.* Philadelphia: American Academy of Political Science, 1955.

LeBon, Gustave. *The Crowd: A Study of the Popular Mind.* New York: Ballentine Books, Inc., 1969. (Many editions of this 1895 book available.)

Lenin, V. I. *State and Revolution.* (Many editions available.)

Lerner, Daniel. *The Passing of Traditional Society.* New York: The Free Press of Glencoe, paperback, 1964.

Lillie, William. *An Introduction to Ethics.* New York: Barnes & Noble, University Paperbacks, 1961.

Lippmann, Walter. *The Public Philosophy*. New York: New American Library, Mentor Books, 1955.

Littell, Franklin H. *Wild Tongues*. London: Collier-Macmillan, Ltd., 1969.

Lowenstein, Ralph L. *Measuring World Press Freedom as a Political Indicator*. Columbia, Mo.: Unpublished Ph.D. Dissertation (University of Missouri, 1967).

Luskin, John. *Lippmann, Liberty, and the Press*. University, Ala.: University of Alabama Press, 1972.

Lynn, Kenneth S. (ed.). *The Professions in America*. Boston: Houghton Mifflin Co., 1965.

Mabbott, J. D. *An Introduction to Ethics*. Garden City, N.Y.: Doubleday & Co., Anchor Books, 1969.

MacIntyre, Alasdair. *Herbert Marcuse: An Exposition and a Polemic*. New York: The Viking Press, 1970.

Macquarrie, John. *Existentialism*. Baltimore: Penguin Books, 1971.

Mannheim, Karl. *Ideology and Utopia*. New York: Harcourt, Brace & Co., 1936.

Manser, Anthony. *Sartre: A Philosophical Study*. New York: Oxford University Press, 1967.

Marcel, Gabriel. *Man Against Mass Society*. Chicago: Henry Regnery Co., Gateway Editions, 1962.

Marcuse, Herbert. *One Dimensional Man*. Boston: Beacon Papeback, 1966.

Marx, Karl. *Capital, The Communist Manifesto, and Other Writings*. Max Eastman, ed. New York: The Modern Library, Inc., 1932.

McCord, William. *The Springtime of Freedom: Evolution of Developing Societies*. New York: Oxford University Press, 1965.

McCormick, John and Mairi MacInnes (eds.). *Versions of Censorship*. Garden City, N.Y.: Doubleday Anchor Books, 1962.

McNelly, John T. and David Berlo (eds.). *Mass Communication and the Development of Nations*. East Lansing: Michigan State University International Communications Institute, 1968.

Means, Richard L. *The Ethical Imperative: The Crisis in American Values*. Garden City, N.Y.: Doubleday, 1969.

Meltzer, M. (ed.). *Thoreau: People, Principles, and Politics*. New York: Hill and Wang, 1963.

Merrill, John C., and Ralph L. Lowenstein. *Media, Messages, and Men: New Perspectives in Communication*. New York: David McKay Co., Inc., 1971.

Meyer, Frank (ed.). *What is Conservatism?* New York: Holt, Rinehart and Winston, 1964.

Mills, C. Wright. *Power, Politics, and People*. New York: Ballantine Books, 1962.

Moore, G. E. *Principia Ethica*. Cambridge, England: University Press, 1966.

Morgan, George W. *The Human Predicament*. New York: Dell Publishing Co., Delta Books, 1968.

Murphy, Jeffrie G. *Kant: The Philosophy of Right*. New York: St. Martin's Press, 1970.

214BIBLIOGRAPHY

Nelson, Harold L. (ed.). *Freedom of the Press from Hamilton to the Warren Court.* Indianapolis: The Bobbs-Merrill Co., Inc., 1967.
Nietzsche, Friedrich. *Beyond Good and Evil.* New York: Random House, Vintage Books, 1966.
Novak, Michael. *Belief and Unbelief: A Philosophy of Self-Knowledge.* New York: Mentor-Omega Books, 1965.
Ortega y Gasset, José. *Man and Crisis.* New York: W. W. Norton Co., Inc., Norton Library, 1962.
——. *Man and People.* New York: W. W. Norton Co., Inc., 1963.
——. *Mission of the University.* New York: W. W. Norton Co., Inc., 1966.
——. *The Revolt of the Masses.* New York: W. W. Norton Co., Inc., 1932.
Patka, Frederick (ed.). *Existentialist Thinkers and Thought.* New York: The Citadel Press, 1966.
Paton, H. J. *The Categorical Imperative: A Study of Kant's Moral Philosophy.* New York: Harper Torchbooks, 1967.
Pieper, Josef. *The Four Cardinal Virtues.* South Bend: Notre Dame University Press, 1966.
Popper, Karl R. *The Open Society and Its Enemies.* Princeton: Princeton University Press, 1930.
Prosser, Michael H. (ed.). *Inter-communication Among Nations and Peoples.* New York: Harper & Row, 1973.
Pye, Lucian (ed.). *Communications and Political Development.* Princeton: Princeton University Press, 1963.
Rader, Melvin M. *Ethics and the Human Community.* New York: Holt, Rinehart, and Winston, 1964.
Rand, Ayn. *Capitalism: The Unknown Ideal.* New York: New American Library, Signet Books, 1967.
——. *For the New Intellectual.* New York: New American Library, Signet Books, 1961.
——.*The New Left: The Anti-Industrial Revolution.* New York: New American Library, Signet Books, 1971.
——. *The Romantic Manifesto.* New York: World, 1969.
——.*The Virtue of Selfishness: A New Concept of Egoism.* New York: New American Library, Signet Books, 1964.
Rao, Y. V. L. *Communication and Development: A Study of Two Indian Villages.* Minneapolis: University of Minnesota Press, 1966.
Reston, James. *The Artillery of the Press.* New York: Harper & Row, Colophon Books, 1967.
Reyburn, Hugh A. *The Ethical Theory of Hegel: A Study of the Philosophy of Right.* Oxford: Clarenden Press, 1921.
Riesman, David, et al. *The Lonely Crowd.* New Haven: Yale University Press Paperbacks, 1969.
Rivers, William L. and Michael J. Nyhan. *Aspen Notebook on Government and the Media.* New York: Praeger Publishers, 1973.
Rivers, William. *The Adversaries.* Boston: Beacon Press, 1970.

Rivers, William, and Wilbur Schramm. *Responsibility in Mass Communications*. New York: Harper & Row, 1969.

Rogers, Arthur K. *Ethics and Moral Tolerance*. New York: Macmillan, 1934.

Roubiczek, Paul. *Ethical Values in the Age of Science*. London: Cambridge University Press, 1969.

———. *Existentialism: For and Against*. London: Cambridge University Press, 1966.

Rourke, Francis E. *Secrecy and Publicity: Dilemmas of Democracy*. Baltimore: Johns Hopkins Press, 1966.

Rucker, Bryce. *The First Freedom*. Carbondale: Southern Illinois University Press, 1968.

Russell, Bertrand. *An Outline of Philosophy*. Cleveland: World Publishing Co., Meridian Books, 1968.

———. *Authority and the Individual*. Boston: Beacon Press, 1960.

———. *Power: A New Social Awareness*. New York: W. W. Norton & Co., Inc., The Norton Library, 1969.

———. *Religion and Science*. London: Oxford University Press, 1935.

———. *The Art of Philosophizing and Other Essays*. New York: Philosophical Library, 1968.

———. *The Will to Doubt*. New York: Philosophical Library, 1958.

Sartre, Jean-Paul. *Existentialism and Human Emotions*. New York: Philosophical Library, 1957.

Sanford, Nevitt. *Self & Society*. New York: Atherton Press, 1966.

Schattschneider, E. E. *Two Hundred Million Americans in Search of a Government*. New York: Holt, Rinehart and Winston, 1969.

Schramm, Wilbur. *Mass Media and National Development*. Stanford: Stanford University Press, 1964.

Siebert, Frederick, Theodore Peterson, and Wilbur Schramm. *Four Theories of the Press*. Urbana: University of Illinois Press, 1963.

Siepmann, Charles A. *Radio, Television and Society*. New York: Oxford University Press, 1950.

Sigmund, Paul E. (ed.). *The Ideologies of the Developing Nations*. New York: Praeger Publishers, 1967.

Sington, Derrick. *Freedom of Communication*. Oxford: Holywell Press Ltd., 1963.

Skinner, B. F. *Beyond Freedom and Dignity*. New York: Bantam/Vintage Books, 1972.

Spinoza, Baruch. *The Ethics: The Road to Inner Freedom*. New York: Philosophical Library—Wisdom Library, 1957.

Stein, Robert. *Media Power: Who is Shaping Your Picture of the World?* Boston: Houghton Mifflin Co., 1972.

Stevenson, Charles L. *Ethics and Language*. New Haven: Yale University Paperbacks, 1965.

Swabey, William C. *Ethical Theory: From Hobbes to Kant*. New York: Philosophical Library, 1961.

Teilhard de Chardin, Pierre. *The Phenomenon of Man.* New York: Harper & Row Torchbooks, 1965.

Thorson, Thomas L. (ed.). *Plato: Totalitarian or Democrat?* Englewood Cliffs, N.J.: Prentice-Hall, Inc., 1963.

Tilton, John E. *Blind Behemoth: A Critical Study of News Media Performance.* Minneapolis: Sun Press, 1972.

Tocqueville, Alexis de. *Democracy in America.* Ed. by Phillips Bradley. New York: Vintage Books, 1959.

Tomkins, Calvin. *Eric Hoffer: An American Odyssey.* New York: E. P. Dutton, 1968.

Tomlin, E. W. F. *The Western Philosophers.* New York: Harper & Row, 1967.

Toulmin, Stephen. *Reason in Ethics.* Cambridge: Cambridge University Press, 1968.

Tuccille, Jerome. *Radical Libertarianism.* New York: Harper & Row, Perennial Library, 1970.

Tucker, Robert C. *Philosophy and Myth in Karl Marx.* Cambridge: University Press, 1969.

Van den Haag, Ernest. *Political Violence & Civil Disobedience.* New York: Harper & Row Torchbooks, 1972.

Von der Mehden, Fred R. *Politics of the Developing Nations.* Englewood Cliffs, N.J.: Prentice-Hall, Inc., 1964.

Waelder, Robert. *Progress and Revolution: A Study of the Issues of Our Age.* New York: International Universities Press, Inc., 1970.

Weber, Ronald (ed.). *The Reporter as Artist: Readings on the New Journalism Controversy.* New York: Hastings House, Publishers, 1974.

Wells, Alan (ed.). *Mass Media and Society.* Palo Alto, Calif.: National Press Books, 1972.

Whalen, Charles W., Jr. *Your Right to Know.* New York: Vintage Books, 1973.

White, Morton. *Social Thought in America: The Revolt Against Formalism.* Boston: Beacon Paperback, 1957.

Whitehead, A. N. *The Function of Reason.* Boston: Beacon Press, 1958.

Wiesman, H. V. *Political Systems: Some Sociological Approaches.* New York: Frederick A. Praeger, 1966.

Wolff, Robert Paul. *Philosophy: A Modern Encounter.* Englewood Cliffs, N.J.: Prentice-Hall, 1971.

———. *The Poverty of Liberalism.* Boston: Beacon Press, 1968.

Wylie, Philip. *The Magic Animal.* New York: Simon & Schuster, Pocket Books, 1969.

Yablonsky, Lewis. *Robopaths.* Baltimore: Penguin Books, Inc., 1972.

Zashin, E. M. *Civil Disobedience and Democracy.* New York: The Free Press, 1972.

Index